Morvern

A Highland Parish

Morvern

A Highland Parish

Norman MacLeod

Edited by Iain Thornber

Birlinn

This edition first published in 2002 by
Birlinn Limited
West Newington House
10 Newington Road
Edinburgh
EH9 1QS

www.birlinn.co.uk

ISBN 1 84158 237 9

British Library Cataloguing-in-Publication Data
A catalogue record for this book is available from
the British Library

The publisher acknowledges subsidy from the

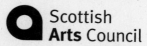

Scottish
Arts Council

towards the publication of this book

Typeset by Edderston Book Design, Peebles
Printed and bound by Creative Print and Design, Wales

CONTENTS

ACKNOWLEDGEMENTS

No man is an island, especially when he sets out to edit a book from a remote Highland parish. I troubled many people during the course of my research and wish to thank the following:

Mr R. A. C. Balfour, Inverness; Sir Hamish MacLeod, Edinburgh; Rev. Ann Winning, Morvern; Mr and Mrs Michael Robertson, Fiunary; Mr Murdo MacDonald, Lochgilphead; Professor Rory Putman, Morvern; Miss Frances Dimond, The Royal Archives, Windsor; Rev Douglas Galbraith, Edinburgh; Mrs Jean Cameron, Moidart; Mrs Jo Currie, Edinburgh; Rev. Sandy Sutherland, Corpach; Mrs May Wilson, Lochaline; Lady Steel, the Borders; The Very Rev. Allan MacLean of Dochgarroch, Glenurquhart; Dr Chris Robinson, Fort William; the editor of the *Oban Times*, Oban; Professor Stewart Brown, Edinburgh; Mrs Susanna Kerr, Edinburgh; The Very Rev. Dr Finlay A. J. MacDonald, Edinburgh; Mrs Margery Livingstone, Lochaline and Lady Joanna Palmer, Berks.

PREFACE

There cannot be many corners left in Scotland which can boast of having so few books written about them as Morvern, against whose picturesque and historical background so many dramas and epic tales were played. Although an area of superlatives, no history has ever been written about Morvern except this one, published in 1867, and *Morvern Transformed* in 1968, which was in essence an economic study centred on the 'big house' and more concerned with legality than morality.

Reminiscences of a Highland Parish was so popular from its first appearance that it went through many editions, including the 1/- edition issued by S. W. Partridge in the *Everyone's Library Series*, which gave to a wider reading public many 'improving' books such as those by Charles Kingsley, Louisa M. Alcott and Harriet Beecher Stowe. It was loved for its piety, for its glimpse of life in a Highland manse and for its family values. Nowadays it is of interest for quite different reasons. A new taste for local history, a consuming fascination with genealogy and a demand for information about the everyday lives of economically deprived Highlanders all combine to make it a 'good read'.

Chapter 8 on the characteristics of the Highlanders is a brilliant essay and a definitive description of a race which was already becoming extinct in MacLeod's own times; it catches the spirit of our ancestors vividly. The value of the book lies in its encapsulation of the past, its humour, its evocation of the scenery of Morvern and surroundings, and its specific appreciation of the remarkable natural intelligence of the indigenous population. It speaks of Morvern but describes a whole breed of West Highlanders. Even more importantly it clarifies the Highlander's view of the clan, a very necessary lesson at a time when notions of what a clan is are becomingly romantically distanced from the reality.

This is a reissue of Norman MacLeod's nineteenth-century bestseller – but with a difference. The names and places which the author attempted to conceal, because of the political correctness of the time, are reconstructed. The allusions are explained, and the whole scene reset in the context of what we know now, and what the author barely knew, of the Morvern clearances. Norman MacLeod's descriptions provide a wonderful window on the way of life in a remote nineteenth-century Highland parish and on the nature of the Gaels who lived there. There are added lists of names for those seeking ancestors and many unpublished photographs, a family tree, and a map.

Norman MacLeod belonged to the most famous family of ministers in Scotland – the MacLeods of Fiunary – which has now given more than 550 years of ordained service to the Church. It has produced no less than six Moderators of the General Assembly of the Church of Scotland, seven Doctors of Divinity, two Deans of the Chapel Royal, two Deans of the Most Ancient and Noble Order of the Thistle and four Royal Chaplains.[1]

Perpetuation of favoured Christian names within the same family and between different generations or branches can lead to considerable confusion. The MacLeods of Fiunary were no exception. In the three generations to which this brief introduction addresses itself, there are for example no fewer than three separate Normans – hence the detailed family tree to which readers are referred immediately.

INTRODUCTION

Morvern is a remote and isolated peninsula in the West Highlands. It lies to the south of Ardnamurchan Point, is bounded by Loch Sunart, Loch Linnhe and the Sound of Mull, and includes the islands of Carna and Oronsay. Situated as it is with a mainly southern exposure, it is a decidedly better favoured district agriculturally than the *Garbh-Criochan,* or the 'Rough Bounds', extending northwards from Loch Moidart to Knoydart.

The landscape of the parish is the result of countless years of geological change and subsequent human imposition. It presents a dramatic blend of upland and lowland, contrasting bleak windswept moors and quiet shady woodlands, the ever variable sea and the placid waters of the trout loch, the tumbling waterfalls and the translucent depths of the salmon rivers. The southern and western coastline of Morvern ascends gradually from the sea, interrupted by a series of escarpments, to a fertile tableland, while that in the south-east from Rudha an Ridire to Eignaig is virtually unbroken by bay or headland as it rises abruptly to 1,650 ft. The northern coast along Loch Sunart is rocky but rarely cliffed, owing to the absence of the great lava pile which dominates the geology of the southern part of the parish. The most prominent topographical features are the deep glens – the *Mor bhearna*, the great, weathered, ice-scoured sea-clefts, which give the district its name. Most notable of these is the hollow running from Loch Teacuis to Loch Aline, containing the fresh-water lochs Doire nam Mairt and Arienas and the River Aline, which has a watershed of only 70 ft above sea level.[2]

The geology of the area is not simple; it is made up of hard metamorphic schist intruded by granite of the Lower Old Red Sandstone age, covered in places with Tertiary basalt originating from massive volcanic activity on the Island of Mull. These lava flows have weathered, producing the spectacular hilltops of Beinn Iadain, Beinn na h' Uamha, Beinn Ghormaig and Beinn Ithearlan. Carboniferous sedimentary rocks exposed south east of Ardtornish

Point have in the past been worked locally as a source of coal, but the extent of the thin seam and the relative inaccessibility of the outcrop has made extraction unprofitable. Lead was mined at Lurga in the Black Glen (Glen Dubh) in the early eighteenth century and a small amount of copper was also produced near Loch Tearnait about the same time. Cretaceous white silica sandstone, used in the manufacturing of high quality glass, occurs at the mouth of Loch Aline and has been worked continuously since the Second World War. With its diverse geology, much of Morvern, especially the Black Glen area, provides an exceptional range of wildlife habitats, which support a huge variety of flora and fauna, including a number of internationally rare arctic-alpine plants, mosses and liverworts.[3]

Man probably reached Morvern about 8,000 years ago, shortly after the end of the last ice age. These Mesolithic hunter-gatherers were few in number and lived in groups in caves and temporary shelters around the edges of the sea-lochs. Some of their flint tools have been found at Acharn and in the hills above Barr. Other cultures followed and overlapped, producing chambered and kerb-cairns with stone coffins, standing stones, funerary urns and metal tools.[4]

Examples of these burial cairns can be found at Rhemore, Killundine, Acharn, Kinlochaline and Claggan. Near Rahoy, on the north shores of Loch Teacuis, there is a 3,000-year-old chambered cairn and a vitrified fort, or dun, which was excavated in 1936-7 and produced a socketed iron axe-head and part of a bronze brooch belonging to the third millennium BC.[5]

The existence of seven other fortified dwellings dating to the same period on rocky promontories along the Sound of Mull show that a turbulent tribal society existed then, as it did later, when a further four important stone castles were erected at Ardtornish, Kinlochaline, Killundine and Drimnin between the thirteenth and seventeenth centuries.[6]

Nothing of the history of Morvern is known in the period between prehistory and the arrival of St Columba on Iona in 563, chiefly because of the absence of any modern archaeological excavation. Local tradition records that it was St Columba himself who brought Christianity to the parish and established the first church at Kiel, a little way above the entrance to Loch Aline. Two grave-markers with simple incised linear crosses found near the mouth of the Killundine River have been ascribed to the Early Christian Period, and a third cross-decorated stone beside the old track that runs over Crois Bheinn from Drimnin to Loch Teacuis, is of similar antiquity.[7]

The raiding, sea-roving Norsemen, who probably arrived some time between the seventh and ninth century, must have found Loch Aline a perfect haven for building and beaching their longships. After three centuries of occupation, it is not surprising that their influence still survives in many local place-names which are a combination of Gaelic and Old Norse. For example, *Aros* on the adjacent Island of Mull is a Scandinavian word meaning 'an estuary', as in the city of Aarhus in Denmark. And in Morvern, *Ardtornish*, 'Promontory of Thor's Headland', and *Achaforsa*, 'field of the waterfall', remind us that the area was once part of the Sea Kingdom of Norway.[8]

The Viking dominance in Argyll was hastened to its closure in the twelfth century by Somerled, a Norse-Celtic warrior chieftain, whose family emerged to lead a rising clan system. Chief amongst these were Dougal, the progenitor of the MacDougalls of Lorn, and Ranald, the forebear of the MacDonald 'Lords of the Isles'. The MacDonalds lived at Ardtornish Castle until shortly after 1493, when they were ousted by various branches of the MacLeans of Duart who built Kinlochaline, Drimnin and Killundine castles. In 1674, through conquest and litigation, the Campbell earls, and later dukes, of Argyll took control of the whole of Mull and two-thirds of Morvern, bringing a degree of sanity and stability to a previously feud-torn countryside.[9]

The Argyll family introduced agrarian reform by replacing dues in work, produce and military service with a cash economy. The second Duke expected his Morvern tenants to be grateful for their emancipation but the 1745 Rising saw most of them supporting the Jacobite Army, and not a single man joined the Hanoverian Argyll Militia. For this act of defiance and as an example to linger-ing Jacobite sympathisers, in March 1746 a detachment of Scots Fusiliers, with naval support from the Sound of Mull, rampaged along the coastline between Drimnin and Ardtornish, destroying

houses, barns and boats and slaughtering every domestic animal
they could find. So thorough was the devastation that the primeval
woods which had been a feature of this coast were reduced to one
red ember, and have never truly recovered.[10]

After the battle of Culloden and the collapse of feudalism, a
traditional way of life came to an end. Communal cattle-raising,
which had been the basis of Morvern's agriculture for centuries,
was gradually replaced by large-scale, but less labour-intensive,
sheep-farming. This change in direction, accompanied by a sharp
rise in population, led to widespread poverty and deprivation. In
1806 George, sixth Duke of Argyll, described as a 'rake, a dandy and
a spendthrift', embarked on a wild social and political extravaganza
and soon found he had lived well beyond his income. His improvi-
dence brought the whole of Morvern onto the market in 1819 and
turned it into a dozen separate estates. In the years that followed,
the new proprietors, with no traditional links to the parish, cleared
several thousand people from their smallholdings to make way for a
few Lowland shepherds, in a manner that was not so very different
from the recent ethnic cleansing in the Balkans. These changes, as
in other parts of the Highlands, were the tragic result of trying to
make a 'Highland gentleman's income support a Lowland gentleman's expenditure', and ended in disaster.[11]

A handful of wealthy landowners, remarkable for the houses
they built and for the removal of sheep to make way for sport,
succeeded the 'improvers' of the first half of the nineteenth century
and made Morvern into a luxury playground for themselves and
their friends. Among the distinguished literary visitors were Alfred,
Lord Tennyson, Sir Walter Scott and Sir Francis Palgrave. While the
guest of the Sellar family at Ardtornish, Tennyson, who had
intended to pay a short visit to Skye but changed his mind,
celebrated his decision with the lines:

> If he did not see Loch Coruisk,
> He ought to be forgiven;
> For though he miss'd a day in Skye,
> He spent a day in Heaven![12]

Meanwhile the tumbrils rolled on. By 1900 fifty-three independent
farms had been replaced by a handful of estates, further reducing

the population to its lowest level since records began, causing a local Gaelic bard to complain:

> *An comhlan beag a dh'fhuirich dhiubh*
> *Chan eil an cor ach cuigeallach,*
> *Fo Sgaithan nan eun Lunnainneach*
> *An doire dubh Loch-Alainn.*[13]

> (The small band who have remained,
> Precarious is their condition,
> Under the wings of the London birds
> In the black wood of Lochaline.)

Today the bulk of the land in Morvern is divided between the Forestry Commission and four private estates – Ardtornish, Laudale, Killundine and Drimnin. None of the proprietors is resident. Some estates continue to keep heavily-subsidised sheep and cattle, but tourism and the servicing of holiday-cottages have replaced agriculture as the main employer.

In contrast to the way of life in Norman MacLeod's day, self-sufficiency has given way to a dependency on the state. Eighteenth- and nineteenth-century eyewitness accounts speak of Morvern as being an area of rich pasture and high quality grazing. Today, however, much of the land has deteriorated through over-grazing by sheep. No fields are ploughed, hay is not made, and few crops are grown other than trees. Salmon are farmed in several sea-lochs, and fruit and vegetables are available from a market garden at the head of Loch Aline, but milk and all other consumables are imported. Underwater diving on historic shipwrecks in the Sound of Mull has become popular and an enterprising centre at Lochaline offers facilities for both amateur and professional divers and archaeologists.

Less than fifty years ago there were eight primary schools in the parish; now there is one at Lochaline. For secondary education it is necessary for students to travel to Tobermory daily, or Fort William weekly. A new high school is being built at Strontian to cover the needs of Ardnamurchan, Sunart and Morvern, but whether it will be a success remains to be seen. There is a resident doctor and a peripatetic district nurse. The Church of Scotland minister holds regular services at Kiel, but, as attendance has fallen off greatly, it

cannot be long before this church is closed and the parish united
with either Ardgour or Ardnamurchan. Little or no Gaelic is
spoken, and because there are now few families living in Morvern
whose association with the place goes back more than three
generations, much of the once rich history of the area has been lost.

The population density of Morvern is now just over two to the
square mile and is concentrated in local authority housing in
Lochaline and Drimnin, with the remainder generally occupying
tied cottages scattered throughout the Peninsula. There is room for
a larger, independent community and greater employment oppor-
tunities in small, manufacturing projects using local skills and
natural resources, but, until land is released for new housing at
affordable prices by the Forestry Commission and the larger private
estates, there is little hope of any improvement in the foreseeable
future.

THE MACLEODS OF FIUNARY

Twenty-nine years after the Duke of Cumberland's soldiers laid waste to Morvern, a young minister from Skye arrived in the parish. His name was Norman MacLeod and he had been appointed by the Presbyterian and Hanoverian loyalist Duke of Argyll to reconcile the many Jacobites living on his estate to the final collapse of the Stewart Cause, and to lead them from Episcopalianism into the established Church.

As the thirty-year-old Norman stepped onto the old stone pier below the manse of Fiunary with Rory, his lame, one-eyed manservant, none of the assembled company could have imagined that not only would the young man they were welcoming be their minister for the next forty-nine years, but that his son would follow him in the same role for a further fifty-eight. The MacLeod of Fiunary family tree is a long and distinguished one and continues to this day, but this book is concerned with only four of its earlier members.

NORMAN MACLEOD (1745–1824), the first of the dynasty to arrive in Morvern, married Jean Morison, 'the girl next door', who bore him five sons and eleven daughters, of whom only three daughters and two sons survived to middle or old age. (See notes 25 and 26.) The young minister did not have an easy life at first. His charge was scattered over 142 square miles, with a coastline of equal length; moreover it was occupied by many hostile Jacobites. However, his engaging personality, his command of the Gaelic language and his understanding of the Highlanders and their manners and customs won through, and before long his 2,000-strong congregation took him to their hearts. Long after his death their sentiments still echoed in the wording of his memorial tablet inside Kiel Church:

> Noble in appearance, excelling in scholarship, an eloquent preacher and a genial and faithful pastor.

Before he died he had the pleasure of seeing his youngest son, John, appointed as his assistant and successor.

NORMAN MACLEOD (1783–1862), whose contributions appear in this book, was an eminent churchman. He left Morvern and worked in Central Scotland and Glasgow, where he devoted himself to the welfare of his fellow Highlanders in a way that has no parallel in modern history. He was born in the Manse of Fiunary, licensed in 1806 by the Presbytery of Mull and preached his first sermon there in the same year. In 1811 he married Agnes, daughter of James Maxwell, the Duke of Argyll's chamberlain for Mull. Of their eleven children only four sons and three daughters reached maturity. In 1824 he received the degree of Doctor of Divinity from the University of Edinburgh and became Moderator of the General Assembly in 1836. He was Dean of the Chapel Royal and one of the Queen's chaplains, in which capacity he preached to Queen Victoria and Prince Albert at Blair Atholl during their second visit to Scotland in 1844.

It is, however, for his work on education and for organising relief during the distress of the potato famines of 1836–37 and 1847 that he is best remembered, and for which he earned the sobriquet *Caraid nan Gaidheal*, 'Friend of the Gael'. During these famines he visited England and addressed several meetings in order to raise money for the inhabitants of the Highlands and Islands who were dying of starvation. A speech he made in Exeter Town Hall produced, before the room was cleared, £10,000 for this purpose. His outstanding services in this field are commemorated in various ways, but his real monument is found in the Gaelic prose of which he was such a master. The standard and style he set may be said to have been second only to the account of the death of Socrates in Plato's *Phaedo* or some well-known chapters in the Gospel of St John, and influenced Gaelic writers for over a century. In the biographical introduction to a choice selection of Norman MacLeod's writings, his son, also Norman, wrote:

> So long as there exists a people on earth speaking the Gaelic and able to appreciate its power and beauty, its eloquence and pathos, linked to worthiest thoughts, so long will the name of Norman MacLeod be remembered, honoured and loved.[14]

Dr Norman Macleod of St Columba's died in the fifty-seventh year of his ministry and was buried in Campsie churchyard in Stirlingshire.

NORMAN MACLEOD (1812–72) author of this book, was born the eldest son of Caraid nan Gaidheal, at Campbeltown, Argyll, where his father was minister. At the age of twelve he was sent to Morvern to board with Samuel Cameron, the parish schoolmaster, in order to learn Gaelic and become familiar with the Highland way of life. His grandfather had died a few months before, but he had pleasant memories of the old man from previous visits to his Uncle John, who had taken over the incumbency. In 1825 his father moved to Campsie and Norman became a pupil at the school there. In 1827 he entered Glasgow College, but it was not until he went to Edinburgh in 1831 that the influence of the great Dr Thomas Chalmers set him on the road to success in dealing with poverty, which was endemic in the industrial cities of Scotland at the time.

After a spell as a tutor in Yorkshire and a year at Weimar in Germany, he returned to Edinburgh to further his studies and in 1838 he was ordained minister of Loudoun, Ayrshire, where he quickly gained the affection of his parishioners and his church became crowded. At the Disruption of 1843 he moved to Dalkeith where, in addition to his parish duties, he began to take a keen interest in foreign missions. In 1851 he married Catherine Mackintosh of Geddes, Nairnshire, and moved to the Barony Church next to Glasgow Cathedral, which had some of the worst slums of the city in its parish. There, among the 87,000 parishioners, his life's work really began. In a flurry of activity and with tireless energy he set about organising schools and missions for the poor, opening refreshment rooms for working men to keep them out of the public houses, arranging meetings to promote adult education, founding the first Congregational Penny Savings Bank, and supervising the building of six new churches.

The poor and the unemployed held him in high and warm affection for, unlike any of his predecessors, he visited them in their overcrowded houses, attended to them when they were sick and defended them when they were in trouble. His geniality was legendary and his readiness to narrate incidents at his own expense was often told. For instance, on his way one day to the Barony Church he found two boys sitting in the street making a building of mud. 'What is that you are making lads?' he asked. 'We're making a church and there's the pulpit.' 'I see,' said Norman, 'but where is the minister?' 'Oh we haven't enough mud to make a minister,' was the crushing reply, and off went Norman, chuckling, to retell the story at his next service.[15]

In 1858 Glasgow University conferred on him the degree of D.D. In 1864 he toured Egypt and Palestine (which he wrote about under the title *Eastward*) and later visited many mission stations in India. Two years later he courted controversy by taking a stance against Puritanism and the traditional Scottish Sabbath. He attacked ultra-Calvinists by announcing,

> They won't enjoy life; they won't laugh without atoning for the sin by a groan; they won't indulge in much hope or joy; they more easily and readily entertain doctrines which go to prove how many may be damned than how many may be saved.[16]

And when he heard ministers in some areas had banned the old songs and tales as being too secular and profane for the pious inhabitants, he was heard to say:

> What next? Are the singing birds to be shot by the kirk sessions?[17]

He was the first editor of *Good Words*, a monthly magazine with a worldwide circulation. He also published many Gaelic books and papers, as well as the now popular hymn, 'Courage, brother! do not stumble', and that best-loved of all Morvern songs, 'Farewell to Fiunary'. His English translations of some of his father's original Gaelic compositions are said to be the finest ever written. Classic amongst these are 'The Emigrant Ship' and 'Mary of Unimore', which are both included in this book. The Rev. Norman MacLeod, or 'Norman' as he was simply referred to by all of Scotland, was a popular minister, who met and preached to Queen Victoria, Prince Albert, Gladstone, David Livingstone, Florence Nightingale and many other famous personalities of his time. He featured in John Wellwood's *Famous Scots Series*, alongside such literary and historical giants as Thomas Carlyle, John Knox, Robert Burns, James Boswell and Hugh Miller.

In 1857 he became chaplain to Queen Victoria, with whom he was a great favourite and who regularly summoned him to Balmoral. His first sermon at Crathie in 1854 was noted by the queen in her journal:

> We went to Kirk as usual at twelve o'clock. The service was performed by the Rev. Norman MacLeod of Glasgow and anything finer I never heard. The sermon, entirely extempore, was quite admirable, so simple and yet so eloquent, and so beautifully put . . . Everyone came back delighted; and how satisfactory it is to come back from church with such feelings![18]

In 1869 he was Moderator of the General Assembly and did much to help the movement for the abolition of patronage in the Church of Scotland; but in 1871 his health began to decline and he died on Sunday, 16 June 1872 in his Glasgow home. He was buried at Campsie. Several monuments were raised to his memory. His Mission Church in Glasgow was made 'the MacLeod Parish Church', and the Barony congregation built a 'MacLeod Memorial Missionary Institute' in a destitute part of the parish. A statue of him was set up in Glasgow and as a token of her respect Queen Victoria placed two beautiful memorial windows in Crathie Church, where he had often preached before her.

At his memorial service in Westminster Abbey, Dean Arthur Stanley summed up perfectly Norman's life when he asked:

> What was it that shed over the close of that career so peaceful, so cheering a light? It was that he was known to have fought the good fight manfully, that he had finished his course with joy, and had done what in him lay to add to the happiness and goodness of the world.

Less eloquently put, perhaps, but just as telling, was the remark made by an old Glasgow woman, blinking in the brilliant sunshine, as she watched his cortège pass by:

> Aye but Providence has been kind to our Norman, giving him such a grand day for his funeral![19]

JOHN MACLEOD (1801-82), was born at Fiunary and known as 'The High Priest of Morvern', because of his magnificent physical presence (he was said to have been six feet, nine inches in height).

No one, according to his nephew Donald MacLeod, could meet him, however cursorily,

> without experiencing a certain wonder at the vision of this notable figure, with its grand head of snow-white hair, towering above the crowd.[20]

He was licensed by the Presbytery of Mull in November 1823 and in 1834 married Margaret, daughter of Donald MacLean of Drimnin and Borreray, by whom he had two sons, John and Norman, and two daughters who died in childhood. He was awarded the degree of Doctor of Divinity by Glasgow University in 1845 and shortly afterwards went on a hugely successful tour of the Presbyterian churches of Canada and America with his nephew Norman of the Barony. As a result of this, and for his work on judicial cases at the bar of the church parliament, where he was considered the brightest and ablest pleader, he was elected Moderator of the General Assembly, Dean of the Most Noble Order of the Thistle and Dean of the Chapel Royal.

John MacLeod's ministry coincided with the Highland Clearances and the changes which occurred in Morvern as a result affected him deeply. His position was almost untenable. On one hand he was acting as an officer for the evictors, and on the other counselling the evictees. Other ministers in similar situations in the Highlands emigrated with their flocks. Why John MacLeod chose not to do so on principle must remain a mystery. From his nephew, Donald, we hear:

> His later years were spent in pathetic loneliness. He had seen his parish almost emptied of its people. Glen after glen had been turned into sheep-walks, and the cottages in which generations of gallant Highlanders had lived and died were unroofed, their torn walls and gables left standing like mourners beside the grave, and the little plots of garden or of cultivated enclosure allowed to merge into the moorland pasture. He had seen every property in the parish change hands, and though, on the whole, kindly and pleasant proprietors came in the place of the old families, yet they were strangers to the people, neither understanding their language nor their ways. The consequence was that they perhaps scarcely realised the havoc produced by the changes they inaugurated. 'At one stroke of a pen,' he said to me, with a look of sadness and indignation, 'two hundred people were ordered off —.

There was not one of these whom I did not know and their fathers before them; and finer men and women never left the Highlands.'

He thus found himself the sole remaining link between the past and the present – the one man above the rank of a peasant who remembered the old days and the traditions of the people. The sense of change was intensely saddened as he went through his parish and passed ruined houses here, there and everywhere. 'There is not a smoke there now,' he used to say with pathos of the glens which he had known tenanted by a manly and loyal peasantry, among whom lived song and story and the elevating influences of brave traditions.[21]

Dr John was a great orator whose Gaelic sparkled with gems of poetic thought and feeling. His diction was chaste, his reasoning close and his eloquence not easily surpassed. As a writer of Gaelic he had no equal and many of the beautiful songs and hymns he composed evince a poetic talent of no mean order. His name was a household word in Argyll, where it was said every inhabitant was proud of him. He received many calls to richer incumbencies but he refused them all, preferring to remain in his native Morvern. One of these was the vacant parish of Loch Broom, considered to be one of the best livings in Scotland. He went there to preach but something occurred which made him feel that the congregation was unfriendly towards him. So he declined the position, to the regret of his patron and of his wife, who had the furniture in the manse prepared for leaving! When he died in his eighty-third year, and the fifty-eighth of his ministry in Morvern, numerous and eloquent were the public appreciations.

The *Oban Times* recorded:

How deeply he was loved by the people of his extensive and scattered parish was amply shown by the many aged men who, on the day of his funeral, had travelled incredible distances over mountains and moor to pay their last token of respect to the pastor who had been for most of their lives their 'guide, philosopher, and friend'. The loving and loyal manner in which they bore him shoulder high from the manse at Fiunary to the burying ground of Kiel, four or five miles off, testified to the deep veneration in which he was held.[22]

A contributor to *The Scotsman* called him the 'Father of the Church of Scotland, who to look at, one might have supposed he had been brought up in kings' palaces rather than in the humble manse of a remote and mountainous parish'.[23] But it was left to John Cameron, the erudite Kirk Session Clerk in Morvern, to have the last word as he recorded the congregation's deep sorrow

> at the removal from them by death of the Rev. John MacLeod, their venerable and revered minister – a man whose gifts and abilities could not fail to raise him to the very highest eminence in any profession he might have chosen. The Session acknowledge that they were in an especial manner favoured in having as their pastor a man of such singularly rare gifts – his talents were known to the world, but his love to his flock, which was boundless, is known and felt by us in ways that can never be known to the world.[24]

The death of the Rev. John MacLeod, and the end of 107 years of unbroken service by the same family brought to a close an important chapter in the history of Morvern and the Church of Scotland. Although his two sons, John and Norman, were both ministers, neither applied for the vacancy and on 13 December 1882 the Rev. Donald Macfarlane from Kintyre was elected and appointed minister of Morvern. Fiunary manse continued to be the home of successive parish ministers until 1957, when it became redundant and was sold by the trustees of the Church of Scotland to Dr George MacLeod, later Lord MacLeod of Fiunary, founder of the Iona Community and grandson of the author of this book, in whose family it still remains.

Iain Thornber
Knock House
Morvern
Argyll

October 2002

MACLEOD OF FIUNARY FAMILY TREE

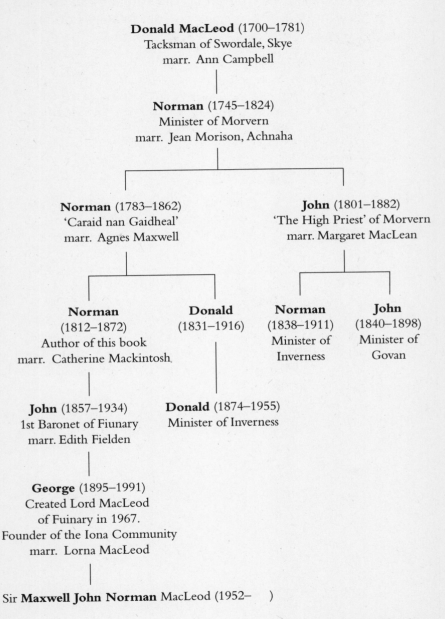

Donald MacLeod (1700–1781)
Tacksman of Swordale, Skye
marr. Ann Campbell

Norman (1745–1824)
Minister of Morvern
marr. Jean Morison, Achnaha

Norman (1783–1862)
'Caraid nan Gaidheal'
marr. Agnes Maxwell

John (1801–1882)
'The High Priest' of Morvern
marr. Margaret MacLean

Norman
(1812–1872)
Author of this book
marr. Catherine Mackintosh

Donald
(1831–1916)

Norman
(1838–1911)
Minister of
Inverness

John
(1840–1898)
Minister of
Govan

John (1857–1934)
1st Baronet of Fiunary
marr. Edith Fielden

Donald (1874–1955)
Minister of Inverness

George (1895–1991)
Created Lord MacLeod
of Fiunary in 1967.
Founder of the Iona Community
marr. Lorna MacLeod

Sir **Maxwell John Norman** MacLeod (1952–   )

Iain Thornber

Chapter 1

PREAMBLE

There, westward away, where roads are unknown to Loch Nevish,
And the great peaks look abroad over Skye to the Westernmost Islands.

The Highlands of Scotland, like many greater things in the world, may be said to be unknown, yet well known. They are known to the thousands of summer tourists who, every year, and from every part of the civilised world, gaze on the romantic beauties of the Trossachs and Loch Lomond, skirt the Hebrides from the Firth of Clyde to Oban, trundle through the wide gorge of Glencoe, chatter among the ruins of Iona, scramble over the wonders of Staffa, sail along the magnificent line of lakes to Inverness, reach the sombre Coolins, and disturb the silence of Coruisk. Pedestrians also, with stick and knapsack, search the more solitary wildernesses and glens of the mainland, from the Grampians to Ross-shire and Caithness. Sportsmen, too, whether real or only make-believe, have their summer quarters in the Highlands dotted over every moor, scattered on hillsides and beside clear streams, with all the irregularity of the boulders of the great northern drift, but furnished with most of the luxuries of an English home. All these strangers, it must be admitted, know something of the Highlands.

The tourists know the names of steamers, coaches, and hotels; and how they were cheated by boatmen, porters, or guides. They have a vague impression of misty mountains, stormy seas, heavy rain, difficult roads, crowded inns, unpronounceable Gaelic names, with brighter remembrances of landscapes whose grandeur they have probably never seen surpassed. Pedestrians can recall lonely and unfrequented paths across broken moorland undulating far away, like brown shoreless seas, and through unploughed and untrodden valleys, where the bark of a shepherd's dog, and much more the sight of a shepherd's hut, were welcomed; and they cannot forget panoramas, from hilltops or from rocky promontories, of lake and river, moor and forest, sea and island, sunshine and cloud, of lonely keeps and ruined homesteads, of infinite sheepwalks and silent glens which seemed to end in chaos – remembrances which will come to them like holy days of youth, to refresh and sanctify, and 'hang about the beatings of the heart' amidst the din and fret of a city life. Sportsmen, too, in a sense, know the Highlands. They have waded up to the shoulders in Highland lakes, nothing visible but hat swathed with flies, and hand wielding the lithe rod and line. They have trod the banks and tried the pools of every famous stream, until the very salmon that are left know their features and their flies, and tremble for their cunning temptations. Or, quitting lake and stream, they have sped with haste to stand upon the Twelfth, at dawn of day, upon the blooming heather. When they visit old shootings, they hail from afar the well-known hillsides and familiar 'ground'. They can tell twenty miles off where the birds are scarce, or where, according to the state of the weather, they can be found, The whole scenery is associated in their memory with the braces that have been bagged, the stags which have been killed, or – oh, horrid memory! – missed, 'when the herd was coming right towards us, and all from that blockhead Charlie, who *would* look if they were within shot'. The keepers, and gillies, and beaters, and the whole tribe of expectants, are also well known, as such, and every furrowed face is to these sportsmen a very poem, an epic, a heroic ballad, a history of the past season of happiness and breezy hills, as well as a prophecy of the morrow which is hoped for with beating heart, that blames the night and urges on the morn.

There are others, too, who may be expected to know something of the Highlands. Low country sheep-farmers, redolent of wool;[25] English proprietors, who as summer visitants occupy the old house or castle of some extinct feudal chief; and antiquaries who have dipped into, or even studied profoundly, the civil and ecclesiastical antiquities of the land. Nevertheless, to each and all such the Highlands may be as unknown in their real life, as the scent of the wild bog myrtle is to the accomplished gentleman who has no sense of smell; or as a Gaelic boat-song in its words and spirit is to a Hindoo pundit.

Some of our readers may very naturally be disposed to ask, with a sneer of contempt, what precise loss any human being incurs from want of this knowledge? The opinion may be most reasonably held and expressed that the summer tourist, the wandering pedestrian, or the autumnal sportsmen, have probably taken out of the Northern wilderness all that was worth bringing into the Southern Canaan of civilised life, and that as much gratitude, at least, is due for what is forgotten as for what is remembered.

Perhaps those readers may be right. And if so, then, for their own comfort as well as for ours we ought to warn them that if they have been foolish enough to accompany us thus far, they should pity us, bid us farewell, and wish us a safe deliverance from the mountains.

Is there any one, let us ask, who reads those lines, and yet who dislikes peat-reek? Any one who puts his fingers in his ears when he hears the bagpipe – the real war-pipe – begin a real pibroch? Any one who dislikes the kilt, the Gaelic, the clans, and who does not believe in Ossian?[26] Any one who has a prejudice to the Mac, or who cannot comprehend why one Mac should prefer a Mac of his own clan to the Mac of any other clan? Any one who smiles at the ignorance of a Highland parson who never reads the *Saturday Review* or the *Westminster,* who never heard about one in ten of the 'schools of modern thought', and who believes, without any mental suffering, that two and two make four? Any one who puts his glass to his eye during prayer in a Highland church, and looks at his fellowtraveller with a smile while the peasants sing their Psalms? Any one who, when gazing on a Highland landscape, descants to his local admirers about some hackneyed Swiss scene *they* never saw, or enumerates a dozen Swiss *Horns,* the Wetterhorn, Schreckhorn, or any other horn which has penetrated into his brain? Forbid that any such terribly clever and well-informed cosmopolitans should 'lose ten tickings of their watch' in reading these reminiscences!

One other class sometimes found in society we would especially beseech to depart: we mean Highlanders ashamed of their country. Cockneys are bad enough, but they are sincere and honest in their idolatry of the Great Babylon. Young Oxonians or young barristers, even when they become slashing London critics, are more harmless than they themselves imagine, and after all inspire less awe than Ben Nevis, or than the celebrated agriculturist who proposed to decompose that mountain with acids, and to scatter the debris as a fertiliser over the Lochaber moss. But a Highlander born, who has been nurtured on oatmeal porridge and oatmeal cakes; who in his youth wore home-spun cloth, and was innocent of shoes and stock-ings; who blushed in his attempts to speak the English language; who never saw a nobler building for years than the little kirk in the glen; and who owes all that makes him tolerable in society to the Celtic blood which flows in spite of him through his veins – for this man to be proud of his English accent, to sneer at the everlasting hills, the old kirk and its simple worship, and to despise the race which has never disgraced him – faugh! Peat-reek is frankincense in comparison with him; let him not be distracted by any of our reminiscences of the old country; leave us, we beseech of thee!

We ask not how old or how young those are who remain with us; we care not what their theory of political economy or their school of modern philosophy may be; we are indifferent as to their evening employment, whether it be darning stockings, sitting idle round the wintry fire in the enjoyment of repose, or occupying, as invalids, their bed or chair. If only they are charitable souls, who hope all things and are not easily provoked; who would like a peep into forms of society, and to hear about people and customs differing in some degree from what they have hitherto been acquainted with; to have an easy chat about a country less known, perhaps, to them than any other in Europe – then shall we gladly unfold to them our reminiscences of a country and people worth knowing about and loving, and of a period in their history that is passing, if, indeed, it has not already passed away.

And now, by way of further preamble to our reminiscences, let us take a birdseye view of the parish. It is not included, by Highland ecclesiastical statists, among what are called the large parishes. We have no idea of the number of square miles, of arable acres, or of waste land, which it contains; but science and the trigonometrical survey will, it is presumed, give those details in due time.[27] When viewed as passing tourists view it, from the sea, it has nothing remarkable about it, and if it is pronounced by these same tourists to be uninteresting, and 'just the sort of scenery one would like to pass when dining or sleeping', we won't censure the judgement. A castled promontory, a range of dark precipices supporting the upland pastures, and streaked with white waterfalls, that are lost in the copse at their base, form a picture not very imposing when

compared with 'what one sees everywhere'. A long ridge of hill
rising some two thousand feet above the sea, its brown sides, up to
a certain height, chequered with green stripes and patches of
cultivation; brown heather-thatched cottages, with white walls; here
and there a mansion, whose chimneys are seen above the trees
which shelter it: these are its chief features along the seaboard of
twenty miles.[28] But how different is the whole scene when one
lands! New beauties reveal themselves, and every object seems to
change in size, appearance and relative position. A rocky wall of
wondrous beauty, the rampart of the old upraised beach which
girdles Scotland, runs along the shore; the natural wild wood of ash,
oak and birch, with the hazel copse, clothe the lower hills and
shelter the herds of wandering cattle; lonely sequestered bays are
everywhere scooped out into beautiful harbours; points and
promontories seem to grow out of the land, and huge dykes of
whinstone fashion to themselves the most picturesque outlines;
clear streams everywhere hasten on to the sea; small glens, perfect
gems of beauty, open up their entrances into the wonders of endless
waterfalls and deep dark pools, hemmed in by steep banks hanging
with ivy, honeysuckle, rowan-trees, and ferns, while on the hillsides
such signs of culture and industry as scattered cottages, small farms
and shepherds' huts, give life to the whole scene.

But to view the parish in all its outward aspect, we must ascend
to the top of — [29]

> I name not its name, lest inquisitive tourist
> Hunt it, and make it a lion, and get it at last into guidebooks.

The upward path soon leaves the cultivated settlements, passes
several streams, winds across tracts of moorland, and at last reaches
the shielings of Corrie Borrodale.[30] One cannot imagine a sweeter
spot than this in which to repose before attempting the proper
ascent of the hill. A stream, clear as a diamond, and singing its hill
song, takes a sweep, and folds within its embrace a bay of emerald
grass, surrounded with blooming heather. Here and there appear
small groups of ruins, mere gatherings of stones, to mark where
man once built his temporary home. Before sheep-farming was
introduced generally into the Highlands, about sixty or seventy
years ago, the cattle ranged through the hills as high up as the grass

grew, and it was necessary, during summer, to follow them thither, to milk them there, and make up stores of butter and cheese for winter use.[31] This led to the building of those summer châlets, which were managed chiefly by women and herd-boys, but visited often, perhaps daily, by the mistress of the farm, who took the dairy under her special charge. Thus it is that when one rests in such a green oasis, his fancy again peoples the waste with the herd-lads 'calling the cattle home', and with the blithe girls who milked the cattle; he sees again the life among the huts, and hears the milking-songs and innocent glee; and when awakened from his reverie by bleating sheep – the only living tenants of the pastures – he is not disposed to admit the present time to be an improvement on the past.

But let us up to that green spot beside the ravine; then to the left along the rocks, then to the right till past the deep 'peat-bogs'; and finally straight up to the Cairn. When we have taken breath, let us look around. This is the very high altar of the parish, and we maintain that all the glories which can be seen from a parish rightfully belong to the parish itself, and are a part of its own rich inheritance.

Let us first look northward. Almost at our feet is a chain of small lakes, round whose green shores, unseen from the Cairn because immediately beneath it, a prosperous tenantry once lived, of whom no trace remains, except those patches of ruins which mark their once happy homesteads.[32] Ruins there are, too, which show us that whatever defects the Church before the Reformation had accumulated, she excelled the Church of the present in the greater number and the greater beauty of her parish churches. There are few sights which more rebuke the vulgar Church parsimony of these later days, or which imbue us with more grateful and generous feelings towards the missionaries of an earlier and more difficult time, than the faith and love which reared so many chapels on distant islands, and so many beautiful and costly fabrics in savage wildernesses, among a people who were too rude to appreciate such works, or the spirit which originated them. These old Highland Church extensionists were not stimulated by party rivalry, public meetings, or newspaper articles. Their praise could not have been from men. How they got the means and money we know not, but this we believe, that:

> They dreamt not of a perishable home
> Who thus could build!

But to our picture again. Opposite to the spectator, and rising abruptly from the valley, is a range of hills, broken into wild scaurs and clothed with copse; while beyond these rise ridge on ridge, like a mighty ocean sea, heaving in gigantic billows onward towards Ben Reshapol, until lost to sight beyond the head of Loch Shiel and among the braes of Lochaber. Sweeping the eye from the north to the west, what a glorious spectacle! The chain of lakes beneath end in the lovely Loch Sunart, with its beauteous bays and wooded islets. Over its farther shore, belonging to that huge parish and huge word Ardnamurchan, and above picturesque hills, the more distant Hebrides rear their heads out of the ocean. Along the horizon southwards are seen, the Scur of Eigg lifting its gigantic pillar, the dark lines of Rum, and the islands of Canna, Coll, and Tiree, with gleams of the ocean between. The long dark, moorland ascent by which we have reached the hilltop, now carries the eye down to the sea. That sea is a strait, worming itself for more than twenty miles between the mainland where we stand, and the island of Mull, which gathers up its hills into a cluster of noble peaks about its centre, with Bentealgh (Bentalve)[33] and Benmore towering over all. A low isthmus[34] right opposite opens up an arm of the sea beyond Mull, with noble headlands, beneath which the man who would see Staffa aright should sail out to the ocean with no strangers save a Highland crew; for not from crowded steamer can he fully understand that pillared island and its cathedral cave. Let us take one other glance to the east, the eye following the Sound of Mull, and our panorama is completed. How nobly the Sound, dotted with vessels, opens up past Ardtornish and Duart Castles, ere it mingles with the broader waters that sweep in eddying tides past the Slate Isles[35], past Jura, Scarba, on to Islay, until they finally spread out into the roll and roar of the shoreless Atlantic. In that western distance may be seen some white smoke that marks Oban, and over it Ben Cruachan, the most beautiful of our western hills, accompanied by its grey companions, 'the shepherds of Etive Glen'.[36]

We back this view from the highest hill in the parish for extent and varied beauty against any view in Europe! It is the Righi of

Argyleshire; and given only what alas! is not easily obtained, a good day, good in transparency, good with 'gorgeous cloudland', good with lights and shadows, the bright blue of the northern sky (more intense than the Italian), looking down and mingling with the sombre dark of the northern hills, dark even when relieved in autumn by the glow of the purple heather – given all this, and we know not where to find a more magnificent outlook over God's fair earth. No reminiscences of the outer world so haunt our memory as those so often treasured up from that grey cairn; and however frequently we have returned from beholding other and more famous scenes, this one has appeared like a first love, only more beautiful than them all.

As we descend from the hill, the minister – how oft has he gone with us there! – tells us stories worth hearing, and as he alone can tell them; stories of a pastor's life, 'from perils in the wilderness, and perils of waters, and perils of the sea'; stories of character, such as the lonely hills and misty moors alone can mould; stories of combats among the wild and primitive inhabitants of the olden time; and stories, too, of the early invaders of the land from Denmark and Norway, sea-kings, or pirates rather, whose names yet linger where they fell in battle, as at *Corrie Borrodale, Corrie Lundie,* and *Ess Stangadal.*[37]

But we have reached 'the manse'; and from thence we must start with our 'Reminiscences of a Highland Parish'.

Chapter 2

THE MANSE[38]

> Say, ye far travelled clouds, far-seeing hills –
> Among the happiest-looking homes of men
> Scatter'd all Britain over, through deep glen,
> On airy uplands, and by forest-rills,
> And o'er wide plains, whereon the sky distils
> Her lark's loved warblings – does aught meet your ken
> More fit to animate the Poet's pen,
> Aught that more surely by its aspect fills
> Pure minds with sinless envy, than the abode
> Of the good Priest: who, faithful through all hours
> To his high charge, and truly serving God
> Has yet a heart and hand for trees and flowers,
> Enjoys the walks his predecessors trod,
> Nor covets lineal rights in lands and towers?'
>
> WORDSWORTH

There lived in the Island of Skye, more than a century ago, a small farmer or 'gentleman tacksman'.[39] Some of his admirably-written letters are now before me; but I know little of his history beyond the fact revealed in his correspondence, and preserved in the affectionate traditions of his descendants, that he was 'a good man', and the first within the district where he lived who introduced the worship of God in his family.

One great object of his ambition was to give his sons the best education that could be obtained for them, and in particular to train his first-born for the ministry of the Established Church of Scotland. His wishes were fully realised, for the noble institution of the parochial school provided in the remotest districts of Scotland teaching of a very high order, and produced admirable classical scholars – such as even Dr Johnson talks of with respect.

Besides the schools, there was an excellent custom then existing among the tenantry in Skye of associating themselves to obtain a good tutor for their sons. The tutor resided alternately at different farms, and the boys from the other farms in the neighbourhood

came daily to him. In this way the burden of supporting the
teacher, and the difficulties of travelling on the part of the boys,
were divided among the several families in the district. In autumn
the tutor, accompanied by his more advanced pupils, journeyed on
foot to Aberdeen to attend the university. He superintended their
studies during the winter, and returned in spring with them to their
Highland homes to pursue the same routine. The then Laird of
MacLeod[40] was one who took a pride in being surrounded by a
tenantry who possessed so much culture. It was his custom to
introduce all the sons of his tenants who were studying in
Aberdeen to their respective professors, and to entertain both
professors and students in his house. On one such occasion, when a
professor remarked with surprise, 'Why, sir, these are all gentlemen!'
Macleod replied, 'Gentlemen I found them, as gentlemen I wish to
see them educated, and as gentlemen I hope to leave them behind
me.'*

The 'gentleman tacksman's' eldest son acted as a tutor for some
time, and then became minister of 'the Highland Parish'.[41] It was
said of him that 'a finer-looking or prettier man never left his native
island'. He was upwards of six feet in height, with a noble countenance which age only made nobler. He was accompanied from Skye
by a servant-lad, whom he had known from his boyhood, called
'Ruari Beg', or little Rory.[42] Rory was rather a contrast to his
master in outward appearance. One eye was blind but the other
seemed to have robbed the sight from its extinguished neighbour to
intensify its own. That grey eye gleamed and scintillated with the
peculiar sagacity and reflection which one sees in the eye of a Skye
terrier, but with such intervals of feeling as human love of the most
genuine kind could alone have expressed. One leg, too, was slightly
shorter than the other, and the manner in which Rory rose on the
longer or sunk on the shorter, and the frequency or rapidity with
which those alternate ups and downs in his life were practised,

---

* 'At dinner I expressed to Macleod the joy which I had in seeing him on such
cordial feelings with his clan. "Government", said he, "has deprived us of our
ancient power; but it cannot deprive us of our domestic satisfactions. I would rather
drink punch in one of their houses [meaning the houses of the people], than be
enabled by their hardships to have claret in my own."' – Boswell's *Life of Johnson*,
vol. iv, p. 275.

became a telegraph of Rory's thoughts when no words, out of respect to his master, were spoken. 'So you don't agree with me, Rory?' 'What's wrong?' 'You think it dangerous to put to sea today?' 'Yes; the mountain-pass also would be dangerous? Exactly so. Then we must consider what is to be done.' These were the sort of remarks which a series of slow or rapid movements of Rory's limbs often drew forth from his master, though no other token was afforded of his inner doubt or opposition. A better boatman, a truer genius at the helm, never took a tiller in his hand; a more enduring traveller never 'gaed ower the moor amang the heather'; a better singer of a boat-song never cheered the rowers, nor kept them as one man to their stroke; a more devoted, loyal and affectionate 'minister's man' and friend never lived than Rory – first called 'Little Rory,' but as long as I can remember, 'Old Rory'. But more of him anon. The minister and his servant arrived in the Highland Parish nearly ninety years ago, almost total strangers to its inhabitants, and alone they entered the manse to see what it was like.

I ought to inform my readers in the south, some of whom – can they pardon the suspicion if it is unjust? – are more ignorant of Scotland and its Church than they are of France or Italy and the Church of Rome – I ought to inform them that the Presbyterian Church is established in Scotland, and that the landed proprietors in each parish are bound by law to build and keep in repair a church, suitable school, and parsonage or 'manse', and also to secure a portion of land, or 'glebe', for the minister. Both the manses and churches have of late years immensely improved in Scotland, so that in many cases they are now far superior to those in some of the rural parishes of England. Much still remains to be accomplished in this department of architecture and taste! Yet even at the time I speak of, the manse was in its structure rather above than below the houses occupied by the ordinary gentry, with the exception of 'the big house' of the Laird.[43] It has been succeeded by one more worthy of the times; but the old manse was nevertheless respectable.[44]

The glebe was the glory of the manse! It was the largest in the county, consisting of about sixty acres, and containing a wonderful combination of Highland beauty. It was bounded on one side by a 'burn',[45] whose torrent rushed far down between lofty steep banks clothed with natural wood, ash, birch, hazel, oak, and rowan-tree,

and poured its dark moss-water over a series of falls, and through
deep pools, 'with beaded bubbles winking at the brim.' It was never
tracked along its margin by any human being, except herd-boys and
their companions, who swam the pools and clambered up the
banks, holding by the roots of trees, starting the kingfisher from his
rock, or the wild cat from his den. On the other side of the glebe
was the sea, with here a sandy beach, and there steep rocks and deep
water; small grey islets beyond;[46] with many birds, curlews, cranes,
divers, and gulls of all sorts, giving life to the rocks and shores.
Along the margin of the sea there stretched such a flat of green
grass as suggested the name which it bore, of 'the Duke of Argyle's
walk'.[47] And pacing along that green margin at evening, what
sounds and wild cries were heard of piping sea-birds, chaffing
waves, the roll of oars, and the song from the fishingboats, which
told of their return home. The green terrace-walk which fringed
the sea was but the outer border of a flat that was hemmed in by the
low precipice of the old upraised beach of Scotland. Higher still was
a second storey of green fields and emerald pastures, broken by a
lovely rocky knoll, called Fingal's Hill, whose grey head, rising out
of green grass, bent towards the burn, and looked down into its
own image reflected in the deep pools which slept at its feet.[48] On
that upper table-land, and beside a clear stream, stood the manse
and garden sheltered by trees. Beyond the glebe began the dark
moor, which swept higher and higher, until crowned by the
mountain-top of which I have already spoken, which looked away
to the Western Islands and to the peaks of Skye.

The minister, like most of his brethren, soon took to himself a
wife, the daughter of a neighbouring 'gentleman tacksman', and the
grand-daughter of a minister, well born, and well bred; and never
did man find a help more meet for him.[49] In that manse they both
lived for nearly fifty years, and his wife bore him sixteen children;
yet neither father nor mother could ever lay their hand on a child
of theirs and say, 'We wish this one had not been.'[50] They were all a
source of unmingled joy to them.

A small farm was added to the glebe, for it was found that the
machinery required to work sixty acres of arable and pasture land
could work more with the same expense.[51] Besides, John Duke of
Argyle made it a rule at that time to give farms at less than their

value to the ministers on his estates; and why, therefore, should not our minister, with his sensible, active, thrifty wife, and growing sons and daughters, have a small one, and thus secure for his large household abundance of food, including milk and butter, cheese, potatoes, meal, with the excellent addition of mutton, and sometimes beef too? And the good man did not attend to his parish worse when his living was thus bettered; nor was he less cheerful or earnest in duty when in his house 'there was bread enough and to spare'.

The manse and glebe of that Highland parish were a colony which ever preached sermons, on week days as well as on Sundays, of industry and frugality, and the domestic peace, contentment and cheerfulness of a holy Christian home. Several cottages were built by the minister and clustered in sheltered nooks near his dwelling. One or two were inhabited by labourers and shepherds; another by the weaver, who made all the carpets, blankets, plaids and finer webs of linen and woollen cloths required for the household; and another by old Jenny, the hen-wife, herself like an old hen, waddling about and *chuckling* among her numerous family of poultry. Old Rory, with his wife and family, was located near the shore, to attend at spare hours to fishing, as well as to be ready with the boat for the use of the minister in his pastoral work.[52] Two or three cottages besides these were inhabited by objects of charity, whose claims upon the family it was difficult to trace. An old sailor had settled down in one, but no person could tell anything about him, except that he had been born in Skye, had served in the navy, had fought at the Nile, had no end of stories for winter evenings, and spinned yarns about the wars and 'foreign parts'. He had come long ago in distress to the manse, from whence he had passed after a time into the cottage, and there lived a dependant on the family until he died twenty years afterwards. A poor decayed gentlewoman, connected with one of the old families of the county, and a tenth cousin of the minister's wife, had also cast herself in her utter loneliness, like a broken wave, on the glebe. She had intended to remain only a few days – she did not like to be troublesome – but she knew she could rely on a relation, and she found it hard to leave, for whither could she go? And those who had taken her in never thought of bidding this sister 'depart in peace, saying, Be ye clothed'; and so she became a neighbour to the sailor, and was always called 'Mrs' Stewart, and was treated with the utmost delicacy and respect, being fed, clothed and warmed in her cottage with the best which the manse could afford; and when she died, she was dressed in a shroud fit for a lady, and tall candles, made for the occasion according to the old custom, were kept lighted round her body. Her funeral was becoming the gentle blood that flowed in her veins; and no one was glad in their heart when she departed, but they sincerely wept, and thanked God she had lived in plenty and had died in peace.[53]

Within the manse the large family of sons and daughters managed, somehow or other, to accommodate not only themselves, but to find permanent rooms also for a tutor and governess; and such a thing as turning any one away from want of room was never dreamt of. When hospitality demanded such a small sacrifice, the boys would all go to the barn, and the girls to the chairs and sofas of parlour and dining-room, with fun and laughter, joke and song, rather than not make the friend or stranger welcome. And seldom was the house without either. The 'kitchen end', or lower house, with all its indoor crannies of closets and lofts, and outdoor additions of cottages, barns and stables, was a little world of its own, to which wandering pipers, parish fools, the parish post, and beggars, with all sorts of odd-and-end characters, came, and where they ate, drank and rested. As a matter of course, the 'upper house' had its own set of guests to attend to. The traveller by sea, whom adverse winds and tides drove into the harbour for refuge; or the traveller by land; or any minister passing that way; or friends on a visit; or, lastly and but rarely, some foreign 'Sassenach' from the Lowlands of Scotland or England, who dared then to explore the unknown and remote Highlands as one now does Montenegro, or the Ural Mountains – all these found a hearty reception.

One of the most welcome visitors was the packman. His arrival was eagerly longed for by all, except the minister, who trembled for his small purse in presence of the prolific pack. For this same pack often required a horse for its conveyance. It contained a choice selection of everything which a family was likely to require from the lowland shops. The haberdasher and linen-draper, the watchmaker and jeweller, the cutler and hairdresser, with sundry other crafts in the useful and fancy line, were all fully represented in the endless repositories of the pack. What a solemn affair was the opening up of that peripatetic warehouse! It took a few days to gratify the inhabitants of manse and glebe, and to enable them to decide how their money should be invested. The boys held sundry councils about knives, and the men about razors, silk handkerchiefs, or, it may be, about the final choice of a silver watch. The servants were in nervous agitation about some bit of dress. Ribbons, like rainbows, were unrolled; prints held up in graceful folds before the light; cheap shawls were displayed on the back of some handsome lass, who served as a model. There never was seen such new fashions or such cheap bargains! And then how 'dear papa' was coaxed by mamma; and mamma again by her daughters. Everything was so beautiful, so tempting, and was discovered to be so necessary! All this time the packman, who was often of the stamp of him whom Wordsworth has made illustrious, was treated as a friend; while the news, gathered on his travels, was as welcome to the minister as his goods were to his family. No one in the upper house was so vulgar as to screw him down, but felt it due to his respectability to give him his own price, which, in justice to those worthy old merchants, I should state was always reasonable.

The manse was the grand centre to which all the inhabitants of the parish gravitated for help and comfort.[54] Medicines for the sick were weighed out from the chest yearly replenished in Glasgow. They were not given in homeopathic doses, for Highlanders, accustomed to things on a large scale, would have had no faith in globules, and faith was half their cure. Common sense and common medicines were found helpful to health. The poor, as a matter of course, visited the manse, not for an order on public charity, but for aid from private charity, and it was never refused in kind, such as meal, wool, or potatoes. As there were no lawyers in the parish, lawsuits were adjusted in the manse; and so were marriages not a few. The distressed came there for comfort, and the perplexed for advice; and there was always something material as well as spiritual to share with them all. No one went away empty in body or soul. Yet the barrel of meal was never empty, nor the cruise of oil extinguished.[55] A 'wise' neighbour once remarked: 'that minister with his large family will ruin himself, and if he dies they will be beggars.' Yet there has never been a beggar among them to the fourth generation. No 'saying' was more common in the mouth of this servant than the saying of his Master, 'It is more blessed to give than to receive.'

One characteristic of that manse life was its constant cheerfulness. One cottager could play the bagpipe, another the violin. The minister was an excellent performer on the violin, and a dance in the evening by his children was his delight. If strangers were present, so much the better. He had not an atom of that proud fanaticism which connects virtue with suffering, as suffering, apart from its cause.*

Here is an extract from a letter written by the minister in his old age, some fifty years ago, which gives a very beautiful picture of the secluded manse and its ongoings.[57] It is written at the beginning of a new year, in reply to one which he had received from his first-born son,[58] then a minister of the Church:

> What you say about the beginning of another year is quite true. But, after all, may not the same observations apply equally well to every new day? Ought not daily mercies to be acknowledged, and God's favour and protection asked for every new day? And are we not as ignorant of what a new day as of what a new year may bring forth? There is nothing in nature to make this day in itself more worthy of attention than any other. The sun rises and sets on it as on other days, and the sea ebbs and flows. Some come into the world and some leave it, as they did yesterday and will do tomorrow. On what day may not one say I am a year older than I was this day last year? Still I must own that the first of the year speaks to me in a more commanding and serious language than any other common day; and the great clock of time, which announced the first hour of this year, did not strike unnoticed by us.
>
> The sound was too loud to be unheard and too solemn to pass away unheeded. '*Non obtusa adio gestamus Pectora boni.*' We in the manse did

---

* A minister in a remote island parish once informed me that, 'on religious grounds', he had broken the only fiddle in the island.[56] His notion of religion, we fear, is not rare among his brethren in the far west and north. We are informed by Mr Campbell, in his admirable volumes on the *Tales of the Highlands*, that the old songs and tales are also being put under the clerical ban in some districts, as being too secular and profane for their pious inhabitants. What next? Are the singing birds to be shot by the kirk sessions?

not mark the day by any unreasonable merriment. We were alone, and did eat and drink with our usual innocent and cheerful moderation. I began the year by gathering all in the house and on the glebe to prayer. Our souls were stirred up to bless and to praise the Lord: for what more reasonable, what more delightful duty than to show forth our gratitude and thankfulness to that great and bountiful God from whom we have our years, and days, and all our comforts and enjoyments. Our lives have been spared till now; our state and conditions in life have been blessed; our temporal concerns have been favoured; the blessing of God co-operated with our honest industry; our spiritual advantages have been great and numberless; we have had the means of grace and the hope of glory; in a word, we have had all that was requisite for the good of our body and soul; and shall not our souls and all that is within us, all our powers and faculties, be stirred up to bless and praise His name!

But to return. This pleasant duty being gone through, refreshments were brought in, and had any of your clergy seen the crowd (say thirty, great and small, besides the family of the manse) they would pity the man who, under God, had to support them all! This little congregation being dismissed, they went to enjoy themselves. They entertained each other by turns. In the evening, I gave them one end of the house, while they danced and sang with great glee and good manners till near day. We enjoyed ourselves in a different manner in the other end. Had you popped in unnoticed, you would see us all grave, quiet and studious. You would see your father reading *The Seasons*; your mother, *Porteous' Lectures*; your sister Anne, *The Lady of the Lake*; and Archy, *Tom Thumb*![59]

Your wee son[60] was a new and great treat to you in those bonny days of rational mirth and joy, but not a whit more so than you were to me at his time of life, nor can he be more so during the years to come. May the young gentleman long live to bless and comfort you! May he be to you what you have been and are to me! I am the last that can honestly recommend you not to allow him to get too strong a hold of your heart, or rather not to allow yourself to *doat too much* upon him. This was a peculiar weakness of my own, and of which I had cause more than once to repent with much grief and sore affliction.[61] But your mother's creed always was (and truly she has acted up to it) to enjoy and delight in the blessings of the Almighty while they were spared to her with a thankful and grateful heart, and to part with them, when it was the will of the gracious Giver to remove them, with humble submission and meek resignation.'

We shall have something more to say in a coming chapter about this pastor and his work in the parish.

Chapter 3

THE BOYS OF THE MANSE AND
THEIR EDUCATION

Life went a-maying
With Nature, Hope, and Poesy
When I was young!
When I was young? – Ah! woeful when?

COLERIDGE

The old minister had no money to leave his boys when he died, and so he wisely determined to give them, while he lived, the treasure of the best education in his power. The first thing necessary for the accomplishment of his object was to obtain a good tutor, and a good tutor was not difficult to get.

James, as we shall call the tutor of the manse boys, was a laborious student, with a most creditable amount of knowledge of the elements of Greek and Latin.[62] When at college he was obliged to live in the top storey of a high house in a murky street, breathing an atmosphere of smoke, fog and gas; cribbed in a hot, close room; feeding on ill-cooked meat (fortunately in small quantities); drinking 'coffee', half water, half chicory; sitting up long after midnight writing essays or manufacturing exercises, until at last dyspepsia depressed his spirits and blanched his visage, except where it was coloured by a hectic flush, which deepened after a fit of coughing. When he returned home after having carried off prizes in the Greek or Latin classes, what cared his mother for all these honours? No doubt she was 'prood o' oor James', but yet she could hardly know her boy, he had become so pale, so haggard, and so unlike 'himsel''. What a blessing for James to get off to the Highlands! He there breathed such air, and drank such water as made him wonder at the bounty of creation without taxation. He climbed the hills and dived into the glens, and rolled himself on the heather; visited old castles, learned to fish, and perhaps to shoot, shutting both eyes at first when he pulled the trigger. He began to write verses, and to fall in love with one or all of the young ladies. That was the sort of life which Tom Campbell the poet passed when sojourning in the West Highlands;[63] ay, for a time in this very parish too, where the lovely spot is yet pointed out as the scene of his solitary musings. James had a great delight not only in imparting the rudiments of language, but also in opening up various high roads and outlying fields of knowledge. The intellectual exercise braced himself, and delighted his pupils.

If ever 'muscular Christianity' was taught to the rising generation, the Highland manse of these days was its gymnasium. After school hours, and on 'play-days' and Saturdays, there was no want of employment calculated to develop physical energy. The glebe and farm made a constant demand for labour which it was joy to the boys to afford. Every season brought its own appropriate and interesting work. But sheep-clipping, the reaping and ingathering of the crops, with now and then the extra glory of a country market for the purchase, and sale of cattle; with tents, games, gingerbread, horse jockeys, and English cattle dealers – these were their great annual feasts,

The grander branches of education were fishing, sailing, shooting – game laws being then unknown – and also what was called 'hunting'.[64] The fishing I speak of was not with line and fly on river or lake, though that was in abundance; but it was sea-fishing with rod and white fly for 'Saith', and mackerel in their season. It was delightful towards evening to pull for miles to the fishing ground in company with other boats. A race was sure to be kept up both going and returning, while songs arose from all hands and from every boat, intensifying the energy of the rowers. Then there was the excitement of getting among a great play of fish, which made the water foam for half a mile round, and attracted flocks of screaming birds who seemed mad with gluttony, while six or seven rods had all at the same time their lines tight, and their ends bent to cracking with the sport, keeping every fisher hard at work pulling in the fine lithe creatures, until the bottom of the boat was filled with scores. Sometimes the sport was so good as to induce a number of boats' crews to remain all night on a distant island, which had only a few sheep, and a tiny spring of water. The boats were made fast on the lee side, and their crews landed to wait

for daybreak. Then began the fun and frolic! – 'skylarking', as the
sailors call it, among the rocks – pelting one another with clods and
wrack, or any harmless substance which could be collected for the
battle, amidst shouts of laughter, until they were wearied, and lay
down to sleep in a sheltered nook, and all was silent but the beating
wave, the 'eerie' cries of birds, and the splash of some sea-monster in
pursuit of its prey. What glorious reminiscences have I, too, of those
scenes, and specially of early morn, as watched from those green
islands.[65] It seems to me as if I had never beheld a true sunrise since;
yet how many have I witnessed! I left the sleeping crews, and
ascended the top of the rock, immediately before daybreak, and
what a sight it was, to behold the golden crowns which the sun
placed on the brows of the mountain monarchs who first did him
homage; what heavenly dawnings of light on peak and scaur, contrasted with the darkness of the lower valleys; what gems of glory in
the eastern sky, changing the cold, grey clouds of early morning into
bars of gold and radiant gems of beauty; and what a flood of light
suddenly burst upon the dancing waves, as the sun rose above the
horizon, and revealed the silent sails of passing ships; and what delight to see and hear the first break of the fish on the waters! With
what pleasure I descended, and gave the cheer which made every
sleeper awake and scramble to their boats, and in a few minutes
resume the work of hauling in our dozens! Then home with a will
for breakfast – each striving to be first on the sandy shore!

Fishing at night with the drag-net was a sport which cannot be
omitted in recording the enjoyments of the manse boys. The spot
selected was a rocky bay, or embouchure of a small stream. The
night was generally dark and calm. The pleasure of the occupation
was made up of the pull, often a long one, within the shadow of the
rocky shore, with the calm sea reflecting the stars in the sky, and
then the slow approach, with gently moving oars, towards the
beach, in order not to disturb the fish; the wading up to the middle
to draw in the net when it had encircled its prey; and the excitement as it was brought into shallow water, the fish shining with
their phosphoric light, until, at last, a grand haul of salmon-trout,
flounders, small cod, and lythe, lay walloping in the folds of the net
upon the sandy beach.

Those fishing excursions, full of incident as they were, did not fully test or develop the powers of the boys. But others were afforded capable of doing so. It was their delight to accompany their father on any boating journey which the discharge of his pastoral duties required. In favourable weather they had often to manage the boat themselves without any assistance. When the sky was gloomy, old Rory took the command. Such of my readers as have had the happiness – or the horror, as their respective tastes may determine – to have sailed among the Hebrides in an open boat, will be disposed to admit that it is a rare school for disciplining its pupils when patient and conscientious to habits of endurance, foresight, courage, decision, and calm self-possession. The minister's boat was about eighteen feet keel, undecked, and rigged fore and aft.[66] There were few days in which the little *Roe* would not venture out, with Rory at the helm; and with no other person would his master divide the honour of being the most famous steersman in those waters. But to navigate her across the wild seas of that stormy coast demanded 'a fine hand' which could only be acquired after years of constant practice, such as a rider for the Derby prides in, or a whipper-in during a long run across a stiff country. If Rory would have made a poor jockey, what jockey would have steered the *Roe* in a gale of wind? I can assure the reader it was a solemn business, and solemnly was it gone about! What care in seeing the ropes in order, the sails reefed, the boys in their right place at the fore and stern sheets, and everything made snug! And what a sight it was to see that old man when the storm was fiercest, with his one eye, under its shaggy grey brow, looking to windward, sharp, calm, and luminous as a spark; his hand clutching the tiller, never speaking a word, and displeased if any other broke the silence, except the minister who sat beside him, assigning this post of honour as a great favour to Rory, during the trying hour! That hour was generally when wind and tide met, and 'gurly grew the sea',[67] whose green waves rose with crested heads, hanging against the cloud-rack, and sometimes concealing the land; while black sudden squalls, rushing down from the glens, struck the foaming billows in fury, and smote the boat, threatening, with a sharp scream, to tear the tiny sail in tatters, break the mast, or blow out of the water the small dark speck that carried the manse treasures. There was one moment of peculiar difficulty and concentrated danger when the hand of a master was needed to save them. The boat had entered the worst part of the tideway. How ugly it looks. Three seas higher than the rest are coming; and you can see the squall blowing their white crests into smoke. In a few minutes they will be down on the *Roe*. 'Look out, Ruari!' whispers the minister. 'Stand by the sheets!' cries Rory to the boys, who, seated on the ballast, gaze on him like statues, watching his face, and eagerly listening in silence. 'Ready!' is their only reply. Down come the seas rolling, rising, breaking; falling, rising again, and looking higher and fiercer than ever. The tide is running like a race-horse, and the gale meets it; and these three seas appear now to rise like huge pyramids of green water, dashing their foam up into the sky. The first may be encountered and overcome, for the boat has good way upon her; but the others will rapidly follow up the thundering charge and shock, and a single false movement of the helm by a hair's-breadth will bring down a cataract like Niagara that would shake a frigate, and sink the *Roe* into the depths like a stone. The boat meets the first wave, and rises dry over it. 'Slack out the main sheet, quick, and hold hard; there – steady!' commands Rory in a low firm voice, and the huge back of the second wave is seen breaking to leeward. 'Haul in, boys, and belay!' Quick as lightning the little craft, having again gathered way, is up in the teeth of the wind, and soon is spinning over the third topper, not a drop of water having come over the lee gunwale. 'Nobly done, Rory!' exclaims the minister, as he looks back to the fierce tideway which they have passed. Rory smiles with satisfaction at his own skill, and quietly remarks of the big waves, 'They have *their* road, and I have mine!' 'Hurrah for the old boat!' exclaims one of the boys. Rory repeats his favourite aphorism – yet never taking his eye off the sea and sky – 'Depend on it, my lads, it is not boats that drown the men, but men the boats!' I take it that the old *Roe* was no bad school for boys who had to battle with the storms and tides of life. I have heard one of those boys tell, when old and grey-headed, and after having encountered many a life storm, how much he had owed to those habits of mind which had been strengthened by his sea life with old Rory.

The 'hunting' I have alluded to as affording another branch of outdoor schooling was very different from what goes under that sporting term in the south. It was confined chiefly to wild cats and otters.[68] The animals employed in this work were terriers. The two terriers of the manse were Gasgach or Hero, and Cuilag or Fly. They differed very considerably in character: Gasgach was a large terrier with wiry black and grey hairs; Cuilag was of a dusky brown, and so small that she could be carried in the pocket of a shooting jacket. Gasgach presumed not to enter the parlour, or to mingle with genteel society; Cuilag always did so, and lay upon the hearth rug, where she basked and reposed in state. Gasgach was a sagacious, prudent, honest police sergeant, who watched the house day and night, and kept the farm dogs in awe, and at their respective posts. He was also a wonderful detective of all beggars, rats, fumarts,[69] wild cats, and vermin of every kind, smelling afar off the battle with man or beast. Cuilag was full of *reticence,* and seemed to think of nothing or do nothing until *seriously* wanted; and then indomitable courage started from every hair in her body. Both had seen constant service since their puppyhood, and were covered with honourable scars from the nose to the tip of the tail; each cut being the record of a battle, and the subject of a story by the boys.

The otters in the parish were both numerous, large, and fierce. There was one famous den called 'Clachoran', or the otter's stone, composed of huge rocks, from which the sea wholly receded during spring tides.[70] Then was the time to search for its inhabitants. This was done by the terriers driving the otter out, that he might be shot while making his way across a few yards of stone and tangle to the sea. I have known nine killed in this one den during a single year. But sometimes the otter occupied a den a few hundred yards inland, where a desperate fight ensued between him and the dogs. Long before the den was reached, the dogs became nervous and impatient, whining, and glancing up to the face of their master, and, with anxious look, springing up and licking his hands. To let them off until quite close to the den was sure to destroy the sport, as the otter would, on hearing them bark, make at once for the sea. Gasgach could, without difficulty, be kept in the rear, but little Cuilag, conscious of her moral weakness to resist temptation, begged to be carried. Though she made no struggle to escape, yet she trembled with eagerness, as, with cocked ears and low cry, she looked out for the spot where she and Gasgach would be set at liberty. That spot reached – what a hurry-scurry, as off they rushed to the den, and sprang in! Gasgach's short bark was a certain sign that the enemy was there; it was the first shot in the battle. If Cuilag followed, the battle had begun. One of the last great battles fought by Cuilag was in that inland den. On gazing down between two rocks which below met at an angle, there, amidst fierce barkings and the muffled sound of a fierce combat, Cuilag's head and the head of a huge otter were seen alternately appearing, as the one tried to seize the throat, and the other to inflict a wound on his little antagonist. At last Cuilag made a spring, and seized hold of the otter about the nose or lip. A shepherd who was present, fearing the dog would be cut to pieces, since the den was too narrow to admit Gasgach (who seemed half apoplectic with passion and inability to force his way in), managed, by a great effort, to get hold of the otter's tail, and to drag him upwards through a hole like a chimney. The shepherd was terrified that the otter, when it got its head out, would turn upon him and bite him – and such a bite as those beautiful teeth can give! – but to his astonishment the brute appeared with Cuilag hanging to the upper lip. Both being flung on the grass, Gasgach came to the rescue, and very soon, with some aid from the boys, the animal of fish and fur was killed and brought in triumph to the manse.

There is a true story about Cuilag which is worth recording. The minister, accompanied by Cuilag, went to visit a friend, who lived sixty miles off in a direct line from the manse. To reach him he had to cross several wild hills, and five arms of the sea or freshwater lochs stretching for miles. The dog, on arriving at her destination, took her place, according to custom, on the friend's hearthrug, from which, however, she was ignominiously driven by a servant, and sent to the kitchen. She disappeared, and left no trace of her whereabouts. One evening, about a fortnight afterwards, little Cuilag entered the manse parlour, worn down to a skeleton, her paws cut and swollen, and she hardly able to crawl to her master, or to express her joy at meeting all her dear old friends once more. Strange to say, she was accompanied into the room by Gasgach, who, after frolicking about, seemed to apologise for the liberty he took, and bolted out to bark over the glebe, and tell the other dogs who had gathered round what had happened. How did Cuilag discover the way home since she had never visited that part of the country before? How did she go round the right ends of the lochs, which had been all crossed by boat on their journey, and then recover her track, travelling twice or thrice sixty miles? How did she live? These were questions which no one could answer, seeing Cuilag was silent. She never, however, recovered that two weeks' wilderness journey. Her speed was ever after less swift, and her grip less firm.[71]

The games of the boys were all athletic – throwing the hammer, putting the stone, leaping, and the like. Perhaps the most favourite game was the 'shinty', called hockey, I believe, in England. This is played by any number of persons, one hundred often engaging in it. Each has a stick bent at the end, and made short or long, as it is to be used by one or both hands. The largest and smoothest field that can be found is selected for the game. The combat lies in the attempt of each party to knock a small wooden ball beyond a certain boundary in his opponent's ground. The ball is struck by any one on either side who can get at it. Few games are more exciting, or demand more physical exertion than a good shinty match.

I have said nothing regarding a matter of more importance than anything touched upon in this chapter, and that is the religious education of the manse boys. But there was nothing so peculiar about it as to demand special notice. It was very real and genuine; and perhaps its most distinguishing feature was that instead of its being confined to tasks, and hard, dry, starched Sundays only, it was spread over all the week, and consisted chiefly in developing the domestic affections by a frank, loving, sympathising intercourse between parents and children; by making home happy to the 'bairns'; by training them up wisely and with *tact*, to reverence *truth* – truth in word, deed, and manner; and to practise *unselfishness* and courteous considerateness towards the wants and feelings of others. These and many other minor lessons were never separated from Jesus Christ, the source of all life. They were taught to know Him as the Saviour, through whose atonement their sins were pardoned, and through whose grace alone, obtained daily in prayer, they could be made like Himself. The teaching was real, and was felt by the boys to be like sunshine on dew, warming, refreshing, and quickening their young hearts; and not like a something forced into the mind, with which it had no sympathy, as a leaden ball is rammed down into a gun-barrel. Once I heard an elderly Highland gentleman say that the first impression he ever received of the reality of religion was in connection with the first death which occurred among the manse boys.[72]

Need I add, in conclusion, that the manse was a perfect paradise for a boy during his holidays! Oh, let no anxious mother interfere at such times with loving grandmother and loving aunts or uncles! No doubt there is a danger that the boy may be 'spoilt'. In spite of the Latin or Greek lesson which his grandpapa or the tutor delights to give him in the morning, his excellent parents write to say that 'too much idleness may injure him'.

Not a bit! The boy is drinking in love with every drink of warm milk given him by the Highland dairymaid, and with every look, and kiss, and gentle hug given him by his dear grannie or aunts. Education, if it is worth anything, draws out as much as it puts in; and this sort of education will strengthen his brain and brace his nerves for the work of the town grammar school, to which he must soon return.

'It does not do to pamper him too much, it may make him selfish,' also write his parents. Quite true as an educational axiom; but his grandmother denies – bless her for it, dear, good woman! – that giving him milk or cream *ad libitum,* with 'scones' and cheese at all hours, is pampering him.

And his aunts take him on their knee, and fondle him, and tell him stories, and sit beside him when he is in bed, and sing songs to him; and there is not a herd or shepherd but wishes to make him happy; and old Rory has him always beside him in the boat, and gives him the helm, and, in spite of the old hand holding the tiller behind the young one, persuades his 'darling', as he calls him, that it is he, the boy, who steers the boat.

Oh! sunshine of youth, let it shine on! Let love flow out fresh and full, unchecked by any rule but what love creates; pour thyself down without stint into the young heart; make his days of boyhood happy, for other days must come of labour and of sorrow, when the memory of those dear eyes, and clasping hands, and sweet caressings, will, next to the love of God from whence they flow, save the man from losing faith in the human heart, help to deliver him from the curse of selfishness, and be an Eden in his memory when driven forth into the wilderness of life.

Chapter 4

THE MANSE BOY SENT TO COLLEGE

It is a great era in most Scotch manses when one of the boys begins his college career. There is first the question of money — the importance of which, over the whole world, and among all races of men, is fully recognised. A large family and a small 'stipend' are not rare phenomena in the Highland manse,[73] and how to clothe, feed, and educate the 'bairns' often seems an insoluble problem. For they do grow so rapidly out of their clothes, and their appetites are so good, 'puir things', as Betty the nurse says. And the eldest girls are every day looking bonnier, as the same unbiased witness asserts, and they require something nice, no doubt; and the younger ones are such romps, and with such high spirits, that they require something which will not easily wear out; and then the boys! — how they wear their shoes, and destroy their clothes, and never think how they can be supplied with new ones. But somehow that most wonderful and most blessed angel in the house, the mother, manages to supply every want, without disturbing her husband at his sermon or in his sleep; and he, good man, seldom knows the genius of contrivance, and the wakeful hours, and the busy thoughts, and the alternate smiles and tears, and the personal self-denial by which, with little means, she accomplishes great ends. It has long been a part of my social creed that, as a rule, the wives are far greater than their husbands, one part of their greatness being that they never allow their husbands to suspect their own inferiority.

But to return to the old manse, and an older generation. When a boy had to go to college, the minister required to exercise all his faculties, and bring every power into play, to raise the necessary funds. What calculations as to what could be spared from his stipend; or how much could be raised from his barley or potato crop, from his cattle, or from his pigs even! Ah! he is now disturbed in his study, and in his sleep; yet the matter of twenty pounds would make him feel like a king — for his boy's sake. And such a boy! — just look at those eyes, as his parents see them, pure and innocent as a

mountain spring; and look at that head, like a granite rock, with
yellow fern drooping over it; and that mouth – oh, that it were
opened in the pulpit! The boy has the make of a grand man in him.
'But twenty pounds!' – the minister mutters in his dream, about
three in the morning, while his wife is staring at the moon then
shining into the room. In spite of every difficulty the good man
succeeds – God's strength is often perfected in his weakness and he
makes no complaint, and owes no man anything.

The night before the boy goes is a night to be remembered by
the family. What a packing of the few clothes! They are very few,
but good, homespun, durable, and blessed, for every thread has the
mark of love in it! What a numbering of shirts and stockings; what
directions about the tender and wise usage of them; what quiet,
confidential talk about the Bible, rolled up in a white handkerchief,
and put into a corner of the trunk; what an extra sobriety about the
family devotions, during which smothered sobs are heard, and a
universal blowing of noses from young brothers and sisters. And
then, on the morning of departure, there is not only the new trunk
to be seen to, with an address upon it which might do for a sign-
board, but a cheese, a 'crock' of butter, a mutton ham, kippered
salmon, and other provisions for use in the lodgings, with a few pots
of jam and jelly for sore throat – his mother says. And then the
parting with all, not forgetting the dogs, which follow to the water's
edge, and with their low whine strike a note in harmony with the
sorrow which all feel, though it is kept down by forced words of
cheer till the last moment. Soon the old manse is out of sight, and
an old world has departed with it, and a new world for good or evil
begun to the boy.

Our Scottish college system is as unlike that of England as the
Presbyterian Church system to the Episcopalian. Each is best suited,
as things are and have been, to their respective countries. The buildings in Glasgow College – soon to be swept away – are unchanged
from a period long antecedent to that in which the manse boy first
entered them. There is still the same old gate, in the dingy yet
solemn-looking walls, entering into the quiet courts, out of the
bustle of the High Street, with its filthy crowds of squalid men and
women, its ragged children, and besotted drunken creatures with
their idiotic looks, and whatever else combines to give to it a look

of vice and poverty, unsurpassed by any street in Europe. But once within the college gate, there are the same lecture rooms in which Adam Smith and Reid taught, and James Watt studied or experimented; and the same stone pavement, to me more sacred, from its peculiar associations with the long past, than the floor of almost any church in Europe.

The students attending our Scotch colleges live anywhere and in any way they please, in so far as the college authorities are concerned. The more respectable, yet certainly not very aristocratic, streets near the University have from time immemorial furnished lodgings to the students, from the flat over the shops up to the attics. A small room, with fire, cooking, attendance, etc., could be obtained for a few shillings weekly; and it was a common custom for the poorer students, for the sake of economy, to share both room and bed with a companion. The following extract from the college life of the eldest son of the manse, dictated, when he was fourscore years, to one of his daughters, as a portion of a domestic autobiography, will give a characteristic idea of the student life and its difficulties in those days, and such as was, and in some respects is still, familiar to not a few of those who have helped to make Scotland what she is:[74]

In November I went to Glasgow College, and the mode of travelling at that time is a strange contrast to the present. On a Monday morning Sandy M'Intyre, with two horses, was ferried across to Mull.[75] My father and I followed, and we got to the ferry of Auchnacraig, near Duart,[76] that night, where we had to remain for a couple of nights, the weather being too stormy for us to proceed. I have a very pleasing recollection of the kindness of our old host,[77] who, on parting, put a five-shilling piece into my pocket, the kindly custom of the time, while he laid his hand on my head and gave me a fatherly blessing. We next crossed to Kerrera, rode to the next ferry, and arrived at Oban in the course of the afternoon, Sandy accompanying us on foot. A pair of saddle-bags on each of our horses carried all our luggage. At Oban the 'Gobhain Sassenach', or English smith, a drunken wit and poet, was sent for to shoe our horses, which he promised to do immediately.[78] But when the horses were expected to be in readiness the 'Gobhain Sassenach' was drunk, so that we were compelled to remain for that night in Oban. Next day we proceeded to Tynuilt,[79] where the landlord met us at the door with a bottle of bitters. Sandy M'Intyre had arrived before us, having taken a short cut across the hill. After a short stay, we pushed on to Port Sonachan,[80] from thence to Inverary. On Saturday afternoon we came to Arrochar, and, having left Sandy and the horses at the inn, we walked to the manse, then occupied by an old college friend of my father's.[81] We found the good man in his study with his Concordance and Pulpit Bible before him, which, on recognising my father, he soon closed and put aside. Very hearty was the welcome which we received. My father preached there next day. On Monday morning we proceeded by Loch Long side and the Gair Loch to Roseneath. At that time there was on the shore of the Gair Loch, now studded with villas on both shores, but one or two houses, and little did I expect that I should ever possess a cottage there.[82] Leaving Sandy and the horses at Roseneath till my father's return and crossing over to Greenock, we reached the house of my grand-uncle, where we passed the night.[83] We arrived at Glasgow on Wednesday forenoon, having been ten days on a journey that can now be accomplished in twice as many hours. I was next morning enrolled as a student in the Latin class, taught at the time by Mr Richardson, a most amiable and accomplished man, whose memory I shall ever revere. I was boarded in a respectable family in the High Street, opposite the Cross, at the rate of twenty pounds in six months, and where I had the advantage of having two amiable and delightful companions.

My first session at college passed rapidly and most agreeably; and upon the evening of the 1st of May,[84] I took my departure for home with twenty shillings in my pocket, and carrying two shirts and two pairs of stockings in a bundle on my back, and with a good oak stick in my hand. I walked to Dumbarton that night, and got drenched to the skin. I was glad to take my place opposite to a large fire in the kitchen, where I dried the contents of my bundle, and made myself as comfortable as circumstances would permit. Having got some slight refreshment, I was shown to my room in the garret flat of the house, tenanted by rats. The waiter removed my shoes lest they should be eaten up! As might be supposed, my sleep was not very comfortable. I started at six next morning for Helensburgh. I was joined on the road by a man, who was followed by a beautiful English terrier, which I agreed to purchase from him for half-a-crown. He gave me a cord by which I could lead him on, but he assured me that I might in a very short time give him his liberty, which I did. Scarcely had I done so, when a loud and peculiar whistle, which the dog quickly recognised, announced to me that I had been swindled, for off set the terrier, and he and my half-crown were for ever lost! I walked on by the banks of the lovely Gair Loch, to the ferry on Loch Long, intending to proceed to Inverary by the Argyle bowling-green.[85] I was joined by a young man, who said that he was going the same way to Inverary. I was glad to have his company, as I had never before travelled across those hills. He ordered some refreshment for himself, but said that he had no change, and the landlord being unable to accommodate him, I paid for his refreshment, and for his share of the ferry. We got to Loch Goilhead, and found a cart proceeding to St Catherine's, and for the sum of sixpence each, I still paying for my companion, we crossed to Inverary. This young man was a most amusing fellow. He asked me to come to tea, and to sleep at his mother's house, giving me her name and place of residence, recommending me, in the meantime, to go to a hotel near, till he should call for me. To this day I have neither seen nor heard of my friend or of his mother. The hotel-keeper informed me afterwards that there was no such family at Inverary!

Early next morning I started for Port Sonachan, with eighteen pence still in my pocket. The inn and ferry at Port Sonachan were at that time kept by a man with whom I had been acquainted: he having at one time been a travelling packman, and in that capacity had made frequent visits to the manse. He received me most cordially, gave me breakfast, and ferried me across, refusing to accept any payment. I certainly did not urge his acceptance in very strong terms. I walked on with a light heart and still lighter purse, till I reached Tynault, where my food cost me a shilling. On leaving Tynault for Oban, I was deluged by a torrent of rain. I overtook a cart within four miles of Oban, and the driver had compassion on me, giving me a seat during the rest of my journey. He was singing an old Gaelic song, but had not the words correctly: fortunately, I was acquainted with them, and I gave him one of the most beautiful of all the verses, and one which he had never heard before. On parting from him, I told him that I was sorry I could not offer him anything for the drive. He said, ' I would not take a farthing though your pockets were full. I am richly rewarded with the beautiful verse which you have taught me.' At the hotel at Oban[86] I found young Maclean of Coll, with whom I was well acquainted.[87] He told me that he expected his barge, and would land me at my father's, meantime that I must be his guest. The barge arrived, and after a couple of days we sailed with fair wind and tide, and the old piper playing to us during the passage. Most joyful was I when once more I reached the manse, and many and affectionate were the salutations with which I was welcomed by its dear and numerous occupants.

Soon after my return, I joined the 'Volunteers', and had great pleasure in attending drill.[88]

There existed at that time a most loyal and martial spirit in the

Highlands, forming an extraordinary contrast to their present feelings as regards the army. There were then three regiments of 'fencibles' raised in the county of Argyle, who were considered the finest-looking men in the army sent to Ireland during the rebellion. Besides the company of Volunteers in each parish, I have still in my possession the names and designation of 110 officers, who held commissions in the army, and with each of whom I was personally acquainted.[89] Many of them were highly distinguished, and some attained to the rank of general officers; and, alas! very many of them perished during the war. I am not aware of a dozen from that country now in the army, and even some of these are on the retired list. I am unwilling to account for this melancholy change. I fear, however, that the clearances which, for years past, have most extensively taken place in these countries, have contributed in some degree to bring about this state of things; but also as likely the outlets afforded by commerce to young men, and the improved education of the country.

It was during the harvest of this year that I became an ardent sportsman, as also an enthusiastic boatman; and I must confess that I spent much more of my time in wandering over the mountains in quest of game, or in sailing on the Sound of Mull with old Rory, than at my classics.

I shall pass over the following sessions at college, as there were very few incidents worthy of remark. I generally lived in lodgings with some companion, having a small parlour and bedroom and truly I must say that we lived most sparingly and moderately. The expense of a session, including professors' fees and some new clothes, cost me from twenty-five to thirty pounds. During two of my last sessions at college in Glasgow, my cousin Neil Campbell,[90] a medical student, was my companion in lodgings, and during the last three months that we were in Glasgow, we had another medical student from the Highlands, of the name of M'Millan, living with us.[91] We were both much attached to this young man. He was obliged for want of funds to leave his lodgings, and had nearly starved himself before doing so. We insisted on his joining us in our room, which was then in the Stockwell; but this additional burden reduced us at times to great extremities, and had it not been for an excellent girl from Oban, who was serving in the house, I do not know what should have become of us.

We often took a walk to the Green, stating that we were to be out at dinner, and took some eggs and potatoes for supper when we returned. M'Millan was a young man of very superior talent, and an ardent student. When the session closed, he was enabled, through the kindness of some Highland gentlemen in Glasgow to whom his case had been made known, to obtain his diploma as surgeon, and he agreed to accompany me home.

He had not been with us above a week when his appointment as assistant-surgeon in the navy was announced to him. The letter which contained his appointment directed him, upon his passing his examination at the Surgeons' Hall, Edinburgh, to draw upon the Treasury for a certain sum of money, and to proceed to Edinburgh immediately. But what was to be done in the meantime? He had not a farthing, and not a moment could be lost. I could not advance him a pound. We told all the circumstances of the case to a carpenter in the parish, and he, with great generosity, advanced upon our mere verbal promise, four pounds, with which we proceeded to Tobermory, where that very evening we found a vessel sailing for Greenock, in which he took his passage.

I am glad to tell you he passed his examination in Edinburgh with éclat, remitted the money we had borrowed from the honest carpenter, and on his arrival in England was placed on board of a frigate, and the first letter I received from him was dated from Van Diemen's Land, of which we knew very little in those days.[92] The ship was on a voyage of discovery, and absent for many years.

Long after, when I was a parish minister, I remarked a stranger whose face interested me much, who waited for me at the, door of the church, and addressed me in very mournful accents in Gaelic, saying that the last sermon he had heard was from my father many years before. I asked his name. He burst into tears, and said, ' I came to see you. I have lost almost every friend I had in the world. I buried my wife and only child not many days ago. Ask for me at the inn, but you must pardon me in the meantime for concealing my name from the only person on earth from whom I expected sympathy.' He was greatly agitated. I assured him that I would go in the morning to see him, but all night I could think of little else than my interview with this mysterious stranger. On calling at the inn next morning, I found that this was my friend M'Millan. He had gone away by an early packet boat for Greenock, leaving a long and affectionate letter, giving me a brief but painful account of his own history since we parted, and stating that he was about to retire to some quiet country town in England, from which he would again write to me. I never heard of him afterwards. He is most honourably mentioned in an account published of the voyage of discovery on which he had been.

But to return to the story of my life at college. I recollect one Saturday night, when we had not one halfpenny among us, I discovered at the bottom of my trunk an otter's skin, with which Neil Campbell and I proceeded to a well-known shop at the head of King Street, and offered it for sale. The person at the counter named for it a sum that we considered far below its value, upon which the good shopkeeper himself came in from the back-shop, and told him that the sum he offered was too little, and, speaking to us with great kindness, he gave us at least a half more than its value. This to us at such a time was a treasure.

On one of those days we were asked to dine with old 'Barnicarry' at the 'Buck's Head'.[93] This generous man was uncle to my companion, and my grand-uncle. We received the message with great joy, as he usually gave us a donation of a guinea when he parted from us. In this hope we were not disappointed, and we returned home to poor M'Millan with great rejoicing, and had a comfortable supper.

Neil had two brothers at sea. Both of them commanded fine West Indiamen. One of them was in the habit of sending us sea biscuits and other articles, especially corned beef, which we liked much. One evening a loud rap came to the door. Our Oban woman went to open it, when we heard a half scream, that brought us to the lobby to see what the matter was. The porter entered, having on his back a pair of large canvas trousers filled with brown sugar, a leg hanging down on each side of his shoulder, which the poor girl supposed was a dead 'subject' for the medical students.[94] This sugar and a quantity of rice he brought along with it was of great service to us. Our kind servant-maid was permitted to take as much as she pleased for her own tea, and we gave several bowlfuls to our landlady. A poor student of the name of M'Gregor, from Lismore, also got a share.[95] This lad was an excellent scholar, and very superior in every way, but exceedingly poor. He lived in a small apartment at the back of a place where they baked oatcake. It was a very small room, containing a bed, a small table and stool, but without any fireplace. Here he contracted disease of the lungs, of which he soon after died. I felt a deep interest in him, and the night I parted from him he told me that he had been much indebted to me for my kindness to him, and that he wished to 'treat' me as expressive of his regard. He did not mention what 'the treat' was to consist of, but, knowing his inability, I objected to his putting himself to any expense on my account. He begged of me to wait for a few minutes, during which he purchased two halfpenny rolls, and, handing me one, he took the other greedily himself! In the course of a year I visited his grave in the island of Lismore, meditating with mournful reflections on the struggle that this most promising young man had made to obtain education enough to become a minister of the gospel. He was eminently pious, and much was I indebted to him for his kind guidance and Christian admonition.

Chapter 5

THE MANSE GIRLS AND THEIR EDUCATION

> Dost thou remember all those happy meetings,
> In summer evenings round the open door;
> Kind looks, kind words, and tender greetings
> From clasping hands, whose pulses beat no more –
> Dost thou remember them?

The manse girls were many.[96] They formed a large family, a numerous flock, a considerable congregation; or, as the minister expressed it in less exaggerated terms, 'a heavy handful'. One part of their education, as I have already noticed, was conducted by a governess. The said governess was the daughter of a 'governor', or commandant of one of the Highland forts – whether Fort Augustus or Fort William[97] I remember not – where he had for years reigned over a dozen rusty guns, and half as many soldiers, with all the dignity of a man who was supposed to guard the great Southern land against the outbreaks and incursions of the wild Highland clans, although, in truth, the said Highland clans had been long asleep in the old kirkyard 'amang the heather', for, as the song hath it:

> No more we'll see such deeds again,
> Deserted is the Highland glen,
> And mossy cairns are o'er the men
> Who fought and died for Charlie.[98]

The 'major' – for the commandant had attained that rank in the first American war – left an only daughter who was small and dumpy in stature, had no money, and but one leg. Yet was she most richly provided for otherwise with every womanly quality, and the power of training girls in 'all the branches' then considered most useful for sensible well-to-do women and wives. She was not an outsider in the family, or a mere teaching machine, used and valued like a mill or plough for the work done, but a member of the household, loved and respected for her own sake. She was so dutiful and kind that the beat of her wooden leg on the wooden stair became musical – a very beating of time with all that was best and happiest in her pupils' hearts. She remained for some years educating the younger girls, until a batch of boys broke the line of feminine succession, and then she retired for a time to teach one or more families in the neighbourhood. But no sooner was the equilibrium of the manse restored by another set of girls, than the little governess returned to her old quarters, and once more stumped through the schoolroom, with her happy face, wise tongue, and cunning hand.

The education of the manse girls was neither learned nor fashionable. They were taught neither French nor German, music nor drawing, while dancing as an art was out of the question – with the wooden leg as the only artist to teach it. The girls, however, were excellent readers, writers, and arithmeticians; and they could sew, knit, shape clothes, and patch to perfection. I need hardly say that they were their own and their mother's only dressmakers, and manifested wonderful skill and taste in making old things look new, and in so changing the cut and fashion of the purchases made long ago from the packman, that Mary's 'everlasting silk' or Jane's merino seemed capable of endless transformations; while their bonnets, by judicious turning, trimming and tasteful placing of a little bit of ribbon, looked always fresh and new.

Contrasted with an expensive and fashionable education, theirs will appear to have been poor and vulgar. Yet in the long course of years, I am not sure but the manse girls had the best of it. For one often wonders what becomes of all this fashionable education in the future life of the young lady. What French or German books does she read as a maid or matron? With whom does she, or can she, converse in these languages? Where is her drawing beyond the Madonna's heads and the Swiss landscape which she brought from school, touched up by the master? What music does she love and practise for the sake of its own beauty, and not for the sake of adding to the hum of the drawing-room after dinner? The manse girls could read and speak two languages, at least Gaelic and English. They could sing, too, their own Highland ditties: wild, but yet as musical as mountain streams and summer winds; sweet and melodious as song of thrush or blackbird in spring, going right to the heart of the listener, and from his heart to his brimming eyes.

And so I am ready to back the education of the poor manse against that of many a rich and fashionable mansion, not only as regards the ordinary 'branches', but much more as developing the mental powers of the girls. At all events, they acquired habits of reflective observation, with a capacity of thoroughly relishing books, enjoying Nature in all her varying scenes and moods, and of expressing their own thoughts and sentiments with such a freshness and force as made them most delightful members of society. A fashionable education, on the other hand, is often a mere tying on to a tree of a number of 'branches' without life, instead of being a developing of the tree itself, so that it shall bear its own branches loaded with beautiful flowers and clustering fruit.

But the manse school included more rooms than the little attic where the girls met around that familiar knot of wood which projected from beneath the neat calico of the major's daughter. The cheerful society of the house; the love of kindred − each heart being as a clear spring that sent forth its stream of affection with equable flow to refresh others − the innumerable requirements of the glebe and farm; the spinning and shearing; the work in laundry, kitchen, and dairy; the glorious outdoor exercise over field and moor, in the glens or by the shore; the ministrations of charity, not with its doled-out alms to beggars only, but with its 'kind words and looks and tender greetings' to the many cottagers around − these all were teachers in the Home School. And thus, partly from circumstances, partly, it must be acknowledged, from rare gifts of God bestowed upon them, they all grew up with a purity, a truthfulness, a love and gladness, which made the atmosphere of the manse one of constant sunshine. Each had her own strong individual character, like trees which grow free on the mountain side. They delighted in books, and read them with head and heart, undisturbed by the slang and one-sided judgments of hack critics. And it occasionally happened that some Southern friend, who in his wanderings through the Highlands enjoyed the hospitality of the manse, sent the girls a new volume of pleasant literature as a remembrance of his visit. These gifts were much valued, and read as volumes are seldom read nowadays. Books of good poetry especially were so often conned by them that they became as portions of their own thoughts.

The manse girls did not look upon life as a vain show, aimless and purposeless; upon everything and every person as 'a bore'; or upon themselves as an insupportable burden to parents and to brothers unless they got husbands! Choice wives they would have made, for both their minds and bodies had attractions not a few; and 'good offers', as they were called, came to them as to others. Young men had been 'daft' about them, and they were too sensible and womanly not to wish for a home they could call their own; yet it never crossed their thoughts that they must marry, just as one must get a pair of shoes. They never imagined that it was possible for any girl of principle and feeling to marry a man whom she did not love, merely because he had a number of sheep and cattle in a Highland farm; or had good prospects from selling tea and sugar in Glasgow; or had a parish as a minister, or a property as a 'laird'. Poor foolish creatures were they not to think so, without one farthing they could call their own; with no prospects from their father, the minister; with no possessions save what he had last purchased for them from the packman? What on earth would come of them or of their mother if the parson drowned some stormy night with Ruari and the *Roe*? Were they to be cast on the tender mercies of this or that brother who had a home over their heads? What, a brother to afford shelter to a sister or could they seriously intend to trust Providence for the future, if they only did His will for the present? Better far, surely, to accept the first good offer; snatch at the woolly hand of the large sheep-farmer, the sweet hand of the rich grocer, the thin, sermon-writing hand of the preacher; nay, let them take their chance even with James, the tutor, who has been sighing over each of them in turn! But no; like 'fools', they took for granted that it never could come wrong in the end to do what was right at the time, and so they never thought it to be absolutely incumbent on them to 'marry for marrying sake'. Neither father nor mother questioned the propriety of their conduct. And thus it came to pass that none of them, save one, who loved most heroically and most truly unto death, ever married.[99] The others became what married ladies and young expectants of that life-climax call – Old Maids.

But many a fireside, and many a nephew and niece, with the children of a second generation, blessed God for them as precious gifts.

I feel that no apology is required for quoting the following extract from a letter written by the pastor, more than sixty years ago, when some of the eldest of the manse girls left home for the first time. It will find, I doubt not, a response in the heart of many a pastor in similar circumstances:

It was, my dear, my very dear girls, at seven in the morning of Thursday, the 31st August, you took your departure from the old quay – that quay where often I landed in foul and fair weather, at night and by day; my heart always jumping before me, anticipating the happiness of joining the delightful group that formed my fireside – a group I may never see collected again. How happy the parents, the fewest in number, who can have their families within their reach! – happier still, when, like you, their families are to them a delight and comfort! You left the well-known shores, and your parents returned with heavy steps, the weight of their thoughts making their ascent to the manse much slower and harder to accomplish than ever they found it before. We sat on the hillside bathed in tears, giving many a kind and longing look to the wherry, which always went further from us, till our dim eyes, wearied of their exertions, could see nothing in its true state; when, behold, cruel Castle Duart[100] interrupted our view, and took out of our sight the boat that carried from us so much of our worldly treasure. Our thousand blessings be with our dear ones, we cried, and returned to the house – to the manse of ———;[101] a house where much comfort and happiness were always to be found; where the friend was friendly treated, and where the stranger found himself at home; where the distressed and the needy met with pity and kindness, and the beggar never went off without being supplied; where the story and the joke often cheered the well-pleased guests, and were often accompanied with the dance and the song, and all with an uncommon degree of elegance, cheerfulness and good humour. But with me these wonted scenes of merriment are now over. The violin and the song have no charms for me; the dance and the cheerful tale delight no more. But hold, minister! what mean you by these gloomy thoughts? Why disturb for a moment the happiness of the dear things you write to, and for whose happiness you so earnestly pray, by casting a damp upon their gay and merry hours? Cease, foolish, and tempt not Providence to afflict you! What! have you not many comforts to make you happy? Is not the friend of your bosom, the loving dutiful wife, and the loving dutiful mother, alive to bless and to comfort you? Is not your family, though somewhat scattered, all alive? Are they not all good and promising? None of them ever yet caused you to blush; and are not these great blessings? Are they not worthy of your most cheerful and grateful acknowledgments? They are, they are, and I bless God for His goodness. But the thought – I cannot provide for these! Take care, minister, that the anxiety of your affection does not unhinge that confidence with which the Christian ought to repose upon the wise and good providence of God! What though you are to leave your children poor and friendless? Is the arm of the Lord shortened that he cannot help? Is His ear heavy that He cannot hear? You yourself have been no more than an instrument in the hand of His goodness; and is His goodness, pray, bound up in your feeble arm? Do you what you can; leave the rest to God. Let them be good, and fear the Lord, and keep His commandments, and He will provide for them in His own way and in His own time. Why, then, wilt thou be cast down, O my soul; why disquieted within me? Trust thou in the Lord! Under all the changes and the cares and the troubles of this life, may the consolations of religion support our spirits. In the multitude of the thoughts within me, Thy comforts, O my God, delight my soul! But no more of this preaching-like harangue, of which, I doubt not, you wish to be relieved. Let me rather reply to your letter, and tell you my news.

It was after this period that he had to mourn the loss of many of his family. And then began for the manse girls the education within the school of sickness and death, whose door is shut against the intrusion of the noisy world, and into which no one can enter, except the Father of all, and 'the Friend who sticketh closer than a brother'.

The first break in a family is a solemn and affecting era in its history; most of all when that family is 'all the world' to its own members. The very thought – so natural to others who have suffered – that this one who has been visited by disease can ever become *dangerously* ill – can ever die – is by them dismissed as a dreadful nightmare. Then follow 'the hopes and fears that kindle hope, an undistinguishable throng'; the watchings which turn night into day, and day into night; the sympathy of sorrow which makes each mourner hide from others the grief that in secret is breaking the heart; the intense realisation, at last, of all that may be – ay, that must be – until the last hours come, and what these are they alone know who have loved and lost. What a mighty change does this first death make in a family, when it is so united, that if one member suffers all suffer! It changes everything. The old haunts by rock or stream can never be as they were; old songs are hushed for years, and if ever sung again, they are like walls for the dead; every room in the house seems, for a time, tenanted more by the dead than by the living; the books are theirs; the seat in church is not empty but occupied by them; plans and purposes, family arrangements and prospects, all seem for a time so purposeless and useless. No one ever calculated on this possibility! The trial which has come verily seems 'strange'. Yet this is, under God, a holy and blessed education. Lessons are then taught, 'though as by fire', which train all the scholars for a higher school. And if that old joyousness and hilarity pass away which belong to a world that seemed as if it could not change – like a very Eden before the Fall – it is succeeded by a deeper life; a life of faith and hope which find their rest in the unchanging rather than the changing present.

Such was the portion of the education which the pastor and his family received for many succeeding years in the old manse; but its memory was ever accompanied by thanksgiving for the true, genuine Christian life and death of those who had died. I need hardly say that the girls, more than the other members of the family, shared these sorrows and this discipline; for whatever men can do in the storm of ocean or battle, women are the ministering angels in the room of sickness and suffering.

Before I turn away from the manse girls, I must say something more of their little governess. She lingered long about the manse, as a valued friend, when her services were no longer needed. But she resolved at last to attempt a school in the low country, and to stamp some uneducated spot with the impress of the wooden knob. Ere doing so, she confided to the minister a story told her by her father, the fort-commandant, about some link or other which bound him to the Argyle family. What that link precisely was, no history records. It may have been that her mother was a Campbell, or that the major had served in a regiment commanded by some member of that noble house, or had picked an Argyle out of the trenches at

Ticonderoga.[102] Anyhow, the commandant fancied that his only
daughter would find a crutch of support, like many others, in 'the
Duke', if he only knew the story. Never up to this time was the
crutch needed; but needed it is now if she is to pursue her life journey in peace. Why not tell the story then to the Duke? quoth the
minister. Why not? thoughtfully ruminated the little governess. And
so they both entered the manse study – a wonderful little sanctum
of books and manuscripts, with a stuffed otter and wildcat, a gun,
compass, coil of new rope, the flag of the *Roe*, a print of the Duke
of Argyle, and of several old divines and reformers, in wigs and
ruffs. There the minister wrote out, with great care, a petition to the
Duke for one of the very many kind charities, in the form of small
annuities, which were dispensed by his Grace. The governess determined to present it in person in Inverary. But the journey thither
was then a very serious matter. To travel nowadays from London to
any capital on the Continent is nothing to what that journey was.
For it could only be done on horseback, and by crossing several
stormy ferries, as wide as the Straits of Dover.[103] The journey was at
last, however, arranged in this way. There lived in one of the many
cottages on the glebe a man called 'old Archy,' who had been a
servant in the family of the pastor's father-in-law.[104] Archy had long
ago accompanied, as guide and servant, the minister's wife, when
she went to Edinburgh for her education. Having been thus trained
to foreign travel, and his fame established as a thoroughly qualified
courier, he was at once selected to accompany, on horseback, the
governess to Inverary. That excellent woman did not, from nervous
anxiety, go to bed the night previous to her departure; and she had
laboured for a fortnight to produce a new dress in which to appear
worthily before the Duke. She had daily practised, moreover, the
proper mode of address, and was miserable from the conviction that
all would be ruined by her saying 'Sir', instead of 'Your Grace'. The
minister tried to laugh her out of her fears, and to cheer her by the
assurance that a better-hearted gentleman lived not than the good
Duke John; and that she must just speak to him as she felt. She
departed with her black trunk slung behind Archy; and also with
extraordinary supplies of cold fowls, mutton, ham, and cheese – not
to speak of letters commendatory to every manse on the road.
What farewells, and kissings, and waving of handkerchiefs, and

drying of eyes, and gathering of servants and dogs at the manse door as the governess rode off on the white horse, Archy following on the brown! The proper arrangement of the wooden leg had been a great mechanical and aesthetic difficulty, but somehow the girls, with a proper disposal of drapery, had made the whole thing quite apropos. Archy too had patched up a saddle of wonderful structure for the occasion.

Time passed, and in a fortnight, to the joy of the household, the white mare was seen coming over the hill with the brown following; and soon the governess was once more in the arms of her friends, and the trunk in those of Archy. Amidst a buzz of questions, the story was soon told with much flutter and some weeping how she had met the Duke near the castle; how she had presented her petition, while she could not speak; how his Grace had expressed his great regard for 'his minister'; and how next day, when she called by appointment, he had signified his intention of granting the annuity.

'It is like himself', was the minister's only remark, while his eyes seemed fuller than usual as he congratulated the little governess on her success; and gave an extra bumper, with many a compliment, to old Archy for the manner in which he had guided the horses and their riders. The little governess taught a school for many years, and enjoyed her annuity till near ninety. During her last days, she experienced the personal kindness and tender goodness of the present 'Argyle', as she had long ago done of the former 'Argyles'.

Chapter 6

THE MINISTER AND HIS WORK

A genuine priest,
The shepherd of his flock; or, as a king
Is styled, when most affectionately praised,
The father of his people. Such is he;
And rich and poor, and young and old, rejoice
Under his spiritual sway.

When his course
Is run, some faithful eulogist may say
He sought not praise, and praise did overlook.
His unobtrusive merit; but his life,
Sweet to himself, was exercised in good
That shall survive his name and memory.

WORDSWORTH

In Dr Macculloch's *Tour to the Highlands of Scotland*[105] we have the most perfect and eloquent descriptions of scenery, but in Dr Johnson's, the truest yet most complimentary delineations of the character and manners of the people.[106] The physical features of the country are, no doubt, abiding, while its social condition is constantly changing, so that we can nowadays more easily recognise the truth of the sketches by the former than by the latter tourist. But the minister of whom I write, and the manners of his time, belonged to the era of Johnson, and not to that of Macculloch.[107]

There is something, by the way, peculiarly touching in that same tour of the old Doctor's, when we remember the tastes and habits of the man, with the state of the country at the time in which he visited it. Unaccustomed to physical exercise, obese in person and shortsighted in vision, he rode along execrable roads; and on a Highland shelty,[108] cautiously felt his way across interminable morasses. He had no means of navigating those stormy seas but an open boat, pulled by sturdy rowers, against wetting spray, or tacking from morning till night amidst squalls, rain, and turbulent tideways. He had to put up in wretched pothouses, sleeping as he did at Glenelg, 'on a bundle of hay, in his riding-coat; while Boswell, being more delicate, laid himself in sheets, with hay over and above him, and lay in linen like a gentleman'. In some of the best houses, he found but clay floors below and peat-reek around, and nowhere did he find the luxuries of his own favourite London. Yet he never growls or expresses one word of discontent or peevishness. Whether this was owing to his having for the first time escaped the conventionalities of city life; or to the fact of the Highlands being then the last stronghold of Jacobinism; or to the honour and respect which was everywhere shown towards himself; or, what is more probable, to the genial influence of fresh air and exercise upon his phlegmatic constitution, banishing its 'bad humours' – in whatever way we may account for it, so it was that he encountered every difficulty and discomfort with the greatest cheerfulness; partook of the fare given him and the hospitality afforded to him with hearty gratitude; and has written about every class of the people with the generous courtesy of a well-bred English gentleman.

His opinion of the Highland clergy is not the least remarkable of his 'testimonies', considering his intense love of Episcopacy, and its forms of public worship, with his sincere dislike of Presbyterianism. 'I saw', he says, writing of the clergy, 'not one in the Islands whom I had reason to think either deficient in learning or irregular in life, but found several with whom I could not converse without wishing, as my respect increased, that they had not been Presbyterians.' Moreover, in each of the distant islands which the Doctor visited, he met ministers with whom even he was able to have genial and scholarly conversation. 'They had attained', he says, 'a knowledge as may be justly admired in men who have no motive to study but generous curiosity, or, what is still better, desire of usefulness; with such politeness as no measure or circle of converse could ever have supplied, but to minds naturally disposed to elegance.' When in Skye, he remarks of one of those clergymen, Mr M'Queen,[109] who had been his guide, that he was 'courteous, candid, sensible, well informed, very learned'; and at parting, he said to him, 'I shall ever retain a great regard for you. Do not forget me.' In another island, the small island of Coll, he paid a visit to Mr Maclean,[110] who was living in a small, straw-thatched, mud-walled hut, 'a fine old man', as the Doctor observed to Boswell, 'well dressed, with as much dignity in his appearance as the Dean of a cathedral!' Mr Maclean had 'a valuable library', which he was obliged, 'from want of accommodation, to keep in large chests'; and this solitary, shut up 'in a green isle amidst the ocean's waves', argued with the awful Southern Don about Leibnitz, Bayle, etc., and though the Doctor displayed a little of the bear, owing to the old man's deafness, yet he acknowledged that he 'liked his firmness and orthodoxy'. In the island of Mull, again, Johnson spent a night under the roof of another clergyman, whom he calls, by mistake, Mr Maclean, but whose name was Macleod,* and of whom he says that he was 'a minister whose elegance of conversation, and strength of judgment, would make him conspicuous in places of greater celebrity'. It is pleasant to know, on such good authority, that there lived at that time, in these wild and distant parts, ministers of such character, manners, and learning.

The minister of our Highland parish was a man of similar culture and character to those of his brethren, two of whom mentioned by the Doctor were his intimate friends. He had the good fortune, let me mention in passing, to meet the famous traveller at Dunvegan Castle;[112] and he used to tell, with great glee, how he found him alone in the drawing-room before dinner, poring over some volume on the sofa, and how the Doctor, before rising to greet him kindly, dashed to the ground the book he had been reading, exclaiming, in a loud and angry voice, 'The author is an ass!'

When the minister came to his parish, the people were but emerging from those old feudal times of clanship, with its loyal feelings and friendships, yet with its violent prejudices and intense clinging to the past, and to all that was bad as well as good in it. Many of his parishioners had been 'out in the '45', and were Prince Charlie men to the core.†

---

* (See also note 111.) The grandfather of the present, and the father of the late Rev. Dr Macleod, of New York, US, both distinguished clergymen.

† (see also note 113) The minister himself was a keen 'Hanoverian.'[114] This was caused by his very decided Protestantism, and also, no doubt, by his devotion to the Dunvegan family, which, through the influence chiefly of President Forbes, had opposed the Pretender. The minister, on a memorable occasion, had his Highland and loyal feeling rather severely tried. It happened thus: When King William IV, like our noble Prince Alfred, was a midshipman in the royal navy, his ship, the *Caesar*, visited the Western Isles. The minister, along with the other public men in the district, went to pay his respects to his Royal Highness. He was most graciously

These were not characterised by much religion. The predecessor of our minister[114] had been commanded by this party not to dare in their hearing to pray for King George in church, or they would shoot him dead. He did, nevertheless, pray, at least in words, but not, we fear, in pure faith. He took a brace of pistols with him to the pulpit, and cocking them before his prayer began, he laid them down before him, and for once at least offered up his petitions with his eyes open. There was no law officer of the crown, not even a justice of the peace at that time in the whole parish. The people were therefore obliged to take the law to some extent in their own hands. Shortly after our minister came to the parish, he wrote stating that 'no fewer than thirty persons have been expelled for theft, not by sentence of the magistrate, but by the united efforts of the better sort of the inhabitants.[116] The good effects of this expulsion have been sensibly felt, but a court of law having been established since then in the neighbourhood, the necessity for such violent means are in a great measure obviated.'[117]

The minister was too far removed from the big world of Church politics, General Assembly debates, controversial meetings and pamphlets, to be a party man. It satisfied him to be a part of the great Catholic Church, and of that small section of it in which he had been born. The business of his Presbytery* was chiefly local, and his work was confined wholly to his parish.

received, and while conversing with the prince on the quarter deck, a galley manned with six rowers pulled alongside. The prince asked him to whom it belonged. On being informed that it belonged to a neighbouring proprietor, the additional remark was made, with a kind smile, 'He was out, no doubt, in the '45? Of course he was! Ah, doctor, all you Highlanders were rebels, every one of you! Ha – ha – ha!' 'Please your Royal Highness,' said the minister, with a low bow, 'I am thankful to say all the Highlanders were not rebels, for had they been so, we might not have had the honour and happiness of seeing your Royal Highness among us now.' The prince laughed heartily and complimented the minister on the felicity of his reply.

* It may interest some of our southern readers to know that the government of the Established Church of Scotland is conducted as follows: (1) Over a single parish is the court called the Kirk Session, composed of lay members, who are ordained for the office as Elders and as Deacons (to attend to the poor). The number of this court varies according to the size and circumstances of the congregation and parish. (2) Over a number of parishes is the Presbytery, composed of all the clergy within a certain district, and a representative Elder from each Session. (3) Over the

After having studied eight years at a university, he entered on his charge with a salary of £40, which was afterwards raised to £80.[118] He ministered to 2,000 souls, all of whom – with the exception of perhaps a dozen families of Episcopalians and Roman Catholics – acknowledged him as their pastor. His charge was scattered over 130 square miles, with a sea-board of 100! This is his own description of the ecclesiastical edifices of the parish at the beginning of his ministry: 'There are two churches so-called, but with respect to decency of accommodation, they might as properly be called sheds or barns.[119] The dimensions of each is no more than forty by sixteen feet, and without seats or bells. It is much to be regretted that since the Reformation little or no attention has been paid to the seating of churches in this country.' No such churches can now be found. How the congregation managed to arrange themselves during service in those 'sheds', I know not. Did they stand? sit on stones or bunches of heather? or recline on the earthen floor? Fortunately the minister was an eloquent and earnest preacher, and he may have made them forget their discomfort. But the picture is not pleasing of a congregation, dripping wet, huddled together in a shed, without seats, after a long walk across the mountains. Sleeping, at all events, was impossible.

It is worth noticing, as characteristic of the times, that during the first period of his ministry there was no copy of the Gaelic Scriptures in existence, except the Irish Bible by Bedell. The clergy translated what they read to the people from the English version. The Highlanders owed much to Gaelic hymns, composed by some of their own poets, and also to metrical translations of the Psalms.*

Presbyteries of a Province is the Synod, composed of all the members of the several Presbyteries; and, finally, over the whole Church is the General Assembly, presided over by a nobleman, representing the Sovereign, and a 'moderator' or chairman, elected by the Church, and composed of representatives, lay and clerical, from every presbytery, and also laymen from the Royal Burghs and Universities. These several courts have many privileges conferred upon them by Act of Parliament. Beyond Scotland, they are no more 'established' than the Church of England. Both Churches are, by Act of Union, placed on an equal footing as regards the State in the Colonies. The government of the Church of Scotland is very similar to that of all the Established Protestant Churches on the Continent.

* It is just as strange that the eldest son of 'the manse' was the first to prepare a metrical translation of the Psalms in Irish, for the use of the Irish Protestant

But even if there had been Bibles, most of the people had not the means of education. What could one or two schools avail in so extensive a parish? To meet the wants of the people, a school would require to be in almost every glen.[121]

But preaching on Sunday, even on a stormy winter's day, was the easiest of the minister's duties. There was not a road in the parish.[122] Along the coast indeed for a few miles there was what was charitably called a road, and, as compared with those slender sheep-tracks which wormed their way through the glens, and across some of the wilder passes, it perhaps deserved the name. By this said road country carts could toil, pitching, jolting, tossing, in deep ruts, over stones, and through the burns like wagons in South Africa, and with all the irregular motion of boats in a storm. But for twenty miles inland the hills and glens were as the Danes had left them.

The paths which traversed those wilds were journeyed generally on foot, but in some instances by 'the minister's horse', one of those sagacious creatures which, with wonderful instinct, seemed to be able, as Ruari used to say, 'to smell out the road' in darkness. It is hardly possible to convey a just impression, except to those acquainted with Highland distances and wildernesses, of what the ordinary labours of such a minister were. Let us select one day out of many of a Highland pastor's work. Immediately after service, a Highlander saluted him, with bonnet off and a low bow, saying, 'John Macdonald in the Black glen is dying, and would like to see you, sir.'[123] After some inquiry, and telling his wife not to be anxious if he was late in returning home, he strode off at 'a killing pace' to see his parishioner. The hut was distant sixteen Highland miles; but what miles! Not such as are travelled by the Lowland or Southern parson, with steps solemn and regular, as if prescribed by law. But

Churches.[120] He also was the chief means of obtaining a new edition of the Gaelic Scriptures for his own countrymen, and of originating and helping on the Education Scheme of the Church of Scotland, which now instructs 20,000 children in the Highlands. In order to supply the hunger for knowledge which these additional means of education would create, he prepared admirable Gaelic schoolbooks, and conducted a monthly magazine in Gaelic for several years, which, it is not too much to say, was, in point of talent, interest, usefulness, and genius, the most precious literary boon ever conferred on the Highlands. A volume of selections from his writings will soon be issued, accompanied by a sketch of his life. I hope this allusion to one so recently departed may be kindly interpreted.

this journey was over bogs, along rough paths, across rapid streams without bridges, and where there was no better shelter than could be found in a Swiss chalet. After a long and patient pastoral visit to his dying parishioner, the minister strikes for home across the hills. But he is soon met by a shepherd, who tells him of a sudden death which had occurred but a few hours before in a hamlet not far off; and to visit the afflicted widow will take him only a few miles out of his course. So be it, quoth the parson, and he forthwith proceeds to the other glen, and mingles his prayers with those of the widow and her children. But the longest day must have an end, and the last rays of the sun are gilding the mountain-tops, and leaving the valleys in darkness. And so our minister, with less elastic step, is ascending towards the steep *Col*, which rises for 2,000 feet with great abruptness, and narrow zigzag path from a chain of lakes up past the *Rhigi* I have already described. But as he nears the summit, down comes thick, palpable, impenetrable mist. He is confident that he knows the road *nearly* as well as the white horse, and so he proceeds with caution over deep moor-hags until he is lost in utter bewilderment. Well, he has before now spent the night under a rock, and waited until break of day. But having eaten only a little bread and cheese since morning, he longs for home. The moon is out, but the light reveals only driving mist, and the mountain begins to feel cold, damp, and terribly lonely. He walks on, feeling his way with his staff, when suddenly the mist clears off, and he finds himself on the slope of a precipice. Throwing himself on his back on the ground, and digging his feet into the soil, he recovers his footing, and with thanksgiving changes his course. Down comes the mist again, thick as before. He has reached a wood – where is he? Ah! he knows the wood right well, and has passed through it a hundred times, so he tries to do so now, and in a few minutes has fallen down a bank into a pool of water. But now he surely has the track, and following it he reaches the spot in the valley from where he had started two hours before! He rouses a shepherd, and they journey together to a ferry by which he can return home by a circuitous route. The boat is there, but the tide is out, for it ebbs far to seaward at this spot, and so he has to wait patiently for the return of the tide. The tide turns, taking its own time to do so; half wading, half rowing, they at last cross the strait. It is now daybreak, and the minister journeys homeward, and reaches the manse about five in the morning.[124]

Such land journeys were frequently undertaken, with adventures more or less trying, not merely to visit the sick, but for every kind of parochial duty – sometimes to baptise, and sometimes to marry. These services were occasionally performed in most primitive fashion at one of those green spots among the hills. Corrie Borrodale, among the old 'shielings', was a sort of halfway house between the opposite sides of the parish.[125] There, beside a clear well, children have been baptized; and there, among the bonnie blooming heather, he has married the Highland shepherd to his bonnie blooming bride. There were also in different districts preaching and 'catechising', as it was called. The catechising consisted in examining on the Church Catechism and Scriptures every parishioner who was disposed to attend.

No sight could be more beautiful than that of the venerable minister seated on the side of a green and sheltered knoll, surrounded by the inhabitants of the neighbouring hamlets, each, as his turn came, answering, or attempting to answer, the questions propounded with gravity and simplicity. A simple discourse followed from the same rural pulpit, to the simple but thoughtful and intelligent congregation. Most touching was it then to hear the Psalms rise from among the moorland, disturbing the 'sleep that is among the lonely hills'; the pauses filled up by the piping of the plover or some mountain bird, and by the echoes of the streams and waterfalls from the rocky precipices. It was a peasant's choir, rude and uncultivated by art, but heard, I doubt not, with sympathy by the mighty angels who sung their own noblest song in the hearing of shepherds on the hills of Bethlehem.

That minister's work was thus devoted and unwearied for half a century. And there is something peculiarly pleasing and cheering to think of him and of others of the same calling and character in every church, who from year to year pursue their quiet course of holy, self-denying labour, educating the ignorant; bringing life and blessing into the homes of disease and poverty; sharing the burden of sorrow with the afflicted, the widow, and the fatherless; reproving and admonishing, by life and word, the selfish and ungodly; and with a heart ever open to all the fair humanities of our nature – a

true 'divine', yet every inch a man! Such men, in one sense, have
never been alone; for each could say with his Master, 'I am not
alone, for the Father is with me.' Yet what knew or cared the great,
bustling, religious world about them? Where were their public
meetings, with reports, speeches, addresses, 'resolutions', or motions
about their work? Where their committees and associations of
ardent philanthropists, rich supporters, and zealous followers?
Where their 'religious' papers, so-called, to parade them before the
world, and to crown them with the laurels of puffs and leading
articles? Alone, he, and thousands like him have laboured, the very
salt of the earth, the noblest of their race!

Chapter 7

PASSING AWAY

I have had playmates, I have had companions,
In my days of childhood, in my joyful school-days
All, all are gone, the old familiar faces.

I have a friend, a kinder friend has no man;
Like an ingrate I left my friend abruptly;
Left him, to muse on the old familiar faces.

Ghost-like I paced round the haunts of my childhood,
Earth seemed a desert I was bound to traverse,
Seeking to find the old familiar faces.

Friend of my bosom, thou more than a brother,
Why wert not thou born in my father's dwelling:
So might we talk of the old familiar faces.

How some they have died, and some they have left me,
And some are taken from me; all are departed,
All, all are gone, the old familiar faces.[126]

The minister, when verging on fourscore, became blind. A son of the manse, his youngest, was, to his joy, appointed to be his assistant and successor in the ministry.[127] I cannot forget the last occasion on which 'the old man eloquent' appeared in the pulpit.[128] The Holy Communion was about to be dispensed, and, before parting forever from his flock, he wished to address them once more. When he entered the pulpit, he mistook the side for the front; but old Rory, who watched him with intense interest, was immediately near him, and seizing a trembling hand placed it on the book-board, thus guiding his master into the right position for addressing the congregation. And then stood up that venerable man, a Saul in height among the people, with his pure white hair falling back from his ample forehead over his shoulders. Few, and loving, and earnest were the words he spoke, amidst the profound silence of a passionately devoted people, which was broken only by their low sobs, when he told them that they should see his face no more. Soon afterwards he died.[129] The night of his death, sons and daughters were grouped around his bed, his wife on one side, old Rory on the other. His mind had been wandering during the day. At evening he sat up in bed, and one of his daughters, who supported his head, dropped a tear on his face. Rory rebuked her and wiped it off; for it is a Highland superstition that no tear should ever drop on the face of a good man dying – is it because it adds to the burden of dying, or is unworthy of the glorious hopes of living? Suddenly the minister stretched forth his hand, as if a child was before him, and said, 'I baptise thee into the name of the Father, the Son, and the Holy Spirit', then, falling back, he expired. It seemed as if it were his own baptism as a child of glory.

The widow did not long survive her husband. She had, with the quiet strength and wisdom of love, nobly fulfilled her part as wife and mother.[130] But who can know what service a wife and mother is to a family, save those who have had this staff to lean on, this pillow to rest on, this sun to shine on them, this best of friends to accompany them, until their earthly journey is over, or far advanced?

Her last years were spent in peace in the old manse, occupied then and now by her youngest son. But she desired, ere she died, to see her first-born in his lowland manse far away, and with him and his children to connect the present with the past.[131] She accomplished her wishes, and left an impress on the young of the third generation which they have never lost during the thirty years that have passed since they saw her face and heard her voice. Illness she had hardly ever known. One morning a grandchild gently opened her bedroom door with breakfast. But, hearing the low accents of prayer, she quietly closed it again, and retired. When she came again, and tapped and entered, all was still. The good woman seemed asleep in peace; and so she was, but it was the sleep of death. She was buried in the Highland kirkyard, beside her husband and nine of her children. There, with sweet young ones, of another generation, who have since then joined them from the same manse, they rest until the resurrection morning, when all will meet 'in their several generations'.

Old Rory next followed his beloved master. One evening, after weeks of illness, he said to his wife, 'Dress me in my best; get a cart ready; I must go to the manse and bless them all, and then die.' His wife thought at first that his strange and sudden wish was the effect of delirium, and she was unwilling to comply. But Rory gave the command in a tone which was never heard except when, at sea or on land, he meant to be obeyed. Arrayed in his Sunday's best, the old man, feeble, pale and breathless, tottered into the parlour of the manse, where the family were soon around him, wondering, as if they had seen a ghost, what had brought him there. 'I bless you all, my dear ones,' he said, 'before I die.' And, stretching out his hands, he pronounced a patriarchal blessing, and a short prayer for their welfare. Shaking hands with each, and kissing the hand of his old and dear mistress, he departed. The family group felt awe-struck – the whole scene was so sudden, strange, and solemn. Next day Rory was dead.

Old Jenny, the hen wife, rapidly followed Rory.[132] Why mention her? Who but the geese or the turkeys could miss her? But there are, I doubt not, many of my readers who can fully appreciate the loss of an old servant who, like Jenny, for half a century has been a respected and valued member of the family. She was associated with the whole household life of the manse. Neither she nor any of those old domestics had ever been mere *things,* but living persons with hearts and heads, to whom every burden, every joy of the family were known. Not a child but had been received into her embrace on the day of birth; not one who had passed away but had received her tears on the day of death; and they had all been decked by her in their last as in their first garments. The official position she occupied as hen wife had been created for her in order chiefly to relieve her feelings at the thought of her being useless and a burden in her old age. When she died, it was discovered that the affectionate old creature had worn next her heart, and in order to be buried with her, locks of hair cut off in infancy from the children whom she had nursed. And here I must relate a pleasing incident connected with her. Twenty years after her death, the younger son of the manse, and its present possessor, was deputed by his church to visit, along with two of his brethren, the Presbyterian congregations of North America. When on the borders of Lake Simcoe he was sent for by an old Highland woman, who could speak her own language only, though she had left her native hills very many years before. On entering her log hut, the old woman burst into a flood of tears, and, without uttering a word, pointed to a silver brooch which clasped the tartan shawl on her bosom. She was Jenny's youngest sister, and the silver brooch which she wore, and which was immediately recognised by the minister, had been presented to Jenny by the eldest son of the manse, when at college, as a token of affection for his old nurse.

Nearly forty years after the old minister had passed away,[133] and so many of 'the old familiar faces' had followed him, the manse boat, which in shape and rig was literally descended from the famous *Roe*, lay becalmed, on a beautiful summer evening, opposite the shore of the glebe. The many gorgeous tints from the setting sun were reflected from the bosom of the calm sea. Vessels, 'like painted ships upon a painted ocean', lay scattered along 'the Sound', and floated double, ship and shadow. The hills on both sides rose pure and clear into the blue sky, revealing every rock and precipice, with heathery knoll or grassy Alp. Fish sometimes broke the smooth unrippled sea, 'as of old the curlews called'. The boating party had gone out to enjoy the perfect repose of the evening, and allowed the boat to float with the tide. The conversation happened to turn on the manse and parish.

'I was blamed the other day', remarked the minister,[134] who was one of the party, 'for taking so much trouble in improving my glebe, and especially in beautifying it with trees and flowers, because, as my cautious friend remarked, I should remember that I was only a life-renter. But I asked my adviser how many proprietors in the parish – whose families are supposed to have a better security for their lands than the minister has for the glebe – have yet possessed their properties so long as our poor family has possessed the glebe? He was astonished, on consideration, to discover that every property in the parish had changed its owner, and some of them several times, since I had succeeded my father!'[135]

'And if we look back to the time since our father became minister,' remarked another of the party, 'the changes have been still more frequent. The only possessors of their first home, in short, in the whole parish, are the families which had no 'possessions' in it!'

'And look', another said, 'at those who are in this boat.[136] How many birds are here out of the old nest!' And strange enough there were in that boat the eldest and youngest sons of the old minister, both born on the glebe, and both doctors of divinity, who had done good, and who had been honoured in their time. There were also in the boat three ordained sons of those old sons born of the manse, in all, five ministers descended from the old minister. The crew was made up of an elderly man, the son of 'old Rory',[137] and of a white-haired man, the son of 'old Archy', both born on the glebe.

But these clergy represented a few only of the descendants of the old minister who were enjoying the manifold blessings of life. These facts are mentioned here in order to connect such mercies with the anxiety expressed sixty years ago by the poor parson himself in the letter to his girls, which I have included here.

One event more remains for me to record connected with the old manse, and then the silence of the hills, in which that lowly home reposes, will no more be broken by any word of mine about its inhabitants except as they are necessarily associated with other 'reminiscences'. It is narrated in the memoir lately published of Professor Wilson,[138] that when the eldest son of our manse came to Glasgow College, in the heyday of his youth, he was the only one who could compete in athletic exercises with the Professor, who was his friend and fellow student. That physical strength, acquired in his early days by the manly training of the sea and hills, sustained his body; while a spiritual strength, more noble still, sustained his soul during a ministry in three large and difficult parishes, which lasted, with constant labour, for more than half a century, and until he was just about to enter on his eightieth year – the day of his funeral being the anniversary of his birth. He had married in early life the daughter of one of the most honourable of the earth, who had for upwards of forty years, with punctilious integrity, managed the estates of the Argyle family in the Western Highlands.[139] Her father's house was opposite the old manse, and separated from it by the 'Sound'.[140] This invested that inland sea which divided the two lovers with a poetry that made the *Roe* and her perilous voyages a happy vision that accompanied the minister until his last hour. For three or four years he had retired from public life, to rest from his labours, and in God's mercy to cultivate the passive more than the active virtues in the bosom of his own family. But when disposed to sink into the silent pensiveness and the physical depression which often attend old age, one topic, next to the highest of all, never failed to rouse him – like a dying eagle in its cage when it sees far off the mountains on which it tried its early flight – and that one was converse about the old parish[141] of his father, and of his youth. And thus it happened that on the very last evening of his life he was peculiarly cheerful, as he told some stories of that long past; and among others a characteristic anecdote of old Rory. How naturally did the prayer of thanksgiving then succeed the memories of those times of peace and of early happiness!

That same night, his first and last love, the 'better half', verily, of his early life, was awoke from her anxious slumbers near him by his complaint of pain. But she had no time to rouse the household ere he, putting his arms round her neck, and breathing the words 'my darling' in her ear, fell asleep. He had for more than twenty-five years ministered to an immense congregation of Highlanders in Glasgow;[142] and his public funeral was remarkable, not chiefly for the numbers who attended it, or the crowds which followed it – for these things are common in such ceremonies – but for the sympathy and sorrow manifested by the feeble and tottering Highland men and women, very many of whom were from the old parish,[143] and who, bathed in tears, struggled to keep up with the hearse, in order to be near, until the last possible moment, one for whom they had an enthusiastic attachment. The Highland hills and their people were to him a passion, and for their good he had devoted all the energies of his long life; and not in vain! His name will not, I think, be lost in this generation, wherever, at least, the Celtic language is spoken; and though this notice of him may have no interest to the Southern reader, who may not know, nor care to know, his name, yet every Gael in the most distant colony who reads these lines will pardon me for writing them. He belongs to them as they did to him.

Chapter 8

SOME CHARACTERISTICS OF THE
HIGHLAND PEASANTRY

I know little from personal observation about the Highlanders in the far North or in the central districts of Scotland, but I am old enough to have very vivid reminiscences of those in the West, and of their character, manners, and customs as these existed during that transition period which began after 'the '45', but has now almost entirely passed away with emigration,[144] the decay of the 'kelp' trade,[145] the sale of so many old properties, and the introduction of large sheep farms, deer forests, and extensive shootings.

I have conversed with a soldier – old John Shoemaker, he was called – who bore arms under Prince Charlie. On the day I met him he had walked several miles, was hale and hearty though upwards of 100 years old, and had no money save ten shillings which he always carried in his pocket to pay for his coffin. He conversed quite intelligently about the olden time with all its peculiarities. I have also known very many who were intimately acquainted with the 'lairds' and 'men' of those days, and who themselves had imbibed all the impressions and views then prevalent as to the world in general, and the Highlands in particular.

The Highlanders whom the tourist meets with nowadays are very unlike those I used to know, and who are now found only in some of the remote unvisited glens, like the remains of a broken-up Indian nation on the outskirts of the American settlements. The porters who scramble for luggage on the quays of Oban, Inverary, Fort William, or Portree; the gillies who swarm around a shooting-box; or even the more aristocratic keepers – that whole *set,* in short, who live by summer tourists or autumnal sportsmen – are to the real Highlander, in his secluded parish or glen, what a commissionaire in an hotel at Innsbruck is to Hofer and his confederates.

The real Highland peasantry are, I hesitate not to affirm, by far the most intelligent in the world. I say this advisedly, after having compared them with those of many countries. Their good breeding must strike every one who is familiar with them. Let a Highland shepherd from the most remote glen be brought into the dining-room of the laird, as is often done, and he will converse with ladies and gentlemen, partake of any hospitality which may be shown him with ease and grace, and never say or do anything *gauche* or offensive to the strictest propriety. This may arise in some degree from what really seems to be an instinct in the race, but more probably it comes from the familiar intercourse which, springing out of the old family and clan feeling, always subsists between the upper and lower classes. The Highland gentleman never meets the most humble peasant whom he knows without chatting with him as with an acquaintance, even shaking hands with him; and each man in the district, with all his belongings, ancestry and descendants included, is familiarly known to every other. Yet this familiar intercourse never causes the inferior at any time, or for a single moment, to alter the dignified respectful manner which he recognises as due to his superior. They have an immense reverence for those whom they consider 'real gentlemen', or those who belong to the 'good families', however distantly connected with them. No members of the aristocracy can distinguish more sharply than they do between genuine blood though allied with poverty, and the want of it though allied with wealth. Different ranks are defined with great care in their vocabulary. The chief is always called lord – 'the lord of Lochiel', 'the lord of Lochbuy'. The gentlemen tenants are called 'men' – 'the man' of such and such a place. The poorest 'gentleman' who labours with his own hands is addressed in more respectful language than his better-to-do neighbour who belongs to their own ranks. The one is addressed as 'you', the other as 'thou'; and should a property be bought by someone who is not connected with the old or good families, he may possess thousands, but he never commands the same reverence as the poor man who has yet 'the blood' in him. The 'pride and poverty' of the Gael have passed into a proverb, and express a fact.

They consider it essential to good manners and propriety never to betray any weakness or sense of fatigue, hunger, or poverty. They are great admirers in others of physical strength and endurance: those qualities which are most frequently demanded of themselves. When, for example, a number of Highland servants sit down to dinner, it is held as proper etiquette to conceal the slightest eagerness to begin to eat; and the eating, when begun, is continued with *apparent* indifference – the duty of the elder persons being to coax the younger, and especially any strangers that are present, to resume operations after they have professed to have partaken sufficiently of the meal. They always recognise liberal hospitality as essential to a 'gentleman', and have the greatest contempt for narrowness or meanness in this department of life. Drunkenness is rarely indulged in as a solitary habit, but too extensively, I must admit, at fairs and other occasions – funerals not excepted – when many meet together from a distance with time on their hands and money in their pockets.

The dislike to make their wants known, or to complain of poverty, was also characteristic of them before the poor law was introduced,[146] or famine compelled them to become beggars upon the general public. But even when the civilised world poured its treasures, twenty years ago, into the Fund for the Relief of Highland Destitution, the old people suffered deeply ere they accepted any help.[147] I have known families who closed their windows to keep out the light, that their children might sleep on as if it were night, and not rise to find a home without food. I remember being present at the first distribution of meal in a distant part of the Highlands. A few old women had come some miles, from an inland glen, to receive a portion of the bounty. Their clothes were rags, but every rag was washed, and patched together as best might be. They sat apart for a time, but at last approached the circle assembled round the meal depot. I watched the countenances of the group as they conversed apparently on some momentous question. This I afterwards ascertained to be which of them should go forward and speak for the others. One woman was at last selected, while the rest stepped back and hung their heads, concealing their eyes with their tattered tartar plaids. The deputy slowly walked towards the rather large official committee, whose attention, when at last directed to her, made her pause. She then stripped her right arm bare, and holding up the miserable skeleton, burst into tears, and sobbed like a child! Yet, during all these sad destitution times, there was not a policeman or soldier in those districts. No food riot ever took place, no robbery was attempted, no sheep was ever stolen from the hills; and all this though hundreds had only shellfish, or 'dulse',[148] gathered on the seashore to depend upon.

The Highlander is assumed to be a lazy animal and not over-honest in his dealings with strangers. I have no desire to be a special pleader in his behalf, with all my national predilections in his favour. But I must nevertheless dissent to some extent from these sweeping generalisations. He is naturally impulsive and fond of excitement, and certainly is wanting in the steady, preserving effort which characterises his Southern brother. But the circumstances of his country, his small 'croft' and want of capital, the bad land and hard weather, with the small returns for his uncertain labour, have tended to depress rather than to stimulate him. One thing is certain, that when he is removed to another clime, and placed in more favourable circumstances, he exhibits a perseverance and industry which make him rise very rapidly.

It must be confessed, however, that Highland honesty is some-times very lax in its dealings with the Sassenach. The Highlander forms no exception, alas, to the tribe of guides, drivers, boatmen, all over Europe, who imagine that the tourist possesses unlimited means, and travels only to spend money. A friend of mine who had been so long in India that he lost the Highland accent, though not the language, reached a ferry on his journey home, and, concealing his knowledge of Gaelic, asked one of the Highland boatmen what his charge was. 'I'll ask the maister,' was his reply. The master being unable to speak English, this faithful mate acted as interpreter. 'What will you take from this Englishman?' quoth the interpreter. 'Ask the fellow ten shillings,' was the reply of the honest master, the real fare being five shillings. 'He says', explained the interpreter, 'that he is sorry he cannot do it under *twenty* shillings, and that's cheap.' Without saying anything, the offer was apparently accepted; but while sailing across, my friend spoke in Gaelic, on which the inter-preter sharply rebuked him in the same language. 'I am ashamed of you!' he said; 'I am indeed, for I see you are ashamed of your country. Och, och, to pretend to me that you were an Englishman! You deserve to pay *forty* shillings – but the ferry is only five!' Such specimens, however, are found only along the great tourist thoroughfare, where they are in every country too common.

I have said that the Highlanders are an intelligent, cultivated people, as contrasted with that dull, stupid, prosaic, incurious condition of mind which characterises so many of the peasantry in other countries. Time never hangs heavily on their hands during even the long winter evenings, when outdoor labour is impossible. When I was young I was sent to live among the peasantry 'in the parish', so as to acquire a knowledge of the language; and living, as I did, very much like themselves, it was my delight to spend the long evenings in their huts, hearing their tales and songs. These huts were of the most primitive description. They were built of loose stones and clay, the walls were thick, the door low, the rooms numbered one only, or in more aristocratic cases two. The floor was clay; the peat fire was built in the middle of the floor, and the smoke, when amiable and not bullied by a sulky wind, escaped quietly and patiently through a hole in the roof. The window was like a porthole, part of it generally filled with glass and part with peat. One bed, or sometimes two, with clean home-made sheets, blankets, and counterpane, a 'dresser' with bowls and plates, a large chest, and a corner full of peat filled up the space beyond the circle about the fire. Upon the rafters above, black as ebony from peat-reek, a row of hens and chickens with a stately cock roosted in a paradise of heat.

Let me describe one of these evenings. Round the fire are seated, some on stools, some on stones, some on the floor, a happy group. Two or three girls, fine, healthy, blue-eyed lasses, with their hair tied up with ribbon snood, are knitting stockings. Hugh, the son of Sandy, is busking hooks; big Archy is peeling willow-wands and fashioning them into baskets; the shepherd Donald, the son of Black John, is playing on the Jews' harp; while beyond the circle are one or two herd boys in kilts, reclining on the floor, all eyes and ears for the stories. The performances of Donald begin the evening, and form interludes to its songs, tales, and recitations. He has two large 'Lochaber trumps', for Lochaber trumps were to the Highlands what Cremona violins have been to musical Europe. He secures the end of each with his teeth, and grasping them with his hands so that the tiny instruments are invisible, he applies the little finger of each hand to their vibrating steel tongues. He modulates their tones with his breath, and brings out of them Highland reels, strathspeys, and jigs – such wonderfully beautiful, silvery, distinct and harmonious sounds as would draw forth cheers and an encore even in St James's Hall. But Donald the son of Black John is done, and he looks to bonny Mary Cameron for a blink of her hazel eye to reward him, while in virtue of his performance he demands a song from her. Now Mary has dozens of songs, so has Kirsty, so has Flory – love songs, shearing songs, washing songs, Prince Charlie songs, songs composed by this or that poet in the parish, and therefore Mary asks, What song? So until she can make up her mind, and have a little playful flirtation with Donald the son of Black John she requests Hugh the son of Sandy to tell a story. Although Hugh has abundance of this material, he too protests that he has none. But having betrayed this modesty, he starts off with one of those tales, the truest and most authentic specimens of which are given by Mr Campbell, to whose admirable and truthful volumes I refer the reader.* When the story is done, improvisatore is often tried, and amidst roars of laughter the aptest verses are made, sometimes in clever satire, sometimes with knowing allusions to the weaknesses or predilections of those round the fire. Then follow riddles and puzzles; then the trumps resume their tunes, and Mary sings her song, and Kirsty and Flory theirs, and all join in chorus, and who cares for the wind outside or the peat-reek inside! Never was a more innocent or happy group.

---

* (See also note 149.) No man knows the Highlanders better than he does – very few so well – and I am glad to quote his opinions, of which I had no recollection while writing the above gossip. He says:

'I have wandered among the peasantry of many countries, and this trip but confirmed my old impression. There are few peasants that I think so highly of, none that I love so well. Scotch Highlanders have faults in plenty, but they have the bearing of Nature's own gentlemen the delicate, natural tact which discovers, and the good taste which avoids, all that would hurt or offend a guest. The poorest is ever the readiest to share the best he has with the stranger; a kind word kindly meant is never thrown away, and whatever may be the faults of this people, I have never found a boor or a churl in a Highland bothy.

'The Highlander sees every year a numerous flood of tourists of all nations pouring through his lochs and glens, but he knows as little of them as they of him. The shoals of herring that enter Loch Fyne know as much of the dun deer on the

This fondness for music from trump, fiddle, or bagpipe, and for song-singing, storytelling, and improvisatore, was universal, and imparted a marvellous buoyancy and intelligence to the people.

These peasants were, moreover, singularly inquisitive, and greedy of information. It was a great thing if the schoolmaster or anyone else was present who could tell them about other people and other places. I remember an old shepherd who questioned me closely how the hills and rocks were formed, as a gamekeeper had heard some sportsmen talking about this. The questions which are put are no doubt often odd enough. A woman, for example, whose husband was anxious to emigrate to Australia, stoutly opposed the step, until she could get her doubts solved on some geographical point that greatly disturbed her. She consulted the minister, and the tremendous question which chiefly weighed on her mind was whether it was true that the feet of the people there were opposite to the feet of the people at home? and if so – what then?

There is one science the value of which it is very difficult to make a Highlander comprehend, and that is mineralogy. He connects botany with the art of healing; astronomy with guidance from the stars, or navigation; chemistry with dyeing, brewing, etc.; but 'chopping bits off the rocks!' as he calls it, this has always been a mystery. A shepherd, while smoking his cutty[150] at a small Highland inn, was communicating to another in Gaelic his experiences of 'mad Englishmen,' as he called them. 'There was one', said the narrator, 'who once gave me his bag to carry to the inn by a short cut across the hills, while he walked by another road. I was wondering myself why it was so dreadfully heavy, and when I got out of his sight I was determined to see what was in it. I opened it, and what do you think it was? But I need not ask you to guess, for

hillside, as Londoners and Highlanders know of each other. The want of a common language here, as elsewhere, keeps Highlands and Lowlands, Celt and Saxon, as clearly separate as oil and water in the same glass.' He remarks with equal truth regarding their stories: 'I have never heard a story whose point was obscenity publicly told in a Highland cottage; and I believe that such are rare. I *have* heard them where the rough polish of more modern ways has replaced the polished roughness of 'wild' Highlanders; and that where even the bagpipes have been almost abolished as profane. I have heard the music of the Cider Cellars in a parlour, even in polished England, where I failed to extract anything else from a group of comfortably dressed villagers.'

you would never find out. It was stones! 'Stones!' exclaimed his companion, opening his eyes. 'Stones! Well, well, that beats all I ever knew or heard of them! And did you carry it?' 'Carry it! Do you think I was as mad as himself? No! I emptied them all out, but I filled the bag again from the cairn near the house, and gave him good measure for his money!'

The schoolmaster has been abroad in the Highlands during these latter years, and few things are more interesting than the eagerness with which education has been received by the people. When the first deputation from the Church of Scotland visited the Highlands and Islands, in a government cruiser put at their disposal, to inquire into the state of education and for the establishing of schools in needy districts, most affecting evidence was afforded by the poor people of their appreciation of this great boon.[151] In one island where an additional school was promised, a body of the peasantry accompanied the deputies to the shore, and bade them farewell with expressions of the most tender and touching gratitude; and as long as they were visible from the boat, every man was seen standing with his head uncovered. In another island where it was thought necessary to change the site of the school, a woman strongly protested against the movement. In her fervour she pointed to her girl and said, 'She and the like of her cannot walk many miles to the new school, and it was from her dear lips I first heard the words of the blessed Gospel read in our house; for God's sake don't take away the school!' Her pleading was successful. Old men in some cases went to school to learn to read and write. One old man, when dictating a letter to a neighbour, got irritated at the manner in which his sentiments had been expressed by his amanuensis. 'I'm done of this!' he at length exclaimed. 'Why should I have my tongue in another man's mouth when I can learn to think for myself on paper? I'll go to the school and learn to write!' And he did so. A class in another school was attended by elderly people. One of the boys in it, who was weeping bitterly, being asked by the teacher the cause of his sorrow, ejaculated in sobs, 'I trapped my grandfather, and he'll no let me up!' The boy was immediately below his grandfather in the class, and having 'trapped', or corrected, him in his reading, he claimed the right of getting above him, which the old man had resisted.

I may notice, for the information of those interested in the education of the Irish- or Welsh-speaking populations, that Gaelic is taught in all the Highland schools, and that the result has been an immediate demand for English. The education of the faculties, and the stimulus given to acquire information, demand a higher aliment than can be afforded by the medium of the Gaelic language alone. But it is not my intention to discourse, in these light sketches, upon grave themes requiring more space and time to do them justice than our pages can afford.

Another characteristic feature of the Highland peasantry is the devoted and unselfish attachment which they retain through life to any of their old friends and neighbours. An intimate knowledge of the families in the district is what we might expect. They are acquainted with all their ramifications by blood or by marriage, and from constant personal inquiries keep up, as far as possible, a knowledge of their history, though they may have left the country for years. I marked, last summer, in the Highlands the surprise of a general officer from India, who was re-visiting the scenes of his youth, as old men, who came to pay their respects to him, inquired about every member of his family, showing a thorough knowledge of all the marriages which had taken place, and the very names of the children who had been born. 'I declare', remarked the general, 'that this is the only country where they care to know a man's father or grandfather! What an unselfish interest, after all, do these people take in one, and in all that belongs to him! And how *have* they found all this out about my nephews and nieces, with their children?' Their love of kindred, down to those in whom a drop of their blood can be traced, is not so remarkable, however, as this undying interest in old friends, whether they be rich or poor. Even the bond of a common name – however absurd this appears – has its influence still in the Highlands. I remember when it was so powerful among old people as to create not only strong predilections, but equally strong antipathies, towards strangers of whom nothing was known save their name. This is feudalism fossilised. In the Highlands there are other connections which are considered closely allied to those of blood. The connection, for instance, between children – it may be of the laird and of the peasant – who are reared by the same nurse, is one of these. Many an officer has

been accompanied by his 'foster-brother'[152] to 'the wars', and has
ever found him his faithful servant and friend unto death. Such an
one was Ewen M'Millan,[153] who followed Col. Cameron, or
Fassiefern[154] – as he was called, Highland fashion, from his place of
residence – to whom Sir Walter Scott alludes in the lines

> Proud Ben Nevis views with awe
> How at the bloody Quatre Bras
> Brave Cameron heard the wild hurrah
> Of conquest as he fell.[155]

The foster-brother was ever beside his dear master, with all the
enthusiastic attachment and devotion of the old feudal times,
throughout the Peninsular campaign, until his death. The 92nd
Regiment was commanded by Fassiefern, and speaking of its
conduct at the Nive, Napier[156] says, 'How gloriously did that
regiment come forth to the charge with their colours flying and
their national music playing as if going to review! This was to
understand war. The man [Col. Cameron], who at that moment,
and immediately after a repulse, though of such military pomp, was
by nature a soldier.' Four days after this, though on each of those
days the fighting was continued and severe, the 92nd was vigorously
attacked at St Pierre, Fassiefern's horse was shot under him, and he
was so entangled by the fall as to be utterly unable to resist a French
soldier, who would have transfixed him but for the fact that the
foster-brother transfixed the Frenchman. Liberating his master, and
accompanying him to his regiment, the foster-brother returned
under a heavy fire and amidst a fierce combat to the dead horse.
Cutting the girths of the saddle and raising it on his shoulders, he
rejoined the 92nd with the trophy, exclaiming, 'We must leave them
the carcass, but they will never get the saddle on which Fassiefern
sat!' The Gaelic sayings 'Kindred to twenty degrees, fosterage to a
hundred', and 'Woe to the father of the foster-son who is unfaithful
in his trust', were fully verified in McMillan's case. I may add one
word about Col. Cameron's death as illustrative of the old Highland
spirit. He was killed in charging the French at Quatre Bras. The
moment he fell, his foster-brother was by his side, carried him out
of the field of battle, procured a cart, and sat in it with his master's
head resting on his bosom. They reached the village of Waterloo,

where M'Millan laid him on the floor of a deserted house by the wayside. The dying man asked how the day went, expressed a hope that his beloved Highlanders had behaved well and that 'his country would believe he had served her faithfully,' and then commanded a piper, who had by this time joined them, to play a pibroch to him, and thus bring near to him his home among the hills far away. Higher thoughts were not wanting, but these could mingle in the heart of the dying Highlander with 'Lochaber no more'.

He was buried on the 17th by M'Millan and his old brave friend Capt. Gordon in the Allée Verte, on the Ghent road. The following year the faithful foster-brother returned, and took the body back to Lochaber; and there it lies in peace beneath an obelisk which the traveller, as he enters the Caledonian Canal from the South, may see near a cluster of trees which shade the remains of the Lochiel family, of which Fassiefern was the younger branch.

It must, however, be frankly admitted that there is no man more easily offended, more thin-skinned, who cherishes longer the memory of an insult, or keeps up with more freshness a personal, family, or party feud, than the genuine Highlander. Woe be to the man who offends his pride or vanity! 'I may forgive, but I cannot forget!' is a favourite saying. He will stand by a friend till the last, but let a breach be once made, and it is most difficult ever again to repair it as it once was. The 'grudge' is immortal. There is no man who can fight and shake hands like the genuine Englishman.

It is difficult to pass any judgment on the state of religion past or present in the Highlands. From the natural curiosity of the High-landers, their desire to obtain instruction, the reading of the Bible, and the teaching of the Shorter Catechism in the schools, they are on the whole better informed in respect to religion than the poorer peasantry of other countries. But when their religious life is suddenly quickened it is apt to manifest itself for a time in enthusiasm or fanaticism, for the Highlander 'moveth altogether if he move at all'. The people have all a deep religious feeling, but that again, unless educated, has been often mingled with superstitions which have come down from heathen and Roman Catholic times. Of these superstitions, with some of their peculiar customs, I may have to speak in another chapter.

The men of 'the '45' were, as a class, half heathen, with strong sympathies for Romanism or Episcopacy, as the supposed symbol of loyalty. I mentioned, in a former sketch, how the parish minister of that time had prayed with his eyes open and his pistols cocked.[157] But I have been since reminded of a fact which I have forgotten, that one of the Lairds who had 'followed Prince Charlie', and who sat in the gallery opposite the parson, had threatened to shoot him if he dared to pray for King George, and, on the occasion referred to, had ostentatiously laid a pistol on the book-board. It was then only that the minister produced his brace to keep the Laird in countenance! This same half-savage Laird was, in later years, made more civilised by the successor of the belligerent parson. Our parish minister, on one occasion, when travelling with the Laird, was obliged to sleep at night in the same room with him in a Highland inn. After retiring to bed, the Laird said, 'Oh, minister, I wish you would tell some tale.' 'I shall do so willingly,' replied the minister; and he told the story of Joseph and his brethren. When it was finished, the Laird expressed his great delight at the narrative, and begged to know where the minister had picked it up, as it was evidently not Highland. 'I got it', quoth the minister, 'in a book you have often heard of, and where you may find many other most delightful and most instructive stories, which, unlike our Highland ones, are all true — in the Bible.'[158]

I will here recall an anecdote of old Rory, illustrative of Highland superstition in its very mildest form. When 'the minister' came to the parish, it was the custom for certain offenders to stand before the congregation during service, and do penance in a long canvas shirt drawn over their ordinary garments. He discontinued this severe practice, and the canvas shirt was hung up in his barn, where it became an object of awe and fear to the farm servants, as having somehow to do with the wicked one.[159] The minister resolved to put it to some useful purpose, and what better could it be turned to than to repair the sail of the *Roe*, which had been torn by a recent squall. Rory, on whom this task devolved, respectfully protested against patching the sail with the wicked shirt; but the more he did so, the more the minister — who had himself almost a superstitious horror for superstition — resolved to show his contempt for Rory's fears and warnings by commanding the patch to be adjusted without delay, as he had that evening to cross the stormy sound.

Rory dared not refuse, and his work was satisfactorily finished, but he gave no response to his master's thanks and praises as the sail was hoisted with a white circle above the boom, marking the new piece in the old garment. As they proceeded on their voyage, the wind suddenly rose, until the boat was staggering gunwale down with as much as she could carry. When passing athwart the mouth of a wide glen which, like a funnel, always gathered and discharged, in their concentrated force, whatever squalls were puffing and whistling round the hills, the sea to windward gave token of a very heavy blast, which was rapidly approaching the *Roe*, with a huge line of foam before it, like the white helmet crests of a line of cavalry waving in the charge. The minister was at the helm, and was struck by the anxiety visible in Rory's face, for they had mastered many worse attacks in the same place without difficulty. 'We must take in two reefs, Rory,' he exclaimed, 'as quickly as possible. Stand by the halyards, boys! Quick and handy.' But the squall was down upon them too sharp to admit of any preparation. 'Reefs will do no good today,' remarked Rory with a sigh. The water rushed along the gunwale, which was taking in more than was comfortable, while the spray was flying over the weather bow as the brave little craft, guided by the minister's hand, lay close to the wind as a knife. When the squall was at its worst, Rory could restrain himself no longer, but opening his large boat knife, sprang up and made a dash at the sail. Whirling the sharp blade round the white patch, and embracing a good allowance of cloth beyond to make his mark sure, he cut the wicked spot out. As it flew far to leeward like a sea bird, Rory resumed his seat, and, wiping his forehead, said: 'Thanks to Providence, that's gone! – and just see how the squall is gone with it!' The squall had indeed spent itself, while the boat was eased by the big hole. 'I told you how it would be. Oh, never, never do the like again, minister, for it's tempting of the devil!' Rory saw he was forgiven, as the minister and his boys burst into a roar of merry laughter at the scene.

One word regarding the attachment of the Highlanders to their native country. 'Characteristic of all savages!' some readers may exclaim; 'they know no better.' Now, I did not say that the Highlanders knew no better, for emigration has often been a very passion with them as their only refuge from starvation. Their love

of country has been counteracted on the one hand by the lash of
famine, and on the other by the attraction of a better land opening
up its arms to receive them, with the promise of abundance to
reward their toil. They have chosen, then, to emigrate, but what
agonising scenes have been witnessed on their leaving their native
land! The women have cast themselves on the ground, kissing it
with intense fervour. The men, though not manifesting their
attachment by such violent demonstrations on this side of the
Atlantic, have done so in a still more impressive form in the
Colonies – whether wisely or not is another question – by
retaining their native language, and cherishing feelings of the
warmest affection for the country which they still fondly call
'home'. I have met in British North America very many who were
born there, but who had no other language than Gaelic. It is not a
little remarkable that in South Carolina there are about fifteen
congregations in which Gaelic is preached every Sunday, by native
pastors, to the descendants of those who emigrated from their
country about a century ago.

> From the dim Shieling on the misty islands
> Mountains divide us, and a world of seas:
> But still our hearts are true, our hearts are Highland,
> And we in dreams behold the Hebrides![160]

   Among the emigrants from 'the Parish', many years ago, was the
Piper of an old family which was broken up by the death of the last
Laird. Poor Duncan Piper[161] had to expatriate himself from the
house which had sheltered him and his ancestors. The evening
before he sailed he visited the tomb of his old master, and played
the family pibroch while he slowly and solemnly paced round the
grave, his wild and wailing notes strangely disturbing the silence of
the lonely spot where his chief lay interred. Having done so, he
broke his pipes, and, laying them on the green sod, departed to
return no more.

Chapter 9

STORIES OF SNOWSTORMS FOR THE FIRESIDE

OLD JENNY OF GLEN IMMEREN

When the sheep were sent to the hills, the shielings were no longer of any use, and so they fell into ruins. But for many a year one hut remained far up in Glen Immeren,[162] inhabited by 'old Jenny'.[163] How she came to live there we never heard. Perhaps she had been there when a child with her father and mother, and with others who had passed from her sight, but not from the eye of her heart; and so she would see forms among the hills that others saw not, and hear voices of the old time whispering in her ear, or echoing among the knolls that others heard not. Thus in the lonely glen Jenny was not alone. And I think she knew One who was more real to her than all those dreams of heart – One who was her Father in heaven, and ever present with her. It is certain, however, that Jenny was singularly respected. When she came down from the glen once a year to the 'big house', the laird's wife brought her into the dining-room and chatted with her, and gave her something from her own hand to eat and drink as a pledge of friendship.[164] The minister visited her regularly, and she came as regularly to see the family, and would remain for days a welcome guest in the kitchen. Besides this, she was often sent for to nurse the sick, and there were few houses which had not received her advice and assistance in time of trouble; for Jenny knew a remarkable collection of 'cures', – that is, medicines made up from plants and roots – as remedies for those accidents and diseases which were common in the country. These 'cures' were at one time familiar to many in the Highlands, and, until educated physicians settled there, they were the only sources of relief to the sufferer; and very good service they did. By such means old Jenny became a sort of public character. No one passed her cottage on the way across the mountains to the thickly-peopled valley on the other side without calling on her and giving her all the news of the district.[165]

A goat and a few hens were all Jenny's property. But then she got wool from one family, and meal from another, and her peats from a third; so that she lived in such comfort as no forced poorlaw ever gave, or can give; for charity did not injure self-respect, and every gift was a sign of kindness. Spring was the trying season, when the winter had almost exhausted all her means of living. The meal was nearly done – potatoes were not then so common among the poor[166] – the pasture was scanty for the goat; and Jenny was some-times forced to take a journey to visit her kind neighbours down near the sea-coast, driven, like a vessel in a storm, for shelter to a friendly harbour. Well, it so happened that one day a dreadful snow-storm came on just as she was planning an excursion to get some meal, and when her hut was almost empty of food, except the little milk she could get from her goat. For a long time that snowstorm was a sort of date in the parish, and people counted so many years before or after 'the great storm'. Never had they seen such a constant and heavy fall, with such deep snowdrifts. When the heavens at last became clear, the whole face of the country seemed changed. It was some time before the thought suddenly occurred to a shepherd – 'What has old Jenny been doing all this time?' No sooner was her name mentioned than she at once became the theme of conver-sation among all the cottages in the Highland hamlet nearest Glen Immeren,[167] and throughout the parish. But for many days, such was the state of the weather that no mortal foot could wade through the snow-wreaths, or buffet the successive storms which swept down with blinding fury from the hills. Jenny was given up as lost! When the minister prayed for her there was deep silence in the small church, and manly sighs were heard. At last, three men re-solved, on the first day the attempt was possible, to proceed up the long and dreary glen to search for Jenny. They carried food in their plaids, and whatever comforts they thought necessary – nay, they resolved to bring the old woman home with them, if they found her alive. So off they went; and many an eye watched those three black dots among the snow, slowly tracking their way up Glen Immeren. At last they reached a rock at an angle, where the glen takes a turn to the left, and where the old woman's cottage ought to have been seen. But nothing met the eye except a smooth white sheet of glittering snow, surmounted by black rocks; and all below was silent as the sky above! No sign of life greeted eye or ear. The men spoke not, but muttered some exclamation of sorrow. 'She is alive!' suddenly cried one of the shepherds: 'for I see smoke.' They pushed bravely on. When they reached the hut, nothing was visible except the two chimneys; and even those were lower than the snow-wreath. There was no immediate entrance but by one of the chimneys. A shepherd first called to Jenny down the chimney, and asked if she was alive; but, before receiving a reply, a large fox sprang out of the chimney, and darted off to the rocks.

'Alive!' replied Jenny. 'But thank God you have come to see me! I cannot say come in by the door; but come down — come down.'

In a few minutes her three friends easily descended by the chimney, and were shaking Jenny's hand warmly.[168] Hurried questions were put and answered.

'Oh, woman! How have you lived all this time?'

'Sit down, and I will tell you,' said old Jenny, whose feelings now gave way to a fit of hysterical weeping.

After composing herself, she continued: ' "How did I live?" you ask, Sandy. I may say, just as I have always lived — by the power and goodness of God, who feeds the wild beasts.'

'The wild beasts, indeed,' replied Sandy, drying his eyes. 'Did you know that a wild beast was in your own house? Did you see the fox that jumped out of your chimney as we entered?'

'My blessings on the dear beast!' said Jenny, with fervour. 'May no huntsman ever kill it, and may it never want food either summer or winter!'

The shepherds looked at one another by the dim light of Jenny's fire, evidently thinking that she had become slightly insane.

'Stop, lads,' she continued, 'till I tell you the story. I had in the house, when the storm began, the goat and hens. Fortunately, I had fodder gathered for the goat, which kept it alive, although, poor thing, it has had but scanty meals. But it lost its milk. I had also peats for my fire, but very little meal; yet I never lived better, and I have been able, besides, to preserve my bonnie hens for summer. I every day dined on flesh meat, too, a thing I have not done for years before; and thus I have lived like a lady.'

Again the shepherds were amazed, and asked in a low voice, as if in pity for her state, 'Where did you get meat, Jenny?'

'From the old fox, Sandy!'

'The fox!' they all exclaimed.

'Ay, the fox,' said Jenny. 'Just the dear old fox, the best friend I ever had. I'll tell you how it was. The day of the storm he looked into the chimney, and came slowly down, and set himself on the rafter beside the hens, yet never once touched them. Honest fellow! he is sorely miscalled; for he every day provided for himself and for me too, like a kind neighbour, as he was. He hunted regularly like a gentleman, and brought in game in abundance for his own dinner – a hare almost every day – and what he left I got, and washed, and cooked, and eat, and so I have never wanted![169] Now he has gone, you have come to relieve me.'

'God's ways are past finding out!' said the men, bowing down their heads with reverence.

'Praise Him,' said Jenny, 'who giveth food to the hungry!'

THE WIDOW AND HER SON

A widow who, I have heard, was much loved for her 'meek and quiet spirit' left her home in 'the parish' early one morning, in order to reach, before evening, the residence of a kinsman who had promised to assist her to pay her rent.[170] She carried on her back her only child. The mountain-track which she pursued passes along the shore of a beautiful salt-water loch; then through a green valley, watered by a peaceful stream which flows from a neighbouring lake. It afterwards winds along the margin of this solitary lake, until, near its further end, it suddenly turns into an extensive copse-wood of oak and birch. From this it emerges halfway up a rugged mountain side; and, entering a dark glen, through which a torrent rushes amidst great masses of granite, it conducts the traveller at last, by a zigzag ascent, up to a narrow gorge, which is hemmed in upon every side by giant precipices, with a strip of blue sky overhead, all below being dark and gloomy.

From this mountain-pass the widow's dwelling was ten miles distant. She had undertaken a long journey, but her rent was some weeks overdue, and the sub-factor threatened to dispossess her.

The morning on which she left her home gave promise of a peaceful day. Before noon, however, a sudden change took place in the weather. Northward, the sky became black and lowering. Masses of clouds came down upon the hills. Sudden gusts of wind began to whistle among the rocks, and to ruffle, with black squalls, the surface of the lake. The wind was succeeded by rain, and the rain by sleet, and the sleet by a heavy fall of snow. It was the month of May, and that storm is yet remembered as the 'great May storm'. The wildest day of winter never beheld snowflakes falling faster, or whirling with more fury through the mountain-pass, filling every hollow and whitening every rock!

Little anxiety about the widow was felt by the villagers, as many ways were pointed out by which they thought she could have escaped the fury of the storm. She might have halted at the home of this farmer, or of that shepherd, before it had become dangerous to cross the hill. But early on the morning of the succeeding day they were alarmed to hear from a person who had come from the place to which the widow was travelling, that she had not made her appearance there.

In a short time about a dozen men mustered to search for the missing woman. At each house on the track they heard with increasing fear that she had been seen pursuing her journey the day before. The shepherd on the mountain could give no information regarding her. Beyond his hut there was no shelter – nothing but deep snow; and between the range of rocks at the summit of the pass the drift lay thickest. There the storm must have blown with a fierce and bitter blast. It was by no means an easy task to examine the deep wreaths which filled up every hollow. At last a cry from one of the searchers attracted the rest, and there, crouched beneath a huge granite boulder, they discovered the dead body of the widow.

She was entombed by the snow. A portion of a tartan cloak which appeared above its surface led to her discovery. But what had become of the child? Nay, what had become of the widow's clothes? for all were gone except the miserable tattered garment which hardly covered her nakedness. That she had been murdered and stripped was the first conjecture suggested by the strange discovery. But in a country like this, in which one murder only had occurred within the memory of man, the notion was soon dismissed from their thoughts. She had evidently died where she sat, bent almost double; but as yet all was mystery in regard to her boy or her clothing. Very soon, however, the mystery was cleared up. A shepherd found the child alive in a sheltered nook in the rock, very near the spot where his mother sat cold and stiff in death. He lay in a bed of heather and fern, and round him were swathed all the clothes which his mother had stripped off herself to save her child! The story of her self-sacrificing love was easily read.

The incident has lived fresh in the memory of many in the parish; and the old people who were present in the empty hut of the widow when her body was laid in it, never forgot the minister's address and prayers as he stood beside the dead. He was hardly able to speak for tears, as he endeavoured to express his sense of that woman's worth and love, and to pray for her poor orphan boy.

More than fifty years passed away, when the eldest son of 'the manse',[171] then old and grey-headed, went to preach to his Highland congregation in Glasgow, on the Sunday previous to that on which the Lord's supper was to be dispensed. He found a comparatively small congregation assembled, for snow was falling heavily, and threatened to continue all day. Suddenly he recalled the story of the widow and her son, and this again recalled to his memory the text: 'He shall be as the shadow of a great rock in a weary land.' He then resolved to address his people from these words, although he had carefully prepared a sermon on another subject.

In the course of his remarks he narrated the circumstances of the death of the Highland widow, whom he had himself known in his boyhood. And having done so, he asked, 'If that child is now alive, what would you think of his heart, if he did not cherish an affection for his mother's memory, and if the sight of her clothes, which she had wrapt round him, in order to save his life at the cost of her own, did not touch his heart, and even fill him with gratitude and love too deep for words? Yet what hearts have you, my hearers, if over the memorials of your Saviour's sacrifice of Himself, which you are to witness next Sunday, you do not feel them glow with deepest love, and with adoring gratitude?'

Some time after this, a message was sent by a dying man requesting to see the minister. The request was speedily complied with. The sick man seized him by the hand, as he seated himself beside his bed, and, gazing intently in his face, said, 'You do not, you cannot recognise me. But I know you, and knew your father before you. I have been a wanderer in many lands. I have visited every quarter of the globe, and fought and bled for my king and country. But while I served my king I forgot my God. Though I have been some years in this city, I never entered a church. But the other Sunday, as I was walking along the street, I happened to pass your church door[172] when a heavy shower of snow came on, and I entered the lobby for shelter, but not, I am ashamed to say, with the intention of worshipping God, or of hearing a sermon. But as I heard them singing psalms, I went into a seat near the door; then you preached, and then I heard you tell the story of the widow and her son.' Here the voice of the old soldier faltered, his emotion almost choked his utterance; but recovering himself for a moment, he cried, 'I am that son!' and burst into a flood of tears. 'Yes,' he continued, 'I am that son! Never, never, did I forget my mother's love. Well might you ask, what a heart should mine have been if she had been forgotten by me! Though I never saw her, dear to me is her memory, and my only desire now is to lay my bones beside hers in the old churchyard among the hills. But, sir, what breaks my heart, and covers me with shame, is this – until now I never saw the love of Christ in giving Himself for me – a poor lost, hell-deserving sinner. I confess it! I confess it!' he cried, looking up to heaven, his eyes streaming with tears. Then pressing the minister's hand close to his breast, he added, 'It was God made you tell that story. Praise be to His holy name, that my dear mother did not die in vain, and that the prayers which, I was told, she used to offer for me, have been at last answered; for the love of my mother has been blessed by the Holy Spirit, for making me see, as I never saw before, the love of the Saviour. I see it, I believe it; I have found deliverance now where I found it in my childhood – in the cleft of the rock – the Rock of Ages!' and, clasping his hands, he repeated with intense fervour, 'Can a mother forget her sucking child, that she should not have compassion on the son of her womb? She may forget; yet will I not forget thee!'

He died in peace.

Chapter 10

TACKSMEN AND TENANTS

The 'upper' and 'lower' classes in the Highlands were not separated from each other by a wide gap. The thought was never suggested of a great proprietor above, like a leg of mutton on the top of a pole, and the people far below, looking up to him with envy. On reviewing the state of Highland society, one was rather reminded of a pyramid whose broad base was connected with the summit by a series of regular steps. The dukes or lords, indeed, were generally far removed from the inhabitants of the land, living as they did for the greater part of the year in London; but the minor chiefs, such as 'Lochnell', 'Lochiel', 'Coll', 'Macleod', 'Raasay', etc., resided on their respective estates and formed centres of local and personal influence.[173] They had good family mansions; and in some instances the old keep was enlarged into a fine baronial castle, where all the hospitality of the far North was combined with the more refined domestic arrangements of the South. They had also their handsome 'barge' or well-built, well-rigged 'smack' or 'wherry', and their stately piper, who played pibrochs with very storms of sound after dinner, or, from the bow of the boat, with the tartan ribbands fluttering from the grand war-pipe, spread the news of the chief's arrival for miles across the water.[174] They were looked up to and respected by the people. Their names were mingled with all the traditions of the country: they were as old as its history, practically as old, indeed, as the hills themselves. They mingled freely with the peasantry, spoke their language, shared their feelings, treated them with sympathy, kindness, and, except in outward circumstances, were in all respects, one of themselves. The poorest man on their estate could converse with them at any time in the frankest manner, as with friends whom they could trust. There was between them an old and firm attachment.

This feeling of clanship, this interest of the clan in their chief, has lived down to my own recollection. It is not many years – for I heard the incident described by some of the clan who took part in the *emeute* – since a new family burial ground was made in an old property by a laird who knew little of the manners or prejudices of the country, having lived most of his time abroad. The first person whom he wished to bury in this new private tomb near 'the big house' was his predecessor, whose lands and name he inherited, and who had been a true representative of the old stock. But when the clan heard of what they looked upon as an insult to their late chief, they formed a conspiracy, seized the body by force, and, after guarding it for a day or two, buried it with all honour in the ancient family tomb on 'The Isle of Saints, where stands the old grey cross'.[175]

The tacksman at that time formed the most important and influential class of society, which has now wholly disappeared in most districts.[176] In no country in the world was such a contrast presented as in the Highlands between the structure of the houses and the culture of their occupants. The houses were of the most primitive description; they consisted of one storey – had only what the Scotch call a *but* and *ben*, that is, a room at each end, with a court between, two garret rooms above, and in some cases a kitchen, built out at right angles behind. Most of them were thatched with straw or heather. Such was the architecture of the house in which Dr Johnson lived with the elegant and accomplished Sir Allan Maclean, in the island of Inch Kenneth. The old house of Glendessary,[177] again in 'the Parish', was constructed, like a few more, of wickerwork; the outside being protected with turf, and the interior lined with wood. 'The house and the furniture', writes Dr Johnson, 'were ever always nicely suited.[178] We were driven once, by missing our passage, to the hut of a gentleman, when, after a liberal supper, I was conducted to my chamber, and found an elegant bed of Indian cotton, spread with fine sheets. The accommodation was flattering; I undressed myself, and found my feet in the mire. The bed stood on the cold earth, which a long course of rain had softened to a puddle.' But in these houses were gentlemen, nevertheless, and ladies of education and high breeding. Writing of Sir Allan Maclean[179] and his daughters, Johnson says: 'Romance does not often exhibit a scene that strikes the imagination more than this little desert in these depths and western obscurity, occupied, not by a gross herdsman or amphibious fisherman, but by a gentleman and two ladies of high rank, polished

manners, and elegant conversation, who, in an habitation raised not
very far above the ground, but furnished with unexpected neatness
and convenience, practised all the kindness of hospitality and the
refinement of courtesy.' It was thus, too, with the old wicker-house
of Glendessary, which has not left a trace behind. The interior was
provided with all the comfort and taste of a modern mansion. The
ladies were accomplished musicians, the harp and piano sounded in
those 'halls of Selma,' and their descendants are now among
England's aristocracy.[180]

These gentlemen Tacksmen were generally men of education;
they had all small but well-selected libraries, and had not only
acquired some knowledge of the classics, but were fond of keeping
up their acquaintance with them. It was not an uncommon pastime
with them when they met together, to try who could repeat the
greatest number of lines from Vigil or Horace, or who among
them, when one line was repeated, could cap it with another line
commencing with the same letter as that which ended the former.
All this may seem to many to have been profitless amusement, but
it was not such amusement as rude and uncultivated boors would
have indulged in; nor was it such as is likely to be imitated by the
rich farmers who now pasture their flocks where hardly a stone
marks the site of those old homes.

I know only one surviving gentleman Tacksman belonging to
the period of which I write, and he is ninety years of age, though in
the full enjoyment of his bodily health and mental faculties. About
forty years ago, when inspecting his cattle, he was accosted by a
pedestrian with a knapsack on his back, who addressed him in a
language which was intended for Gaelic. The Tacksman, judging
him to be a foreigner, replied in French, which met no response but
a shake of the head, the Tacksman's French being probably as bad as
the tourist's Gaelic. The Highlander then tried Latin, which kindled
a smile of surprise, and drew forth an immediate reply. This was
interrupted by the remark that English would probably be more
convenient for both parties. The tourist, who turned out to be an
Oxford student, laughing heartily at the interview, gladly accepted
the invitation of the Tacksman to accompany him to his thatched
home, and share his hospitality. He was surprised on entering 'the
room' to see a small library in the humble apartment. 'Books here!'

he exclaimed, as he looked over the shelves. 'Addison, Johnson, Goldsmith, Shakespeare – what! Homer, too?' The farmer, with some pride, begged him to look at the Homer. It had been given as a prize to himself when he was a student at the University.

It was men like these who supplied the Highlands with clergy, physicians, lawyers, and the army and navy with many of their officers. It is not a little remarkable that the one island of Skye, for example, should have sent forth from her wild shores since the beginning of the last wars of the French Revolution, twenty-one lieutenant-generals and major-generals; forty-eight lieutenant-colonels; 600 commissioned officers; 10,000 soldiers; four governors of colonies; one governor-general; one adjutant-general; one chief baron of England; and one judge of the Supreme Court of Scotland. I remember the names of sixty-one officers[181] being enumerated, who, during 'the war', had joined the army or navy from farms which were visible from one hilltop in 'the Parish'. These times have now passed away. The Highlands furnish few soldiers or officers. Even the educated clergy are becoming few.

One characteristic of these Tacksmen which more than any other forms a delightful reminiscence of them, was their remarkable kindness to the poor. There was hardly a family which had not some man or woman who had seen better days for their guest, during weeks, months, perhaps years. These forlorn ones might have been very distant relations, claiming that protection which a drop of blood never claimed in vain; or former neighbours, or the children of those who were neighbours long ago; or, as it often happened, they might have had no claim whatever upon the hospitable family, beyond the fact that they were utterly destitute, yet could not be treated as paupers, and had in God's Providence been cast on the kindness of others, like waves of the wild sea breaking at their feet. Nor was there anything 'very interesting,' about such objects of charity. One old gentleman beggar I remember, who used to live with friends of mine for months, was singularly stupid, often bad-tempered. A decayed old gentlewoman, again, who was an inmate for years in one house, was subject to fits of great depression, and was by no means entertaining. Another needy visitor used to be accompanied by a female servant. When they departed after a sojourn of a few weeks, the servant was generally laden with wool, clothing, and a large allowance of tea and sugar, contributed by the hostess for the use of her mistress, who thus obtained supplies from different families during summer which kept herself and her red-haired domestic comfortable in their small hut during the winter. 'Weel, weel,' said the worthy host, as he saw the pair depart, 'it's a puir situation that of a beggar's servant, like yon woman carrying the bag and poke.' Now this hospitality was never dispensed with a grudge, but with all tenderness and nicest delicacy. These 'genteel beggars' were received into the family, had comfortable quarters assigned to them in the house, partook of all the family meals, and the utmost care was taken by old and young that not one word should be uttered, nor anything done, which could for a moment suggest to them the idea that they were a trouble, a bore, an intrusion, or anything save the most welcome and honoured guests. This attention, according to the minutest details, was almost a religion with the old Highland 'gentleman' and his family.

The poor of the parish, strictly so called, were, with few exceptions, wholly provided for by the Tacksmen.[182] Each farm, according to its size, had its old men, widows, and orphans depending on it for their support. The widow had her free house, which the farmers and the 'cottiers' around him kept in repair. They drove home from 'the Moss' her peats for fuel; her cow had pasturage on the green hills. She had land sufficient to raise potatoes, and a small garden for vegetables. She had hens and ducks, too, with the natural results of eggs, chickens and ducklings. She had sheaves of corn supplied her, and these, along with her own gleanings, were threshed at the mill with the Tacksman's crop. In short, she was tolerably comfortable, and very thankful, enjoying the feeling of being the object of true charity, which was returned by such labour as she could give, and by her hearty gratitude.

But all this was changed when those Tacksmen were swept away to make room for the large sheep farms, and when the remnants of the people flocked from their empty glens to occupy houses in wretched villages near the seashore, by way of becoming fishers – often where no fish could be caught.[183] The result has been that 'the Parish', for example, which once had a population of 2,200 souls, and received only £11 per annum from public (Church) funds for the support of the poor, expends now under the poor law upwards of £600 annually, with a population diminished by one half, and with poverty increased in a greater ratio. This, by the way, is the result generally, when money awarded by law, and distributed by officials, is substituted for the true charity prompted by the heart, and dispensed systematically to known and well-ascertained cases, that draw it forth by the law of sympathy and Christian duty. I am quite aware of how poetical this doctrine is in the opinion of some political economists, but in these days of heresy in regard to older and more certain truths, it may be treated charitably.

The effect of the poor law, I fear, has been to destroy in a great measure the old feelings of self-respect which felt it to be a degradation to receive any support from public charity when living, or to be buried by it when dead. It has loosened, also, those kind bonds of neighbourhood, family relationship, and natural love which linked the needy to those who could and ought to supply their wants, and which was blessed both to the giver and receiver. Those who ought on principle to support the poor are tempted to cast them on the rates, and thus to lose all the good derived from the exercise of Christian almsgiving. The poor themselves have become more needy and more greedy, and scramble for the miserable pittance which is given and received with equal heartlessness.[184]

The temptation to create large sheep-farms has no doubt been great. Rents are increased, and more easily collected. Outlays are fewer and less expensive than upon houses, etc. But should more rent be the highest, the noblest object of a proprietor? Are human beings to be treated like so many things used in manufactures? Are no sacrifices to be demanded for their good and happiness? Granting even, for the sake of argument, that profit, in the sense of obtaining more money, will be found in the long run to measure what is best for the people as well as for the landlord, yet may not the converse of this be equally true – that the good and happiness of the people will in the long run be found the most profitable? Proprietors, we are glad to hear, are beginning to think that if a middle-class tenantry, with small arable farms of a rental of from £20 to £100 per annum, were again introduced into the Highlands, the result would be increased rents. Better still, the huge glens, along whose rich straths no sound is now heard for twenty or thirty miles but the bleat of sheep or the bark of dogs, would be tenanted, as of yore, with a comfortable and happy peasantry.[185]

In the meantime, emigration has been to a large extent a blessing to the Highlands, and to a larger extent still, a blessing to the colonies. It is the only relief for a poor and redundant population. The hopelessness of improving their condition, which rendered many in the Highlands listless and lazy, has in the colonies given place to the hope of securing a competency by prudence and industry. These virtues have accordingly sprung up, and the results have been comfort and independence. A wise political economy, with sympathy for human feelings and attachments, will, we trust, be able more and more to adjust the balance between the demands of the old and new country, for the benefit both of proprietors and people. But I must return to the old tenants.

Below the 'gentlemen' Tacksmen were those who paid a much lower rent, and who lived very comfortably, and shared hospitably with others the gifts which God gave them. I remember a group of men tenants in a large glen which now 'has not smoke in it', as the Highlanders say, throughout its length of twenty miles.[186] They had the custom of entertaining in rotation every traveller who cast himself on their hospitality. The host on the occasion was bound to summon his neighbours to the homely feast. It was my good fortune to be a guest when they received the present minister of 'the Parish', while *en route* to visit some of his flock. We had a most sumptuous feast – oat-cake, crisp and fresh from the fire; cream, rich and thick, and more beautiful than nectar, whatever that may be; blue Highland cheese, finer than Stilton; fat hens, slowly cooked on the fire in a pot of potatoes, without their skins, and with fresh butter – 'stoved hens', as the superb dish was called; and, though last, not least, tender kid, roasted as nicely as Charles Lamb's cracklin' pig.[187] All was served up with the utmost propriety, on a table covered with a pure white cloth, and with all the requisites for a comfortable dinner, including the champagne of elastic, buoyant, and exciting mountain air. The manners and conversation of those present would have pleased the best-bred gentleman. Everything was so simple, modest, unassuming, unaffected, yet so frank and cordial. The conversation was such as might be heard at the table of any intelligent man. Alas! there is not a vestige remaining of their homes. I know not whither they have gone, but they have left no representatives behind. The land in the glen is divided between sheep, shepherds, and the shadows of the clouds.

There were annual festivals of the Highland tenantry, which deeply moved every glen, and these were the Dumbarton and Falkirk 'Trysts', or fairs for cattle and sheep.[188] What preparations were made for these gatherings, on which the rent and income of the year depended! What a collecting of cattle, small and great; of drovers, and of dogs! – the latter being the most interested and excited of all who formed the caravan. What speculations as to how the 'market' would turn out. What a shaking of hands in boats, wayside inns, and on decks of steamers by the men in homespun cloth, gay tartans, or in the more correct new garbs of Glasgow or Edinburgh tailors! What a pouring in from all the glens, increasing at every ferry and village, and flowing on a river of tenants and proprietors, small and great, to the market! What that market was I know not from personal observation, nor desire to know.

> Let Yarrow be unseen, unknown,
>   If now we're sure to rue it,
> We have a vision of our own,
>   Ah, why should we undo it?[189]

The impression left in early years is too sublime to be tampered with. I have a vision of miles of tents, of flocks, and herds, surpassed only by those in the wilderness of Sinai; of armies of Highland sellers trying to get high prices out of the Englishmen, and Englishmen trying to get low prices out of the Highlandmen – but all in the way of 'fair dealing'.

When any person returned who had been himself at the market, who could recount its ups and downs, its sales and purchases, with all the skirmishes, stern encounters, and great victories; it was an eventful day in the Tacksman's dwelling! A stranger not initiated into the mysteries of a great fair might have supposed it possible for anyone to give all information about it in a brief business form. But there was such an enjoyment in details, such a luxury in going over all the prices, and all that was asked by the seller and refused by the purchaser, and asked again by the seller, and again refused by the purchaser, with the nice financial fencing of 'splitting the difference', or giving back a 'luck's penny',[190] as baffles all description. It was not enough to give the prices of three-year-olds and four-year-olds, yell cows, crock ewes, stirks, stots, lambs, tups, wethers, shots, bulls, etc.,[191] but the stock of each well-known proprietor, or breeder, had to be discussed. Colonsay's bulls, Corrie's sheep, Drumdriesaig's heifers, or Achadshenaig's wethers, had all to be passed under careful review.[192] Then following discussions about distinguished 'beasts' which had 'fetched high prices; their horns, their hair, their houghs, and general 'fashion', with their parentage. It did not suffice to tell that this or that great purchaser from the south had given so much for this or that 'lot', but his first offer, his remarks, his doubts, his advance of price, with the sparring between him and the Highland dealer, must all be particularly recorded, until the final shaking of hands closed the bargain. And after all was gone over, it was a pleasure to begin the same tune again with variations. But who that has ever heard an after-dinner talk in England about a good day's hunting, or a good race, will be surprised at this endless talk about a market?

I will close this chapter with a story told of a great sheep-farmer – not one of the old 'gentleman tenants' verily! – who, though he could neither read nor write, had nevertheless made a large fortune by sheep-farming, and was open to any degree of flattery as to his abilities in this department of labour.[193] A purchaser, knowing his weakness, and anxious to ingratiate himself into his good graces, ventured one evening over their whisky toddy to remark, 'I am of opinion, sir, that you are a greater man than even the Duke of Wellington!' 'Hoot toot!' replied the sheep farmer, modestly hanging his head with a pleasing smile and taking a large pinch of snuff. 'That is too much – too much, by far – by far.' But his guest, after expatiating for a while upon the great powers of his host in collecting and concentrating upon a Southern market a flock of sheep, suggested the question, 'Could the Duke of Welling-ton have done that?' The sheep-farmer thought a little, snuffed, took a glass of toddy, and replied, 'The Duke of Wellington was, no doot, a clever man; very, very clever, I believe. They tell me he was a good sojer, but then, d'ye see, he had reasonable men to deal with – captains, and majors, and generals that could understand him – every one of them, both officers and men; but I'm not so sure after all if he could manage say twenty thousand sheep, besides black cattle, that could not understand one word he said, Gaelic or English, and bring every hoof o' them to Fa'kirk Tryst! I doot it – I doot it! But I have often done that.' The inference was evident.

Chapter 11

MARY CAMPBELL'S MARRIAGE

Mary Campbell was a servant in the old manse, about sixty years ago, and was an honest and bonnie lassie.[194] She had blue eyes and flaxen hair, with a form as 'beautiful as the fleet roe on the mountain', a very Malvina to charm one of the heroes of old Ossian.[195] Her sweetheart was not, however, an 'Oscar of the Spear', a 'Cuchullin of the car', or a Fingal who 'sounded his shield in the halls of Selma', but was a fine-looking shepherd lad named Donald Maclean, who 'wandered slowly as a cloud' over the hills at morning after his sheep, and sang his songs, played his trump, and lighted up Mary's face with his looks at evening. For two years they served together; and, as in all such cases, these years seemed as a single day. Yet no vows were exchanged, no engagement made between them. Smiles and looks, improvised songs full of lovers' chaffing, joining together as partners in the kitchen dance to Archy M'Intyre's fiddle, showing a tendency to work at the same hay-rick, and to reap beside each other on the same harvest rigs, and to walk home together from the kirk – these were the only significant signs of what was understood by all, that bonnie Mary and handsome Donald were sweethearts.

It happened to them as to all lovers since the world began; the old history was repeated in the want of smoothness with which the river of their affection flowed on its course. It had the usual eddies and turns which belong to all such streams, and it had its little falls, with tiny bubbles, that soon broke and disappeared in rainbow hues, until the agitated water rested once more in a calm pool, dimpled with sunlight, and overhung with wild flowers.

But a terrible break and thundering fall at last approached with rich Duncan Stewart, from Lochaber! Duncan was a well-to-do small tenant, with a number of beeves and sheep, was a thrifty, money-making bachelor, who never gave or accepted bills for man or for beast, but was contented with small profits, and ready cash secured at once and hoarded in safety with Carrick, Brown, and

Company's Ship Bank, Glasgow, there to grow at interest while he was sleeping – though he was generally 'wide awake'. He was a cousin of Mary's, 'thrice removed,' but close enough to entitle him to command a hearing in virtue of his relationship when he came to court her; and on this very errand he arrived one day at the manse where, as a matter of course, he was hospitably received – alas! for poor Donald Maclean.

Duncan had seen Mary but once, but having made up his mind, which it was not difficult for him to do, as to her fair appearance, and having ascertained from others that she was in every respect a most properly-conducted girl, and a most accomplished servant, who could work in the field or dairy, in the kitchen or laundry, that beside the fire at night her hands were the most active in knitting, sewing, carding wool, or spinning, he concluded that she was the very wife for Duncan Stewart of Blairdhu. But would Mary take him? A doubt never crossed his mind upon that point. His confidence did not arise from his own good looks, for they, to speak charitably, were doubtful, even to himself. He had high cheek-bones, small teeth not innocent of tobacco, and a large mouth. To these features there was added a sufficient number of grey hairs sprinkled on the head and among the bushy whiskers, to testify to many more years than those which numbered the age of Mary. But Duncan had money – a large amount of goods laid up for many years – full barns and sheepfolds. He had a place assigned to him at the Fort William market, such as a well-known capitalist has in the city Exchange. He was thus the sign of a power which tells in every class of society. Are no fair merchant's daughters, we would respectfully ask, affected in their choice of husbands by the state of their funds? Has a coronet no influence over the feelings? Do the men of substance make their advances to beauties without it, with no sense of the weight of argument which is measured by the weight of gold in their proffered hand? Do worth and character and honest love, and *sufficient* means, always get fair play from the fair, when opposed by rivals having less character and less love, but with more than *sufficient* means? According to the reader's replies to these questions will be his opinion as to the probability of Duncan winning Mary, and of Mary forsaking poor Donald and accepting his 'highly respectable' and wealthy rival.

It must be mentioned that another power came into play at this juncture of affairs, and that was an elder sister of Mary's who lived in the neighbourhood of the farmer, and who was supposed by the observing dames of the district to have 'set her cap' at Duncan. But it was more the honour of the connection than love which had prompted those gentle demonstrations on the part of Peggy. She wished to give him the hint, as it were, that he need not want a respectable wife for the asking; although of course she was quite happy and contented to remain in her mother's house, and help to manage the small croft, with its cow, pigs, poultry, and potatoes. Duncan, without ever pledging himself, sometimes seemed to acknowledge that it might be well to keep Peggy on his list as a reserve corps, in case he might fail in his first plan of battle. The fact must be confessed, that such marriages 'of convenience' were as common in the Highlands as elsewhere. Love, no doubt, in many cases, carried the day there as it will do in Greenland, London, or Timbuctoo. Nevertheless, the dog-team, the blubber, the fishing-tackle, of the North will, at times, tell very powerfully on the side of their possessor, who is yet wanting in the softer emotions; and so will the cowries and cattle of Africa, and the West-end mansion and carriage of London. The female heart will everywhere, in its own way, acknowledge that 'love is all very well, when one is young, but—' and with that prudential 'but', depend upon it, the blubber, cowries, and carriage are sure to carry the day, and leave poor Love to make off with clipped wings!

Duncan of Blairdhu so believed when he proposed to Mary, through the minister's wife, who had never heard the kitchen gossip about the shepherd, and who was delighted to think that her Mary had the prospect of being so comfortably married. All the pros and cons having been set before her, Mary smiled, hung her head, pulled her fingers until every joint cracked, and after a number of 'could not really says', and 'really did not knows', and 'wondered why he had asked her', and 'what was she to do', etc., followed by a few hearty tears, she left her mistress, and left the impression that she would in due time be Mrs Duncan Stewart. Her sister Peggy appeared on the scene, and, strange to say, urged the suit with extraordinary vehemence She spoke not of love, but of honour, rank, position, comfort, influence, as all shining around on the Braes of Lochaber. Peggy never heard of the shepherd, but had she done so, the knowledge would have only moved her indignation. Duncan's cousinship made his courtship a sort of family claim – a social right. It was not possible that her sister would be so foolish, stupid, selfish, as not to marry a rich man like Mr Stewart. Was she to bring disgrace on herself and people by refusing him? Mary was too gentle for Peggy, and she bent like a willow beneath the breeze of her appeals. She would have given worlds to have been able to say that she was engaged to Donald; but that was not the case. Would Donald ask her? She loved him too well for her to betray her feeling so as to prompt the delicate question, yet she wondered why he was not coming to her relief at such a crisis. Did he know it? Did he suspect it?

Donald, poor lad, was kept in ignorance of all these diplomatic negotiations; and when at last a fellow-servant expressed his suspicions, he fell at once into despair, gave up the game as lost, lingered among the hills as long as possible, hardly spoke when he returned home at night, seemed to keep aloof from Mary, and one evening talked to her so crossly in his utter misery that next morning, when Duncan Stewart arrived at the manse, Peggy had so arranged matters that Mary before the evening was understood to have accepted the hand of the rich farmer.

The news was kept secret. Peggy would not speak. Mary could not. Duncan was discreetly silent, and took his departure to arrange the marriage, for which the day was fixed before he left. The minister's wife and the minister congratulated Mary; Mary gave no response, but pulled her fingers more energetically and nervously than ever. This was all taken as a sign of modesty. The shepherd whistled louder than before for his dogs, and corrected them with singular vehemence; he played his trumps with greater persever-ance, sang his best songs at night, but there was no more dancing, and he did not walk with Mary from the kirk; and the other servants winked and laughed, and knew there was 'something atween them', then guessed what it was, then knew all about it; yet none presumed to tease them. There was a something which kept back all intrusion, but no one seemed to know what that something was.

The marriage dress was easily got up by the manse girls, and each of them added some bonnie gift to make Mary look still more bonnie. She was a special favourite, and the little governess with the work of her own hands contributed not a little to Mary's wardrobe.

All at once the girls came to the conclusion that Mary did not love Duncan. She had no interest in her dress; she submitted to every attention as if it were a stern duty; her smile was not joyous. Their suspicions were confirmed when the cook, commonly called Kate Kitchen, confided to them the secret of Mary's love for the shepherd – all, of course, in strict confidence but every fair and gentle attempt was made in vain to get her to confess. She was either silent, or said there was nothing between them, or she would do what was right, and so on; or she would dry her eyes with her apron, and leave the room. These interviews were not satisfactory, and so they were soon ended; a gloom gathered over the wedding; there was a want of enthusiasm about it; everyone felt drifting slowly to it without any reason strong enough for pulling in an opposite direction. Why won't Donald propose? His proud heart is breaking, but he thinks it too late, and will give no sign. Why does not Mary refuse Duncan – scorn him, if you will, and cling to the shepherd? Her little proud heart is also breaking, for the shepherd has become cold to her. He ought to have asked her, she thinks, before now, or even now proposed a runaway marriage, carried her off, and she would have flown with him, like a dove, gently held in an eagle's talon, over hill and date, to a nest of their own, where love alone would have devoured her. But both said, 'Tis too late!' Fate, like a magic power, seemed to have doomed that she must marry Duncan Stewart.

The marriage was to come off at the house of a tacksman, an uncle of the bride's, about two miles from the manse, for the honour of having a niece married to Blairdhu demanded special attention to be shown on the occasion.[196] A large party was invited, a score of the tenantry of the district, with the minister's family, and a few of the gentry, such as the sheriff[197] and his wife, the doctor, and some friends who accompanied Duncan from Lochaber: big Sandy Cameron from Lochiel; Archy, son of Donald, from Glen Nevis; and Lachlan, the son of young Lachlan, from Corpach. How they all managed to dispose of themselves in the but and ben, including the centre closet, of Malcolm Morrison's house, has never yet been explained. Those who have known the capacity of

Highland houses – the capacity to be full, and yet to be able to accommodate more – have thought that the walls possessed some expansive power, the secret of which has not come down to posterity. On that marriage day a large party was assembled. On the green, outside the house, were many Highland carts, which had conveyed the guests; while the horses, their forelegs being tied together at the fetlock, with ungainly hops cropped the green herbage at freedom, until their services were required within the next twelve hours. Droves of dogs were busy making one another's acquaintance, collie dogs and terriers – every tail erect or curled, and each, with bark or growl, asserting its own independence. Groups of guests, in homespun clothes, laughed and chatted round the door, waiting for the hour of marriage. Some of 'the ladies' were gravely seated within, decked out in new caps and ribands, while servant-women, with loud voices and louder steps, were rushing to and fro, as if in desperation, arranging the dinner. This same dinner was a very ample one of stoved hens and potatoes, legs of mutton, roast ducks, corned beef, piles of cheese, tureens of curds and cream, and oat cakes piled in layers. Duncan Stewart walked out and in, dressed in a full suit of blooming Stewart tartan, with frills to his shirt, which added greatly to his turkey-cock appearance.

But where was the bride? She had been expected at four o'clock, and it was now past five. It was understood that she was to have left the manse escorted by Hugh, son of big John M'Allister. The company became anxious. A message of inquiry was at last despatched, but the only information received was that the bride had left the manse at two o'clock, immediately after the manse party. A herd-boy was again despatched to obtain more accurate tidings, and the governess whispered in his ear to ask particularly about the whereabouts of Donald the shepherd. But the boy could tell nothing, except that Hugh and the bride had started on horseback three hours before; and as for Donald, he was unwell in bed, for he had seen him there rolled up in blankets, with his face to the wall. The excitement became intense. Duncan Stewart snuffed pro-digiously; Malcolm, Mary's uncle, uttered sundry expressions by no means becoming; Peggy, full of alarming surmises, wrung her hands, and threw herself on a bed in the middle closet. The ladies became perplexed; the sheriff consulted the company as to what should be done. The doctor suggested the suicide of the bride. The minister suspected more than he liked to express.

But two men, mounted on the best horses, and taking a gun with them – why, no one could conjecture – started off in great haste to the manse. The timid bird had flown, no one knew whither. The secret had been kept from every human being. But if she was to leave the parish it could only be by a certain glen, across a certain river, and along one path, which led to the regions beyond.[198] They conjectured that she was *en route* for her mother's home, in order to find there a temporary asylum. To this glen, and along this path, the riders hurried with the gun. The marriage party in the meantime 'took a refreshment', and made M'Pherson, the bagpiper, play reels and strathspeys, to which the young folk danced, while the older people assured Duncan Stewart that the mystery would soon be satisfactorily cleared up. Duncan pretended to laugh at the odd joke – for a joke he said it was. Peggy alone refused to be comforted. Hour after hour passed, but no news of the bride. The ladies began to yawn; the gentlemen to think how they should spend the night; until at last all who could not be accommodated within the elastic walls by any amount of squeezing, dispersed, after house and barn were filled, to seek quarters at the manse or among the neighbouring farms.

The two troopers who rode in pursuit of Mary came at last, after a hard ride of twenty miles, to a small inn, which was the frontier house of the parish, and whose white walls marked, as on a peninsula, the ending of one long uninhabited glen, and the commencement of another.[199] As they reached this solitary and wayside place, they determined to put up for the night. The morning had been wet, and clouds full of rain had gathered after sunset on the hills. On entering the kitchen of the 'change house', they saw some clothes drying on a chair opposite the fire, with a 'braw cap' and ribands suspended near them, and dripping with moisture. On making inquiry they were informed that these belonged to a young woman who had arrived there shortly before, behind Hugh, son of big John M'Allister of the manse, who had returned with the horse by another road over the hill. The woman was on her way to Lochaber, but her name was not known. Poor Mary was caught! Her pursuers need not have verified their conjectures by entering her room and upbraiding her in most unfeeling terms, telling her, before locking the door in order to secure her, that she must accompany them back in the morning and be married to Duncan Stewart, as sure as there was justice in the land. Mary spoke not a word, but gazed at them as in a dream.

At early dawn she was mounted behind one of these moss-troopers, and conducted in safety to the manse, as she had requested to see the family before she went through the ceremony of marriage. That return to the manse was an epoch in its history. The shepherd had disappeared in the meantime, and so had Hugh M'Allister. When Mary was ushered into the presence of the minister, and the door was closed, she fell on her knees before him, and bending her forehead until she rested it on his outstretched hand, she burst forth into hysterical weeping. The minister soothed her, and bid her tell him frankly what all this was about. Did she not like Stewart? Was she unwilling to marry him? 'Unwilling to marry him!' cried Mary, rising up, with such flashing eyes and dramatic manner as the minister had never seen before in her, or thought it possible for one so retiring and shy to exhibit. 'I tell you, sir, I would sooner be chained to a rock at low water, and rest there until the tide came and choked my breath, than marry that man!'[200] and Mary, as if her whole nature was suddenly changed, spoke out with the vehemence of long-restrained freedom breaking loose at last in his own inherent dignity. 'Then, Mary, dear,' said the minister, patting her head, 'you shall never be married against your will, by me or anyone else, to mortal man.' 'Bless you, dear, dear sir,' said Mary, kissing his hand.

Duncan heard the news. 'What on earth, then,' he asked, 'is to be done with the dinner?' for the cooking had been stopped. To his Lochaber friends he whispered certain sayings borrowed from sea and land – as, for example, that there were 'as good fish in the sea as ever came out of it' – 'that she who winna when she may, may live to rue another day', and so on. He spoke and acted like one who pitied as a friend the woman whom he thought once so wise as to have been willing to marry Blairdhu. Yet Blairdhu's question was a serious one, and was still unanswered: 'What was to become of the dinner?' Mary's uncle suggested the answer. He took Duncan aside, and talked confidentially and earnestly to him. His communications were received with a smile, a grunt, and a nod of the head, each outward sign of the inward current of feeling being frequently repeated in the same order. The interview was ended by a request from Duncan to see Peggy. Peggy gave him her hand, and squeezed his with a fervour made up of hysterics and hope. She wept, however, real tears, pouring forth her sympathies with the bride-groom in ejaculatory gasps, like jerks for breath, when mentioning a man of his res – pect – a – bil – i – ty.' Before night, a match was made up between Duncan and Peggy: she declaring that it was done to save the credit of her family, though it was not yesterday that she had learned to esteem Mr Stewart; he declaring that he saw clearly the hand of Providence in the whole transaction – that Mary was too young, too inexperienced for him, and that the more he knew her, the less he liked her. The hand of Providence was not less visible when it conveyed a dowry of £50 from Peggy's uncle with his niece. The parties were 'proclaimed' in church on the following Sunday and married on Monday – and so the credit of both the family and the dinner was saved.

But what of Mary? She was married to the shepherd, after explanations and 'a scene', which, as I am not writing fiction, but truth, I cannot describe, the details not having come to me in the traditions of the parish.

Donald enlisted as a soldier in some Highland regiment, and his faithful Mary accompanied him to the Peninsula. How he managed to enlist at all as a married man, and she to follow him as his wife, I know not. But I presume that in those days, when soldiers were recruited by officers who had personally known them and their people, and to whom the soldier was previously attached, many things were permitted and favours obtained which would be impossible now. Nor can I tell why Mary was obliged to return home. But the rules or necessities of the service during war demanded this step. So Mary once more appeared at the manse in the possession of £60 which she had earned and saved by working for the regiment, and which Donald had entrusted, along with an only daughter, to his wife's care. The money was invested by the minister. Mary, as a matter of course, occupied her old place in the family, and found every other servant, but Donald, where she had left them years before. No one received her with more joy than

Hugh M'Allister, who had been her confidant – and best man. But what stories and adventures Mary had to tell! And what a high position she occupied at the old kitchen fireside. Everything there was as happy as in the days of auld lang syne, and nothing wanting save Donald's blithe face and merry trumps.

Neither Mary nor Donald could write, nor could they speak any language except Gaelic. Their stock of English was barely sufficient to enable them to transact the most ordinary business. Was it this want, and the constant toil and uncertain marches of a soldier during war, which had prevented Donald from writing home to his wife? For, alas, two long years passed without her having once heard from him!

After months of anxious hope had gone by, Mary began to look old and careworn. The minister scanned the weekly newspaper with intense anxiety, especially after a battle had been fought, to catch her husband's name among the list of the dead or wounded. He had written several times for information, but with little effect. All he could hear was that Donald was alive and well. At last the news came that he was married to another woman. A soldier journeying homewards from the same regiment, and passing through the parish, had said so to several persons in the village after he had had 'his glass'. But the soldier was gone long before he could be cross-questioned. Mary heard the news, and though scorning the lie, as she said it was, she never alluded to the fearful story. Still the secret wound was evidently injuring her health; her cheek became paler, 'the natural force abated' while at her work, and Kate Kitchen had on more than one occasion discovered tears dropping on the little girl's face as her mother combed her hair, or laid her down to sleep.

There was not a person in the house who did not carry poor Mary's burthen, and treat her with the utmost delicacy. Many an expression calculated to strengthen her faith in God, and to comfort her, was uttered at family prayers, which she always attended. Yet she never complained, never asked any sympathy; she was quiet, meek, and most unselfish, like one who tried to bear alone her own sorrow, without troubling others. She worked diligently, but never joined in the chorus song which often cheered the hours of labour. She clung much to Hugh M'Allister, who, like a shield, cast aside from her the cruel darts which were shot in the parish by insinuations of Donald's unfaithfulness, or the repetition of the story 'told by the soldier'.

The fifth year of desolation had reached midsummer, and it was clear that Mary was falling into permanent bad health. One day, having toiled until the afternoon at the making of a haystack, she sat down to rest upon some hay near it. Above, lads and lasses were busy trampling, under the superintendence of Hugh M'Allister. Hugh suddenly paused in the midst of his work, and gazing steadfastly for a minute or two at a distant person approaching the manse from the gate, said, with a suppressed voice, and a 'Hush!' which commanded silence, 'If Donald Maclean is in life, that's him!' Every eye was directed to the traveller, who, with a knapsack on his back, was slowly approaching. 'It's a beggar,' said Kate Kitchen. 'It's like Donald, after all,' said another, as the sounds of the traveller's feet were heard on the narrow gravel walk. 'It is him, and none but him!' cried Hugh as he slid down to the ground, having seen Donald's face as he took off his cap and waved it. Flying to Mary, who had been half asleep from fatigue, he seized her by the hand, raised her up, and, putting his brawny arm round her neck, kissed her; then brushing away a tear from his eye with the back of his rough hand, he said, 'God bless you! this is better than a thousand pounds, any day!' Mary, in perplexity and agitation, asked what he meant, as he dragged her forward, giving her a gentle push as they both came round the haystack which concealed Donald from their view. With a scream she flew to him, and as they embraced in silence, a loud cheer rose from the stack, which was speedily hushed in silent sobs even from the strong men.

What an evening that was at the manse! If ever Donald heard the falsehood about his second marriage, there was no allusion to it that night. He had returned to his wife and child with honourable wounds, a Waterloo medal, and a pension for life.[201] He and Mary settled down again at the manse for many months, and the trump was again heard as in the days of yore. On the last night of the year Donald insisted on dancing once more with Mary, in spite of his lame leg and the laughter of his girl.

I will not follow their adventures further, beyond stating that they removed to Glasgow; that Donald died, and was buried thirty years ago in the old churchyard of 'the parish';[202] that the daughter was married, but not happily; that Mary fought a noble, self-denying battle to support herself by her industry, and her army savings, the capital of which she has preserved until now.

When nearly eighty years of age she went on a pilgrimage to visit Donald's grave. 'Do you repent marrying him,' I asked her on her return, 'and refusing Duncan Stewart?' 'Repent!' she exclaimed, as her fine old face was lighted up with sunshine; 'I would do it all again for the noble fellow!'

Mary lived in Glasgow till her death, respected by all who knew her.

Chapter 12

CHURCHYARDS AND FUNERALS

The Highland churchyard is a spot which seldom betrays any other traces of human art or care than those simple headstones which mark its green graves. In very few instances is it enclosed; its graves generally mingle with the mountain pasture and blooming heather, and afford shelter to the sheep and lamb from the blast of winter and the heat of summer. But although not consecrated by holy prayer and religious ceremony, these are, nevertheless, holy spots in the hearts and memories of the peasantry, who never pass them without a subdued look, which betokens a feeling of respect for the silent sleepers. To deck a father's or mother's grave would be, in the estimation of the Highlander, to turn it into a flower-garden. He thinks it utter vanity to attempt to express his grief or respect for the departed by any ornament beyond the tombstone, whose inscription is seldom more than a statistical table of birth and death.[203]

Many of those Highland churchyards, so solitary and so far removed from the busy haunts of men, are, nevertheless, singularly touching and beautiful. Some are on green islands whose silence is disturbed only by the solemn thunder of the great ocean wave, or the ripple of the inland sea; some are in great wide glens round the ruins of a chapel, where prayers were once offered by early missionaries who with noble aim and holy ambition penetrated these wild and savage haunts; while others break the green swards about the parish church on ground where God has been worshipped since the days of St Columba.

One of the most beautiful I ever visited is on a small green island in Loch Shiel in Argyleshire.[204] The loch for nearly twenty miles is as yet innocent of roads on either shore, so that the tourist who visits the place has to navigate the lake in a rude country boat; and if he attempts to sail, he must do so with blankets attached probably to the oar, and then trust to a fair wind. Yet what can be more delicious than thus to glide along the shore with a crew that won't speak till they are spoken to, and in silence gaze upon the ever-varying scene – to skim past the bights and bays with their reedy margins – the headlands tufted with waving birch – the gulfy torrents pouring down their foaming waterfalls and 'blowing their trumpets from the steeps' – with the copse of oak and hazel, that covers the sides of the mountain from the deep dark water up to the green pasture, and beyond, the bare rocks that pierce the blue.

Not unlikely the crew, when they take to their oars, will sing 'Ho Morag', in honour of Prince Charlie, 'the lad wi' the Philabeg', who on the green alluvial plain at the head of the loch[205] – where his monument now stands – first unfurled his banner, to regain the British crown; and if you don't know this romantic episode in history, the boatmen with pride will point out the glens where the Camerons, Macdonalds, Stewarts, and Macleans poured down their kilted clans, the last old guard of the feudal times, to do battle for 'the yellow-haired laddie'; and unless you cordially believe (at least until you leave Loch Shiel) that you would have joined them on that day, with the probability even of losing your head and your common sense, you are not in a fit state of spirit to enjoy the scene.

Halfway up this lake, and at its narrowest portion, there is a beautiful green island, which stretches itself so far across as to leave but a narrow passage for even the country boat. Above it, and looking down on it, rises Ben Reshobal for 2,000 feet or more, with its hanging woods, grey rocks, dashing streams, and utter solitude.[206] On the island is an old chapel, with the bell – now we believe preserved by the laird – which long ago so often broke the silence of these wilds on holy days of worship or of burial.[207] There lie chiefs and vassals, fierce cateran robbers of sheep and cattle, murderers of opposing clans, with women and children, Catholic and Protestant, Prince Charlie men, and men who served in army and navy under George the Third. Yet the only monument we remember consisted of a wooden stake driven into the ground, with no other carving on it than D. W. 1746.[208] How silent is the graveyard! You sit down among the ruins and hear only the bleat of sheep), the whish-whish of the distant waterfalls, the lapping of the waves, or the wind creeping through the archways and mouldering windows. The feuds and combats of the clans are all gone, the stillness and desolation of their graves alone remain.

But 'the Parish' churchyard is not much less picturesque.[209] It is situated on a green plateau of table-land which forms a ledge between the low seashore and mountain background. A beautiful tall stone cross from Iona adorns it;[210] a single gothic arch of an old church remains as a witness for the once consecrated ground, and links the old 'cell' to the modern building, which in architecture – shame to modern Lairds – is to the old one what a barn is to a church.[211] The view, however, from that churchyard of all God's glorious architecture above and below makes one forget those paltry attempts of man to be a fellow-worker with Him in the rearing and adorning of the fitting, and the beautiful. There is not in the Highlands a finer expanse of inland seas, of castled prom-ontories, of hills beyond hills, until cloudland and highland mingle, of precipice and waterfall, with all the varied lights and shadows which heathy hillsides, endless hilltops, dark corries, ample bays and rocky shores, can create at morn, noonday, or evening from sun and cloud – a glorious panorama extending from the far west beyond the giant point of Ardnamurchan, 'the height of the great ocean', to the far east, where Ben Cruachan and 'the Shepherds of Etive Glen'[212] stand sentinels in the sky. No sea king could select a more appropriate resting place than this, from whence to catch a glimpse, as his spirit walked abroad beneath the moonlight, of galleys coming from the Northland of his early home; nor could an old saint find a better resting place,[213] if he desired that after death the mariners, struggling with stormy winds and waves, might see his cross from afar, and thence snatch comfort from this symbol of faith and hope 'in extremis'; nor could any man, who in the frailty of his human nature shrunk from burial in lonely vault, and who wished rather to lie where birds might sing, and summer's sun shine, and winter's storms lift their voices to God, and the beautiful world be ever above and around him, find a spot more congenial to his feelings than the kirkyard of 'the Parish'.

The Highlander has a love which amounts to a decided super-stition to lie beside his kindred. The Celt is intensely social in his love of family and tribe. It is long ere he takes to a stranger as bone of his bone and flesh of his flesh. When sick in the distant hospital, he will, though years have separated him from home and trained him to be a citizen of the world, yet dream in his delirium of the old burial ground. To him there is in this idea a sort of homely feeling, a sense of friendship, a desire for a congenial neighbourhood, which, without growing into a belief of which he would be ashamed, unmistakeably circulates as an instinct in his blood, and cannot easily be dispelled. It is thus that the poorest Highlanders always endeavour to bury their dead with kindred dust. The pauper will save his last penny to secure this boon.

A woman from 'the mainland', somewhere in Kintail, was married to a highly respectable man in one of the Hebrides which need not be specified. When she died, twelve of her relations, strong men, armed with oak sticks, journeyed sixty miles to be present at her funeral. They quietly expressed their hope to her husband that his wife should be buried in her own country and beside her own people. But on ascertaining from him that such was not his purpose they declared their intention to carry off the body by force. An unseemly struggle was avoided only through the husband being unable to find anyone to back him in his refusal to what was deemed by his neighbours a reasonable request. He therefore consented, and accompanied the body sixty miles to the old churchyard.

This feeling is carried to a length which is too ludicrous to be dignified even by the name of superstition. A Highland porter, who carried our bag but the other day, and who has resided for thirty years in the low country, sent his amputated finger to be buried in the graveyard of the parish beside the remains of his kindred! It is said that a bottle of whisky was sent along with the thumb that it might be entombed with all honour! – but I don't vouch for the truth of the latter part of the story. I never heard who dug the grave of the thumb – whether it was 'I says the owl' – nor who attended the funeral, nor what monument was erected over the respected member. But there, nevertheless, the thumb lies, to be some day joined by the whole body.

This desire of being interred with kindred dust or with 'the faithful ones', as they express it, is so strong, that I have known a poor man selling all his potatoes, and reducing himself to great suffering, in order to pay the expense of burying his wife in a distant churchyard among her people, and that, too, when the minister of his parish offered to bury her at his own expense in the churchyard of the parish in which the widower resided. Only last year a pauper in the parish of K— begged another poor neighbour to see her buried beside her family. When she died, twelve men assembled, carried her ten miles off, dug her grave, and paid all the expenses of her funeral, which, had she been buried elsewhere, would have been paid by the parish.

It is still a very common belief among the peasantry that shadowy funeral processions precede the real ones, and that 'warnings' are given of a common death by the crowing of cocks, the ticking of the death watch, the howling of dogs, voices heard by night, the sudden appearance of undefined forms of human beings passing to and fro, etc.

It has also been the custom of the poorest persons to have all their dead clothes prepared for years before their death, so as to insure a decent orderly interment. To make these clothes was a task often imposed upon the ladies or females in a parish who were good at their needle. The pattern of the shroud was fixed, and special instructions were given regarding it by the uninitiated. Such things are common even now among Highland families who have emigrated to Glasgow. A few months ago a highly respectable lady, when she found that her illness was dangerous, gave a confidential servant the key of a box, where, in the event of death, all would be found that was required to dress her body for the grave.

The old wrapping of the body was woollen cloth, and the Gaelic term used to express it, *Ollanach*, which may be translated 'woollening', is still used to describe the dressing of the body before burial.* The old stone coffin is dug up in the Highlands as

---

* I cannot at this moment quote from authority, but I have somewhere read that in some English Parliament, if I remember rightly, in the reign of Henry VII, it was enacted, in the interest no doubt of the wool trade, that corpses should be dressed in woollen grave-clothes.

Two correspondents have been obliging enough to favour me with communications as to the laws enacted in England and Scotland, on the wrapping of dead bodies in woollen for burial.

An English correspondent writes –

'The Act to which you refer for the encouragement of the woollen trade, was passed 30 Charles II. stat. 1, c. 3, 1678. The Act was unpopular and fell into disuse, and was finally repealed 54 Geo. III, c. 108, 1814.

'The Rev. G. F. Townsend (of Burleigh Street Church, Strand) refers to this in his

elsewhere, but the coffins hollowed out of the solid log – one of which was discovered a few years ago in Lochaber – seem, as far as I know, to have been peculiar to the Highlands. The Gaelic terms still in use for a coffin, *Caisil Chro*, the 'wattle enclosure', points to

History of Leominster, published October, 1862, of which place he was vicar, and gives some curious extracts from their parish register on this subject. He also gave me one of the original certificates – and I now present it to you, as it may be of some little service to you.

"Pope, you may remember, refers to the custom

'Odious! in woollen: 'twould a saint provoke!'
Were the last words the fair Narcissa spoke:
'No! let a charming chintz and Brussels lace
Wrap my cold hands and shade my lifeless face!'"

The following is the quaint certificate referred to:

'Mrs. Eliz. Watcham, of the Borough of Leominster, in the county of Hereford, maketh Oath, That Mr. Solomon Long, of the Borough aforesaid, of the County aforesaid, lately deceased, was not put in, wrapt, or wound up, or Buried in any Shirt, Shift, Sheet or Shroud, made or mangled with Flax, Hemp, Silk, Hair, Gold or Silver, or other than what is made of Sheeps-Wooll only: Nor in any Coffin lined or faced with any Cloth, Stuff, or any other Thing whatsoever, made or mingled with Flax, Hemp, Silk, Hair, Gold, or Silver, or any other Material, contrary to the late Act of Parliament for Burying in Woollen, but Sheeps-Wooll only. Dated the Third Day of October, in the Third Year of the Reign of our Sovereign Lord George the Second, by the Grace of GOD, King, of Great Britain, France and Ireland, Defender of the Faith, Annoq; Dom' 1729.

'Sealed and Subscribed by us who
were present, and Witnesses
to the Swearing of the above
said Affidavit.
'PENELOPE POWELL.
ELIZ. ˣ JONES.

'I, Caleb Powell do hereby Certify, that the Day and Year abovesaid, the said Eliz. Watcham came before me, and made such Affidavit as is above specified, according to the late Act of Parliament, Intituled, an 'Act for Burying in Woollen, Witness my Hand, the Day and Year first above-written.'

"CALEB POWELL."

A Scotch correspondent writes us on the same subject:

'There are various old Scottish statutes regulating the cloth to be used at burials. One is the statute of James VII. 1686, cap. 16, enacting that no '*corps*' should be buried in any cloth but 'plain linen, or cloth of hards, made and spun within the

what we doubt not was equally peculiar to the Highlands, that of surrounding the dead body with slender branches of trees, and bending them firmly together with *withes* or twisted rods of hazel or willow, and thus interring it.

From the time of death till that of interment the body is watched day and night. A plate of salt is always placed upon the breast. Candles are also frequently lighted around it. When the body, on the day of funeral, is carried a considerable distance, a cairn of stones is always raised on the spots where the coffin has rested, and this cairn is from time to time renewed by friends and relatives.[214] Hence the Gaelic saying or prayer with reference to the departed, 'Peace to thy soul, and a stone to thy cairn!' – thus expressing the wish that the remembrance of the dead may be cherished by the living.

The bagpipe is sometimes still played at funerals.[215] Five or six years ago, a medical man greatly beloved and respected for his skill, and kindness to the poor, died at Fort William from fever, caught in the discharge of his duties in close, ill-ventilated huts.[216] The funeral was attended by about 1,400 people. Strong men were weeping, and women threw themselves on the ground in the agony of their impassioned sorrow. Three pipers headed the procession, playing the wild and sad lament of 'I'll never, I'll never, I'll never return'. The whole scene has been described as having been most deeply

Kingdom', and specially *prohibiting* the use of Holland or other linen-cloth made in other Kingdoms, and all silk, hair or *woolen,* gold or silver, or any other stuff whatsoever, than what is made of flax or hards, spun and wrought within the Kingdom.' And two responsible parties in the parish had to certify in the case of every burial that the statute had been complied with; and had to bring a certificate to that effect to the minister of the parish who was then to record the same. The statute was re-enacted, with some sumptuary clauses in 1695, but both were repealed in the *last* Scottish parliament (1707, c. 14) before the union. – That act *forbade* the use of linen at burials; and ordered that 'hereafter no corps of any person of what condition or quality soever shall be buried in linen of whatever kind; and that *where linen has been made use of about dead bodies formerly, plain woolen cloath or stuff shall only be made use of in all time coming'.*

'The preambles of the first two statutes declare the object to be the encouragement of linen manufacture in the kingdom and the prevention of the exportation of money for foreign goods, and the preamble of Queen Anne's Act (1707), declares its object to be the encouragement of 'the manufacture of wool within the kingdom.'

affecting. Many tourists who have ascended Ben Nevis will remember that green and beautiful churchyard near Fort William which looks up to the overhanging mountain, and down upon the sea and Inverlochy Castle, with the dark peat-moss of the Lochy beyond, and, further still, the hills of Lochiel.

But after these digressions I must return to the churchyard of 'the Parish'.

There are two graves which lie side by side across the ruins of the old archway I have spoken of.[217] The one is an old stone coffin, the other a grassy hillock — and I shall tell what I have heard, and what I know about their inhabitants.

Chapter 13

THE OLD STONE COFFIN

OR

THE TOMB OF THE SPANISH PRINCESS[218]

In the year 1588, the good ship *Florida*, one of the Spanish Armada, was driven into the harbour of Tobermory, in Mull, by the great storm which scattered that proud fleet.[219] The ship was visited by the chief of the Macleans of Duart, the remains of whose castle are still among the most picturesque objects in the Sound of Mull. The clan had a feud at the time with the clan MacIan, of Ardnamurchan, immediately opposite Tobermory harbour, and for some 'consideration' or other, Maclean induced a party of Spanish soldiers to aid him in attacking his rival. Having revenged himself by the powerful and unexpected aid of the Spaniards, he failed to implement his bargain with them, and shortly afterwards, whether through treachery or not is uncertain, the *Florida* was blown up. The body of a female was washed on shore and buried in a stone coffin in the consecrated ground of 'the Parish'. She has ever since been dignified by the name of 'the Spanish Princess'.

Oliver Cromwell sent a vessel to the Highlands, commanded by a Captain Pottinger, to coerce some of the rebellious Highland Popish chiefs.[220] This vessel was wrecked upon a rock opposite Duart, and only a few years ago the spot was examined, in which, according to tradition, Pottinger's body was buried, when human remains were discovered. Some of the guns of the vessels have also, I believe, been seen.

So much for true history;* now for the Highland tale founded on these facts. It is literally translated from the *ipsissma verba* of an old woman.

---

* In the year 1740, Spaldin, the diver, was sent by the British Government to regain some of the treasure which was supposed to have been sunk in the *Florida*. He succeeded only in obtaining ten of the guns, which are now at Inverary Castle. We

'In the time that is gone, the daughter of the king of Spain, in her sleep of the night, beheld in a dream a hero so splendid in form and mien as to fill her whole heart with love. She knew that he was not of the people of Spain, but she knew not what his race, his language, or his country was. She had no rest by day, or by night, seeking for the beautiful youth who had filled her heart, but seeking him in vain. At last she resolved to visit other lands, and got a ship built – a great ship with three masts, and with sails as white as the young snow one night old. She went to many countries and to many lands, and whenever she reached land she invited all the nobles of the neighbourhood to come on board her great ship. She entertained them royally. There was feasting, and wine and music, dice and dancing. All were glad to be her guests, and very many gave her the love of their hearts; but among them all she found not her love, the hero of her bright night-dream (her whisper). She went from one harbour to another, from one kingdom to another. She went to France, and to England. She went to Ireland and to Lochlinn. She went to the "Green Isle of the Ocean at the end of the land of the world" (Scandinavia). She made feasting and music wherever she went. Around her all was gaiety and gladness – the song and the harp – the wine, and the voice of laughter – hilarity and heartiness, but within her breast all was dark, and cold, and empty.

'At length, passing by the land under the wave (the flat island of Tiree), she came near the kingdom of Sorcha (Ardnamurchan), and after this to "Mull of the great mountains", to the harbour of all harbours, curved like a bent bow, sheltered from every wind and every wave.[221] Here the great ship of the three masts and of the white sails cast her anchor, and here, as in all other ports, the

ourselves have a portion of one of the black oak planks which was raised at the time.

Mr. Gregory, in his learned and accurate history of the Highlands, confirms the tradition of Maclean of Duart having been instrumental in destroying the *Florida*. He states that Spain, being at that time at peace with Scotland, though at war with England, demanded reparation for the savage and inhospitable conduct of Maclean of Duart, and that the records of council in Edinburgh show that the Highland chief had to confess his guilt and sue for pardon, as one who had justly forfeited his life.

daughter of the King of Spain sent invitations to all the nobles of the neighbouring country to visit her on board her ship. Here many a bold steersman of the Berlinns, who quailed not before ocean's wrath, many a brave swordsman who rejoiced in the field of slaughter, and many a daring rider who could quell the wildest steed, with the owner of many a hospitable house whose door was never shut, and many a leader of numerous hosts who never turned their face from the foe, came on board the great ship. But all were strangers unto her, until at length the Lord of Duart, the chief of the numerous, the warlike, the renowned Macleans, shone upon her sight.²²² Then did her heart leap with joy, and soon turn to rest in gladness; for he was her vision of the night, and the desire of her heart, in quest of whom she had travelled to so many lands.

'It was then that there was the magnificent and royal entertainment. There was red wine in "*cup, còrn,* and *cuach*" (cup, goblet, and bicker.²²³) There was music of sweetest sound. Sorrow was laid down, and joy was lifted on high. The daughter of the King of Spain had a sunbeam in the heart, and brightness in the countenance. The Lord of Duart was so blinded by her beauty and her nobleness that he saw not the black gulf before him. He surrendered himself entirely to her loveliness, and great was the happiness of their converse. He forgot that in the strong black castle of frowning Duart he had left a youthful bride. On board of the great ship days passed like moments in the midst of enjoyment; but not faster flew the days than rumour flew to Duart, proclaiming to the forsaken Lady of the castle the unfaithfulness of her Lord. The colour left her cheeks, sleep departed from her eyes, gnawing jealousy entered her heart, and fierce revenge filled her mind. Often as she turned on her pillow, as often turned she a new plan in her head for the destruction of her who had robbed her of her love; but none of these did satisfy her. At long and at last (at length and at worst), she contrived a plan which succeeded in drawing the Lord of Duart, and him alone, to the land; and, one of her most attached followers,★ being on board the ship, set fire to the store of powder,

★ 'Most attached follower', *Cota-eneais* – 'coat of the waist', and *Léine chrios* – 'shirt of the girdle', are the terms used in Gaelic to denote a thoroughly devoted follower. It was customary of old, when a lady married beyond her father's clan, as was

which, with sound louder than the thunder of the skies, rent the great ship of the three masts and the snow white sails into ten thousand pieces, bringing death and utter destruction on all who were on board, and, saddest woe! on the beautiful and loving daughter of the King of Spain.

'The Lady of Duart rejoiced. Her Lord wished not to show his grief, nor to keep in remembrance the wandering love he had given to a stranger. Thus, though he sent followers to gather the remains of the fair daughter of the King of Spain, and to bury her in holy ground, and though they laid her bones in the (Cill) churchyard of the holy Columba (Callum Cille) in Morven, she was committed to the dust without priest or prayer – without voice of supplication or psalm of repose – silently and secretly in the blackness of midnight.

'It chanced, shortly after this, that two young men in Morven, bound in ties of closest friendship, and freely revealing to one another all that was in their hearts, began to speak with wonder of the many great secrets of the world beyond the grave. They spoke, and they spoke of what was doing in the habitation of the spirits beyond the thick veil that hides the departed from the friends who sorrow so sorely after them. They could not see a ray of light – they could discover nothing. At length they mutually promised and vowed that whichever of them was first called away would, while engaged in the dread task of *Faire 'Chlaidh,* or, "Watching of the churchyard",* tell to the survivor all that he could reveal regarding the abode of the departed; and here the matter was left.

'Not long after it fell out that one of them, full as his bone was of marrow, yielded to the sway of death. His body, after being

generally the case, that she took with her two or more of her family followers, who always formed a sort of bodyguard to her, considering themselves entirely at her disposal, and at her command were ready to stab husband or son. Many strange interminglings of names and races have thus arisen. In the very centre of Lochaber there are several Burkes and Boyles. On inquiry I found that these had come from Ireland ages ago as the followers of an Irish lady, who had married MacDonald of Kippoch. There the descendants still are.

* This is a curious idea. In many parts of the Highlands it is believed to this day that the last person buried has to perform the duty of sentinel over the churchyard, and that to him the guardianship of the spirits of those buried before is in some degree committed. This post he must occupy until a new tenant of the tomb releases him.

carried *Deas iul** (according to the course of the sun) around the stone cross in the churchyard of Callum Cille (Columba), in Morven, and allowed to rest for a time at the foot of that cross, was laid amid the dust of his kindred.[224] His surviving comrade, Evan of the Glen, mourned sore for the loss of his friend; and much awe and fear came upon him as he remembered the engagement made between them; for now the autumn evening was bending (or waning), and like a stone rolling down a hill is the faint evening of autumn. The hour of meeting drew nigh, and regard to the sacredness of a promise made to him who was now in the world of ghosts, as well as regard for his own courage, decided him to keep the tryst (meeting). With cautious, but firm, step he approached the Cill, and looked for his departed friend, to hear the secrets of the land of ghosts. Quickly as his heart beat at the thought of meeting the spirit of his friend, he soon saw what made it quiver like the leaf of the aspen tree. He saw the grey shade of him who had, at one time, been his friend and his faithful comrade; but he saw all the 'sheeted spectres' of the populous churchyard moving in mournful

It is not esteemed as an enviable position, but one to be escaped if possible; consequently, if two neighbours die on the same day, the surviving relatives make great efforts to be first closing the grave over their friend.

A ludicrous but striking illustration of this strange notion occurred three years ago in the parish of A—. An old man and an old woman, dwelling in the same township, but not on terms of friendship – for the lady Kate Ruadh (or Red-headed Kate) was more noted for antipathies than attachments – were both at the point of death. The good man's friends began to clip his nails – an office always performed just as a person is dying. He, knowing that his amiable neighbour was, like himself, on the verge of the grave, roused himself to a last effort, and exclaimed, 'Stop, stop; you know not what use I may have for all my nails, in compelling Kate Ruadh to keep *Faire 'Chlaidh* (to watch the churchyard), in place of doing it myself!'

* Carried *Deas iul* – 'a turn the right or the south way'; i.e. following the course of the sun. This is said to be a Druidical practice, followed in many places to this day. Very recently it was customary in the churchyard of 'the Parish' to carry the bier around the stone cross which stands there, and to rest it for a few minutes at its base before committing the body to the grave. It is still customary with people, if any food or drink goes wrong in the throat, to exclaim *Deas iul,* apparently as a charm; and sending the bottle round the table in the course of the sun, is as common in the south as in the north. The south seems to have been held in high estimation by the Celts. Thus the *right* hand is termed the *south* hand: *Deas.* The same word is used to signify 'the being prepared or ready', 'the being expert', and 'being handsome in person'.

procession around the boundary of their dark abodes, while his friend seemed to lead the dread and shadowy host. But his eye was soon drawn by the aspect of utter woe presented by one white form which kept apart from the rest, and moved with pain which cannot be told. Forgetful of what had brought him to the Cill, he drew near this sight of woe, and heard a low and most plaintive song, in which the singer implored the aid of him whose 'ship was on the ocean', bewailed her miserable condition, in a land of strangers, far from father and from friends, laid in the grave without due or holy rites, and thus she moaned:

> Worm and beetle, they are whistling
>   Through my brain – through my brain;
> Imps of darkness they are shrieking
>   Through my frame – through my frame.

'Evan, whose heart was ever soft and warm towards the unhappy, asked her the cause of her grief, and whether he could lighten it. She blessed him that he, in the land of the living, had spoken to her in the land of the dead; for now she said she might be freed from evil, and her spirit might rest in peace.

'She told him that she was Clara Viola, daughter of the King of Spain. She told him of the bright vision of her youthful dream, and how, after drawing her over many an ocean, and bringing her to many lands, it had, like the *Dreag*,★ the shooting star of night, suddenly vanished in darkness, or, like the flame of the *sky-fire* (lightning), quickly ended in thunder and in ruin. She pointed out the grave into which she had been cast without holy rites. She implored of him to raise her bones – to wash them in the holy well of Saint Moluag in Lismore;[225] thereafter to carry them to the kingdom of Spain; and she described a place where he would get a chest full of gold, and a chest full of silver.

'With many fears, but with the courage of a hero, he accomplished what the Princess asked of him. He washed her bones in the Sainted Well of Moluag, in Lismore, and her name is now attached

---

★ *Dreag* signifies the death of a Druid, and is the common name still for a bright meteor or shooting star, implying the belief that the spirits of the Druids departed in fiery chariots.

(bound) to the spring, Tobar Clár Mheolain (pronounced Clàur Ve-o-len), the Well of Clara Viola.* Thereafter he set off for the kingdom of Spain, and though it was a long way off, he was not long in reaching it. He soon made his way to the palace of the King of Spain, and that was the palace of many windows, of many towers, of many doors, doors which were never closed – the great house of feasts and of royal hospitality. He was received with honour. He got the chest full of gold, and the chest full of silver, and many a reward besides. But when the King of Spain heard how his beautiful daughter had been treated in Albin (Scotland), his heart swelled with wrath, and his face flamed with fury. He ordered his three strongest and most destructive ships of war to be immediately fitted out, his three best and bravest captains to command them, to sail as fast as possible to the three best harbours in Scotland, one in the Kyles of Bute, one in the "Horse-shoe" of Kerrera, and one in the Bay of Tobermory, Mull, and there to load them all with the limbs of Scottish men and of Scottish women.

'One ship did come to Tobermory Bay, and fearful she looked, as with masts bending, and great guns roaring, she leaped and bellowed along the Sound of Mull. She was commanded by Captain Pottinger. He was skilful in sailing, firmer in fighting, and besides had great knowledge of magic (Druidism). He spoke the direst threats against the people of Mull, and said that he would sweep the island with a besom – that he would leave it bare.

'The people of Mull were seized with great fear, and the Lord of Duart, though dreading no ordinary foe, had many things to move him. He found no rest in or out of his house. He sorrowed for the past, and he dreaded what was to come. Not thinking any human power of avail against the great and deadly warship of Spain, commanded by a man deep in magic, he and his men sought evil from magic also (Druidism), and with effectual spells and charms, gathered all the witches of Mull, the *Doideagan Muileach*,[227] to one meeting place. He told them of the dire threat of Captain Pottinger, and begged them to raise a wind which would sink his ship, even in

---

* (See also note 226.) A well in the churchyard of St Moluag, in Lismore, does actually bear this name, '*Tobar Claur-Ve-o-len*' – but I cannot in the least certify that it is derived from that of the Spanish princess.

the harbour that was better than any other harbour. The *Doideag* asked him if Captain Pottinger, when uttering his threat of devastation, had said "With God's help?" He did not. "Good is that," said she.

'She and her companions began their work. What every *ubag*, *obag*, and *gisreag* (charm, incantation, and canting) they used I know not ("Christ's cross between us and them all," says the narrator); but I know that she tied a straw rope to a *Braa* (a quern-stone), passed the rope over one of the rafters of the house, and raised the *Braa*) quern-stone as far as she could. As the quern-stone rose the wind rose; but all the strength of the *Doideag* could not raise it high, for Captain Pottinger could put weight on the stone and keep it down. She summoned her sisters from various quarters: one *Laovag*, *Thirisdeach* from Tiree, *Maol-Odhar* from Kintyre, and *Cas a' Mhogain riabhaich* from Cowal.⋆ They came to her aid and pulled at the rope. They could not raise it higher. Some of them flew through the air to the ship, and in the shape of cats ascended the rigging. They numbered nine. Captain Pottinger said he was stronger than these – that he feared them not. They increased to fifteen, reached the very top of the mast, and scrambled along all the yard-arms, and up and down the shrouds. Captain Pottinger was stronger than these yet, and defied them all.

'At last the *Doideag*, seeing her work like to fail, called on a very strong man, Domhnull Dubh Laidir (Black Donald the Strong) to hold the rope and keep the quern-stone from falling lower. He

⋆ The names of the witches may be thought of very little consequence; but it is interesting to observe that these are names all implying some personal deformity or peculiarity, and show that the witches were more objects of dislike than respect. *Doideag* means little frizzle, applied to anything dry and withered, but more especially to frizzled hair; *Laovag* signifies hoofie, clootie, or spindle-shanked. *Cas a' Mhogain riabhaich*, the foot of the russet, or brindled old stocking – Osan is the ordinary term for stocking; *Mogan*, Scottice *Hoggan*, a ragged stocking without a sole; *Maol-odhar*, bald and dun; *Gormal mhor*, the great blue-eye, is the only one who has a respectable name.

One of my story-tellers gave a different list of the witches engaged in this work. *Luideag, Agus Doideag, Agus Corrag Nighinn Ian Bhain, Cas a' mhogain Riabhaich a Gleancomham, Agus Gormshuil mhor bhàr na Maighe, Raggie* and *Frizzle*, and the finger of White John's Daughter; that is '*Hogganfoot* from Glenco, and Great Blue-Eye from Moy' (in Lochaber).

seized the rope with the grasp of death, and with his muscles stretched and strained he held fast the quern-stone.

'The *Doideag* quickly flew to Lochaber to beg for the assistance of Great Gormal of Moy, whose powers were more than that of all the others put together. Gormal yielded to the request, and no sooner did she spread her wings on the air than the tempest raged and roared, blowing the sea to spindrift, tearing the trees from the ground, and splintering the adamant rock. Captain Pottinger felt that evil was approaching, resolved to leave the bad neighbourhood, and ordered his cable to be cut with speed. His sailors began to do so with gladness; but when the hatchet was raised aloft to strike the blow, the wind blew the iron head off the handle before it could reach the cable. Not an axe-head would remain on the haft. Gormal soon reached the harbour. In the likeness of a cat, larger than ever was seen before, she climbed to the top of the mast and sang

> Aha, Captain Pottinger, thou didst boast
> Last year to desolate Mull's coast,
> But now Hoo-hoo! thy ship is lost!

And with this, Captain Pottinger and his men, and the great deadly warship of Spain, sank down into the depths.'

And so ends the Highland story!

Chapter 14

THE GRASSY HILLOCK
OR
THE GRAVE OF FLORY CAMERON

We might expect to find peculiar types of character among a people who possess, as the Highland Celts do, a vivid fancy, strong passions, and keen affections; who dwell among scenery of vast extent and great sublimity; who are shut up in their secluded valleys, separated even from their own little world by mountains and moorlands or stormy arms of the sea; whose memories are full of the dark superstitions and wild traditions of the olden time; and who are easily impressed by the mysterious sights and sounds created by mists and clouds and eerie blasts, among the awful solitudes of nature; and who cling with passionate fondness to home and family, as to the very life and soul of the otherwise desert waste around them. But I never met, even in the Highland, with a more remarkable example of the influence of race and circumstances than was Flora, or rather Flory Cameron.[228]

The first time I saw her was when going to the school of 'the Parish,' early on an autumnal morning. The school was attached to the church[229] and the churchyard was consequently near it. The churchyard, indeed, with its headstones and flat stones, its walled tombs and old ruined church, was fully appreciated by us, as an ideal place for our joyous games, especially for 'hide and seek', and 'I spy'. Even now, in spite of all the sadder memories of later years, I can hardly think of the spot without calling up the blithe face of some boy peering cautiously over the effigy of an old chief, or catching the glimpse of a kilt disappearing behind a headstone, or hearing a concealed titter beside a memorial of sorrow.

As I passed the churchyard for the first time in the sober dawning of that harvest day, I was arrested by seeing the figure of a woman wrapt in a Highland plaid, sitting on a grave, her head bent and her hands covering her face, while her body slowly rocked to and fro. Beside her was a Highland terrier that seemed asleep on the grave. Her back was towards me, and I slipped away without disturbing her, yet much impressed by this exhibition of grief.

On telling the boys what I had seen, for the grave and its mourners were concealed at that moment from our view by the old ruin, they, speaking in whispers, and with an evident feeling of awe or of fear, informed me that it was 'Flory the witch', and that she and her dog had been there every morning since her son had died months before; and that the dog had been a favourite of her son's, and followed the witch wherever she went. I soon shared the superstitious fear for Flory which possessed the boys; for, though they could not affirm, in answer to my inquiries, that she ever travelled through the air on a broomstick, or became a hare at her pleasure, or had ever been seen dancing with demons by moonlight in the old church, yet one thing was certain, that the man or woman whom she blessed was blessed indeed, and that those whom she cursed were cursed indeed. 'Was that really true?' I eagerly asked. 'It is true as death!' replied the boy, Archy Macdonald, shocked by my doubt; 'for,' said he, 'did not black Hugh Maclean strike her boy once at the fair, and did she not curse him when he went off to the herring fishery? and wasn't he and all in the boat drowned? True! ay, it's true.' 'And did she not curse', added little Peter M'Phie, with vehemence, 'the ground officer for turning old Widow M'Pherson out of her house? Was he not found dead under the rock? Some said he had been drunk; but my aunt, who knew all about it, said it was because of Flory's curse, nothing else, and that the cruel rascal deserved it too.' And then followed many other terrible proofs of her power, clinched with the assurance from another boy that he had once heard 'the maister himself say, that he would any day far rather have her blessing than her curse!'

This conversation prepared me to obey with fear and trembling a summons which I soon afterwards unexpectedly received. Flory had one day, unseen by me, crossed the playground, when we were too busy to notice anything except the ball for which we were eagerly contending at our game of shinty. She heard that I was at the school, and seeing me, sent a boy to request my presence. As I came near her, the other boys stood at a respectful distance, watching the interview. I put out my hand frankly, though tremblingly, to greet her. She seized it, held it fast, gazed at my face, and I at hers. What she saw in mine I know not, but hers is still vividly before me in every line and expression. It was in some respects very strange and painfully impressive, yet full of affection, which appeared to struggle with an agonised look of sorrow that ever and anon brought tears down her withered cheeks. Her eyes seemed at one time to retire into her head, leaving a mere line between the eye-lashes, like what one sees in a cat when in the light; they then would open slowly, and gradually increase until two large black orbs beamed on me, and I felt as if they drew me into them by a mysterious power. Pressing my hand with one of hers, she stroked my head fondly, muttering to herself all the time, as if in prayer. She then said, with deep feeling, 'Oh, thou calf of my heart! my love, my darling, son and grandson of friends, the blessed! let the blessing of the poor, the blessing of the widow, the blessing of the heart be on thee, and abide with thee, my love, my love!' And then, to my great relief, she passed on. In a little while she turned and looked at me, and, waving a farewell, went tottering on her way, followed by the dog. The boys congratulated me on my interview, and seemed to think I was secure against any bodily harm. I think the two parties in our game that day competed for my powerful aid.

I often saw Flory afterwards, and instead of avoiding her, felt satisfaction rather in having my hand kissed by her, and in receiving the blessing, which in some kind form or other she often gave. Never, during the autumn and winter months when I attended that Highland school, did she omit visiting the grave on which I first saw her. The plashing rain fell around her, and the winds blew their bitter blast, but there she sat at early morning for a time to weep and pray. And even when snow fell, the black form of the widow, bent in sorrow, was only more clearly revealed. Nor was she ever absent from her seat below the pulpit on Sunday. Her furrowed countenance with the strange and tearful eyes, the white *mutch* with the black ribbon bound tightly round the head, the slow rocking motion, with the old, thin, and withered body – all are before me, though nearly forty years have passed since then.

In after years, the present minister of 'the Parish' told me more about Flory than I then knew.[230] The account given to me by the boys at school was to some extent true. She was looked upon as a person possessing an insight into the character of people and their future, for her evil predictions had in many cases been fulfilled. She had remarkable powers of discernment, and often discovered elements of disaster in the recklessness or wickedness of those whom she denounced; and when these disasters occurred in any form, her words were remembered, and her predictions attributed to some supernatural communications with the evil one. Although the violence of her passion was so terrible when roused by any act of cruelty or injustice, that she did not hesitate to pour it forth on the objects of her hate, in solemn imprecations expressed in highly-wrought and poetic language, yet Flory herself was never known to claim the possession of magic powers.* 'She spoke', she said, 'but the truth, and cursed those only who deserved it, and had they not all come true?' Her violent passion was her only demon possession.

Flory was not by any means an object of dislike. She was as ardent and vehement in her attachments as in her hates, and the former were far more numerous than the latter. Her sick and afflicted neighbours always found in her a sympathising and

---

* In many Highland parishes – aye, and in Scotch and English ones too – there were persons who secretly gave charms to cure diseases and prevent injuries to man or beast. These charms have come down from Popish times. A woman still lives in 'the Parish' who possessed a charm which the minister was resolved to obtain from her, along with the solemn promise that she would never again use it. We understand that if any charm is once repeated to and thus possessed by another, it cannot, according to the law which regulates those powers of darkness, be used again by its original owner. It was with some difficulty that the minister at last prevailed on 'the witch' to repeat her charm. She did so, in a wild glen in which they accidentally met. She gave the charm with loud voice, outstretched arm, and leaning against the stem of an old pine tree, while the minister quietly copied it into his note-book, as he sat on horseback. 'Here it is, minister,' she said, 'and to you or your father's son alone would I give it, and once you have it, it will pass my lips no more:

> The charm of God the Great:
> The free gift of Mary
> The free gift of God:
> The free gift of every Priest and Churchman
> The free gift of Michael the Strong;
> That would put strength in the sun.

Yet all this echo of old ecclesiastical thunder was but 'a charm for sore eyes'! Whether it could have been used for greater, if not more useful purposes, I know not.

comforting friend. With that strange inconsistency by which so much light and darkness, good and evil, meet in the same character, Flory, to the minister's knowledge, had been the means of doing much good in more than one instance by her exhortations and her prayers, to those who had been leading wicked lives; while her own life as a wife and a mother had been strictly moral and exemplary. She had been early left a widow, but her children were trained up by her to be gentle, obedient, and industrious, and she gave them the best education in her power.

But it was God's will to subdue the wild and impassioned nature of Flory by a series of severe chastisements. When a widow, her eldest son, in the full strength of manhood, was drowned at sea; and her only daughter and only companion died. One son alone, the pride of her heart, and the stay of her old age, remained, and to him she clung with her whole heart and strength. He deserved, and returned, her love. By his industry he had raised a sufficient sum of money to purchase a boat, for the purpose of fishing herring in some of the Highland lochs – an investment of capital which in good seasons is highly advantageous. All the means possessed by Donald Cameron were laid out on this boat, and both he and his mother felt proud and happy as he launched it free of debt and was able to call it his own. He told his mother that he expected to make a little fortune by it, that he would then build a house, and get a piece of land, and that her old age would be passed under his roof in peace and plenty. With many a blessing from Flory the boat sailed away. But Donald's partner in the fishing speculation turned out a cowardly and inefficient seaman. The boat was soon wrecked in a storm. Donald, by great exertion, escaped with his life. He returned to his mother a beggar, and so severely injured that he survived the wreck of his boat and fortune but a few weeks.

There was not a family in the parish which did not share the sorrow of poor Flory.

I have the account of his funeral now before me, written by one present, who was so much struck by all he saw and heard on that occasion that he noted down the circumstances at the time.[231] I shall give them in his own words:

'When I arrived at the scene of woe, I observed the customary preparations had been judiciously executed, all under the immedi-

ate superintendence of poor Flory. On entering the apartment to
which I was conducted, she received me with perfect composure
and with all that courteous decorum of manner so common in her
country. Her dress she had studiously endeavoured to render as suitable to the occasion as circumstances would admit. She wore a
black woollen gown of a peculiar, though not unbecoming, form,
and a very broad black riband was tightly fastened round her head,
evidently less with regard to ornament than to the aching pain
implanted there by accumulated suffering. According to the custom
of the country she drank to the health of each individual present,
prefacing each health with a few kind words. In addressing the
schoolmaster, who had been assiduous in his parish attentions
towards her, she styled him the "Counsellor of the dying sufferer,
the comforter of the wounded mourner". Another individual
present she addressed as "the son of her whose hand was bountiful,
and whose heart was kind", and in like manner, in addressing me,
she alluded very aptly and very feelingly to the particular relation in
which I then stood towards her. She then retired with a view of
attending to the necessary preparations amongst the people assembled without the house. After a short interval, however, she
returned, announcing that all was in readiness for completing the
melancholy work for which we had convened. Here she seemed
much agitated. Her lips and even her whole frame seemed to quiver
with emotion. At length, however, she recovered her former
calmness, and stood motionless and pensive until the coffin was
ready to be carried to the grave. She was then requested to take her
station at the head of the coffin, and the black cord attached to it
was extended to her. She seized it for a moment, and then all self-
possession vanished. Casting it from her, she rushed impetuously
forward, and clasping her extended arms around the coffin, gave
vent to all her accumulated feelings in the accents of wildest
despair. As the procession slowly moved onwards, she narrated in a
sort of measured rhythm her own sufferings, eulogised the character of her son, and then, alas! uttered her wrath against the man to
whose want of seamanship she attributed his death. I would it were
in my power to convey her sentiments as they were originally
expressed. But though it is impossible to convey them in their
pathos and energy, I shall endeavour to give a part of her sad and

bitter lamentation by a literal translation of her words. Her first allusion was to her own sufferings.

> Alas! alas! woe's me, what shall I do?
> Without husband, without brother,
> Without substance, without store:
> A son in the deep, a daughter in her grave,
> The son of my love on his bier –
> Alas! alas! woe's me, what shall I do?
>
> Son of my love, plant of beauty,
> Thou art cut low in thy loveliness
> Who'll now head the party at their games on the plains of Ardtornish?
> The swiftest of foot is laid low.
> Had I thousands of gold on the sea-covered rock,
> I would leave it all and save the son of my love.
> But the son of my love is laid low –
> Alas! alas! woe's me, what shall I do?
>
> Land of curses is this! – where I lost my family and my friends,
> My kindred and my store,
> Thou art a land of curses for ever to me –
> Alas! alas! what shall I do?
>
> And, Duncan, thou grandson of Malcolm,
> Thou wert a meteor of death to me;
> Thine hand could not guide the helm as the hand of my love.
> But, alas! the stem of beauty is cut down,
> I am left alone in the world,
> Friendless and childless, houseless and forlorn –
> Alas! alas! woe's me, what shall I do?

'Whilst she chanted forth these and similar lamentations, the funeral procession arrived at the place of interment, which was only about a mile removed from her cottage. The grave was already dug. It extended across an old Gothic arch of peculiar beauty and simplicity.[232] Under this arch Flory sat for some moments in pensive silence. The coffin was placed in the grave, and when it had been adjusted with all due care, the attendants were about to proceed to cover it. Here, however, they were interrupted. Flory arose, and motioning to the obsequious crowd to retire, she slowly descended into the hollow grave, placed herself in an attitude of devotion, and continued for some time engaged in prayer to the Almighty.

'The crowd of attendants had retired to a little distance, but being in some degree privileged, or at least considering myself so, I remained leaning upon a neighbouring gravestone as near to her as I could without rudely intruding upon such great sorrow. I was, however, too far removed to hear distinctly the words which she uttered, especially as they were articulated in a low and murmuring tone of voice. The concluding part of her address was indeed more audibly given, and I heard her bear testimony with much solemnity to the fact that her departed son had never provoked her to wrath, and had ever obeyed her commands. She then paused for a few moments, seemingly anxious to tear herself away, but unable to do so. At length she mustered resolution, and after impressing three several kisses on the coffin, she was about to rise. But she found herself again interrupted. The clouds which had hitherto been lowering were now dispelled, and just as she was slowly ascending from the grave, the sun burst forth in full splendour from behind the dark mist that had hitherto obscured its rays. She again prostrated herself, this time under the influence of a superstitious belief still general in the Highlands, that bright sunshine upon such occasions augurs well for the future happiness of the departed. She thanked God "that the sky was clear and serene when the child of her love was laid in the dust". She then at length arose, and resumed her former position under the old archway, which soon re-echoed the ponderous sound of the falling earth upon the hollow coffin.

'It was indeed a trying moment to her. With despair painted on her countenance, she shrieked aloud in bitter anguish, and wrung her withered hands with convulsive violence. I tried to comfort her, but she would not be comforted. In the full paroxysm of her grief, however, one of the persons in attendance approached her. "Tears", said her friend, "cannot bring back the dead. It is the will of Heaven – you must submit." "Alas!" replied Flory, "the words of the lips – the words of the lips are easily given, but they heal not the broken heart!" The offered consolation, however, was effectual thus far, that it recalled the mourner to herself, and led her to subdue for the time every violent emotion. She again became alive to every- thing around, and gave the necessary directions to those who were engaged in covering up the grave. Her directions were given with unfaltering voice, and were obeyed by the humane neighbours with unhesitating submission. On one occasion indeed, and towards the close of the obsequies, she assumed a tone of high authority. It was found that the turf which had been prepared for covering the grave was insufficient for the purpose, and one of the attendants was not quite so fastidious as his countrymen, who in such cases suffer not the smallest inequality to appear, proposed that the turf should be lengthened by adding to it. The observation did not escape her notice. Flory fixed her piercing eye upon him that uttered it, and after gazing at him for some moments with bitter scorn, she indignantly exclaimed, "Who talks of patching up the grave of my son? Get you gone! Cut a green sod worthy of my beloved." This imperative order was instantly obeyed. A suitable turf was procured, and the grave was at length covered up to the entire satisfaction of all parties. She now arose, and returned to her desolate abode, supported by two aged females, almost equally infirm with herself, and followed by her dog.

'But Flory Cameron did not long remain inactive under suffering. With the aid of her good friend, the parish schoolmaster,[233] she settled, with scrupulous fidelity, all her son's mercantile transactions; and with a part of the very small reversion of money accruing to herself she purchased a neat freestone slab, which she has since erected as the "Tribute of a widowed mother to the memory of a dutiful son."[234] Nor has her attention been limited to the grave of her son. Her wakeful thoughts seem to have been the subject of her midnight dreams. In one of the visions of the night, as she herself expressed it, her daughter appeared to her, saying that she had honoured a son and passed over a daughter. The hint was taken. Her little debts were collected; another slab was provided on which to record the name and merits of a beloved daughter; and to his honour I mention it, that a poor mason employed in the neighbourhood entered so warmly into the feeling by which Flory was actuated that he gave his labour gratuitously in erecting this monument of parental affection.[235] But though the violence of her emotion subsided, Flory Cameron's grief long remained. In church, where she was a regular attendant, every allusion to family bereavement subdued her, and often, when that simple melody arose in which her departed son was wont very audibly to join, she used to sob bitterly, uttering with a low tone of voice, "Sweet was the voice of my love in the house of God." Frequently I have met her returning from the burying ground at early dawn and at evening twilight, accompanied by her little dog, once the constant attendant of her son; and whilst I stood conversing with her I have seen the daisy which she had picked from the grave of her beloved, carefully laid up in her bosom. But her grief is now assuaged. Affliction at length tamed the wildness of her nature, and subdued her into a devotional frame. She ceased to look for earthly comfort, but found it in Christ. She often acknowledged to me with devout submission that the Lord, as He gave, had a right to take away, and that she blessed His name; and that as every tie that bound her to earth had been severed, her thoughts rose more habitually to the home above, where God her Father would at last free her from sin and sorrow and unite her to her dear ones.'

Flory continued to visit the grave of her children as long as her feeble steps could carry her thither. But her strength soon failed, and she was confined to her poor hut. One morning, the neighbours, attracted by the howling of her dog, and seeing no smoke from her chimney, entered unbidden and found Flory dead and lying as if in calm sleep in her poor bed. Her body was laid with her children beneath the old arch and beside the stone coffin of the Spanish Princess.

Chapter 15

THE SCHOOLMASTER

The Parish Schoolmaster of the past belonged to a class of men and to an institution peculiar to Scotland. Between him and the Parish clergyman there was a close alliance formed by many links. The homes and incomes of both, though of very unequal value, were secured by Act of Parliament, and provided by the heritors of the Parish. Both held their appointments for life, and could be deprived of them only for heresy or immorality, and that by the same kind of formal 'libel', and trial before the same ecclesiastical court. Both were members of the same church, and had to subscribe the same confession of faith; both might have attended the same university, nay, passed through the same curriculum of eight years of preparatory study.

The Schoolmaster was thus a sort of prebendary or minor canon in the Parish cathedral — a teaching presbyter and coadjutor to his preaching brother. In many cases 'the master' was possessed of very considerable scholarship and culture, and was invariably required to be able to prepare young men for the Scotch universities, by instructing them in the elements of Greek, Latin, and Mathematics. He was by education more fitted than any of his own rank in the Parish to associate with the minister. Besides, he was mostly always an elder of the kirk, and the clerk of the kirk session; and, in addition to all these ties, the school was generally in close proximity to the church and manse. The master thus became the minister's right hand and confidential adviser, and the worthies often met. If the minister was a bachelor — a melancholy spectacle too often seen! — the Schoolmaster more than any other neighbour cheered him in his loneliness. He knew all the peculiarities of his diocesan, and knew especially when he might 'step up to the Manse for a chat' without being thought intrusive. If, for example, it was Monday — the minister's Sunday of rest — and if the day was wet, the roads muddy, the trees dripping, and the hens miserable, seeking shelter under carts in the farmyard, he knew well that ere evening came, the minister would be glad to hear his rap break the stillness of the

Manse. Then seated together in the small study before a cheerful fire, they would discuss many delicate questions affecting the manners or morals of the flock, and talk about the ongoings of the Parish, its births, marriages, and deaths; its poor, sick, dying sufferers; the state of the crops, and the prospects of good or bad 'Fiars prices', and the prospects of good or bad stipends, which they regulated; the chances of repairs or additions being obtained for Manse, church, or school; preachers and preachings; Church and State politics – both being out-and-out Tories; knotty theological points connected with Calvinism or Arminianism; with all the minor and more evanescent controversies of the hour. Or, if the evening was fine, they would walk in the garden to examine the flowers, or more probably the vegetables, and dander over the glebe to inspect the latest improvements, when the master was sure to hear bitter complaints of the laziness of 'the minister's man' John, whom he had been threatening to turn off for years, but who accepted the threats with as great ease of mind as he did his work. Before parting they partook, perhaps, of a humble supper of eggs and toasted cheese, soft as thick cream, washed down by one glass of Edinburgh ale, or, to be perfectly honest, one tumbler of whisky toddy, when old Jenny was told to be sure that the water was boiling.

A schoolmaster who had received licence to preach, and who consequently might be presented to a parish, if he could get one, belonged to the aristocracy of his profession. Not that he lived in a better house than his unlicensed and less educated brother, or received higher emoluments, or wore garments less glittering and japanned from polished old age. But the man in the pulpit was taller than the man in the school, addressed larger pupils, and had larger prospects.

Among those schoolmasters who were also preachers, it was possible, I dare say, to find a specimen of the Dominie Sampson class, with peculiarities and eccentricities which could easily account for his failure as a preacher, and his equally remarkable want of success as a teacher. There were also a few, perhaps, who had soured tempers, and were often crabbed and cross in school and out of it. But don't be too severe on the poor Dominie! He had missed a church from want of a patron, and, it must be acknowledged, from want of the gift of preaching, which he bitterly termed 'the gift of the gab'. In college he had taken the first rank in his classes: and no wonder, then, if he is a little mortified in seeing an old acquaintance who had been a notorious dunce obtain a good living through some of those subtle and influential agencies and 'pow'r o' speech i' the poopit', neither of which he could command, and who – oleaginous on the tiends – slowly jogged along the smooth road of life on a paunchy, sleek horse, troubled chiefly about the great number of his children and the small number of his 'chalders' – it is no wonder, I say, that he is mortified at this, compelled, poor fellow, to whip his way, tawse in hand, through the mud of A B C and Syntax, Shorter Catechism, and long division, on a pittance of some sixty pounds a year.

Nay, as it often happened, the master had a sore at his heart of which few knew. When he was a tutor long ago in the family of a small Laird, he fell in love with the Laird's daughter Mary, whose mind he had first wakened into thought, and first led into the land of poetry. She was to have married him, but not until he got a parish, for the Laird would not permit his fair star to move in any orbit beneath that of the Manse circle. And long and often had the parish been expected, but just when the presentation seemed to be within his nervous grasp, it had vanished through some unexpected mishap, and with its departure hope became more deferred, and the heart more sick, until Mary at last married, and changed all things to her old lover. She had not the pluck to stand by the master when the Laird of Blackmoss was pressing for her hand. And then the black curly hairs of the master turned to grey as the dream of his life vanished, and he awoke to the reality of a heart that can never love another, and to a school with its A B C and Syntax. But some- how the dream comes back in its tenderness as he strokes the hair of some fair girl in the class and looks into her eyes; or it comes back in its bitterness, and a fire begins to burn at his heart, which very possibly passes off like a shock of electricity along his right arm, and down the black tawse, finally discharging itself with a flash and a roar into some lazy mass of agricultural flesh who happens to have a vulgar look like the Laird of Blackmoss, and an unprepared lesson!

It often happened that those who were uncommonly bad preachers were, nevertheless, admirable teachers, especially if they had found suitable wives, and were softened by the amenities of domestic life; above all, when they had boys of their own to 'drill'. The parish school then became a school of no mean order. The glory of the old Scotch teacher of this stamp was to *ground* his pupils thoroughly in the elements of Greek and Latin. He hated all shams, and placed little value on what was acquired without labour. To master details, to stamp grammar rules and prosody rules, thoroughly understood, upon the minds of his pupils as with a pen of iron; to move slowly, but accurately through a classic, this was his delight, not his work only, but his recreation, the outlet for his tastes and energies. He had no long-spun theories about education, nor ever tried his hand at adjusting the fine mechanism of boys' motives. 'Do your duty and learn thoroughly, or be well licked', 'Obedience, work, and no humbug', were the axioms which expressed his views. When he found the boys honest at their work, he rejoiced in his own. And if he discovered one who seemed bitten with the love of Virgil or Homer; if he discovered in his voice or look, by question or answer, that he 'promised to be a good classic,' the Dominie had a tendency to make that boy a pet. On the annual examination by the Presbytery, with what a pleased smile did he contemplate his favourite in the hands of some competent and sympathising examiner! And once a year on such a day the Dominie might so far forget his stern and iron rule as to chuck the boy under the chin, or clap him fondly on the back.

I like to call those old teaching preachers to remembrance. Take them all in all they were a singular body of men: their humble homes, and poor salaries, and hard work, presenting a remarkable contrast to their manners, abilities, and literary culture. Scotland owes to them a debt of gratitude that never can be repaid; and many a successful minister, lawyer, and physician is able to recall some one of those old teachers as his earliest and best friend, who first kindled in him the love of learning, and helped him in the pursuit of knowledge under difficulties.

In cities the Schoolmaster may be nobody, lost in the great crowd of professional and commercial life, unless that august personage, the Government Inspector, appears in the school, and links its master and pupil teachers to the august and mysterious Privy Council located in the official limbo of Downing Street. But in a country parish, most of all in a Highland parish, to which we must now return, the Schoolmaster or 'Master' occupied a most important position.

The Schoolmaster of 'the Parish' [236] half a century ago was a strong built man, with such a face, crowned by such a head, that taking face and head together, one felt that he was an out-and-out man. A Celt he evidently was, full of emotion, that could be roused to vehemence, but mild, modest, subdued, and firm — a granite boulder covered with green moss, and hanging with flower, heather, and graceful fern. He had been three years at Glasgow University, attending the Greek, Latin, and logic classes. How he, the son of a very small farmer, had supported himself is not easily explained. His fees, which probably amounted to £6, were the heaviest item in his outlay. The lodgings occupied by him were in the High Street, and he lived nearer the stars than men of greater ambition in Glasgow. His landlady, overlooking these peculiar privileges, charged but 4s. or 5s. a week for everything, including coals, gas, cooking, and attendance. He had brought a supply of potatoes, salt herrings, sausages, and salt fish from the Highlands, and a ham which seemed immortal from the day it was boiled. It was wonderful how the student with a few pounds eked out his fare, with the luxuries of weak coffee and wheaten bread for breakfast, and chop or mince-meat for dinner. And thus he managed, with a weekly sum which an unskilled labourer would consider wretched wages, to educate himself for three years at the University. He eventually became the schoolmaster, elder, session clerk, precentor, postmaster, and catechist of 'the Parish', offices sufficient perhaps to stamp him as incompetent by the Privy Council Committee acting under 'a Minute', but nevertheless capable of being all duly discharged by 'the Master'.

The school of course was his first duty, and there he diligently taught some fifty or sixty scholars in male and female petticoats for five days in the week, imparting knowledge of the 'usual branches', and also instructing two or three pupils, including his own sons, in Greek, Latin, and Mathematics. I am obliged to confess that neither the teacher nor the children had the slightest knowledge of physiology, chemistry, or even household economy. It is difficult to know, in these days of light, how they got on without it: for the houses were all constructed on principles opposed in every respect to the laws of health as we at present understand them, and the cooking was confined chiefly to potatoes and porridge. But whether it was the Highland air which they breathed, or the rain which daily washed them, or the absence of doctors, the children who ought to have died by rule did not, but were singularly robust and remarkably happy. In spite of bare feet and uncovered heads they seldom had colds, or, if they had, as Charles Lamb says, 'they took them kindly'.

His most important work, next to the school, was catechising. By this is meant, teaching the *Shorter Catechism* of the church to the adult parishioners. The custom was at certain seasons of the year, when the people were not busy at farm work, to assemble them in different hamlets throughout 'the Parish': if the weather was wet, in a barn; if fine, on the green hill side, and there by question and answer, with explanatory remarks, to indoctrinate them into the great truths of religion. Many of the people in the more distant valleys, where even the small 'side schools' could not penetrate, were unable to read, but they had ears to hear, and hearts to feel, and through these channels they were instructed. These meetings were generally on Saturdays when the school was closed. But on all days of the week the sick who were near enough to be visited – that is, within ten miles or so – had the benefit of the master's teaching and prayers.

The Schoolmaster, as I have said, was also postmaster. But then the mail was but weekly, and by no means a heavy one. It contained only a few letters for the sheriff[237] or the minister, and half-a-dozen to be delivered as opportunity offered to outlying districts in 'the Parish', and these, with three or four newspapers a week old,[238] did not occupy much of his time. The post, moreover, was never in a hurry. 'Post haste' was unknown in those parts: the 'Poste restante' being much more common. The 'runner' was a sedate walker, and never lost sight of his feelings as a man in his ambition as a post. Nor was the master's situation as Precentor a position like that of organist in Westminster or St Paul's. His music was select, and confined to three or four tunes. These he modulated to suit his voice and taste, which were peculiar and difficult to describe. But the people understood both, and followed him on Sundays as far as

TOP.
Rev Dr Norman Macleod
(1812–1872) author of
Morvern – A Highland Parish
(Unless otherwise stated, all
photographs are from the Iain
Thornber Collection)

MIDDLE.
Old Rory's Cottage, Fiunary
see note 52

BOTTOM.
Fiunary Manse c. 1890
see note 44

TOP.
Ardtornish Towers c. 1920, standing at the head
of Loch Aline. Built 1884–91 by Thomas Valentine
Smith from the proceeds of gin and wool.
see introduction

MIDDLE.
Kiel graveyard c. 1900 with the ruins of the medieval
church in the foreground and the old smiddy beyond,
which was demolished in 1914.
see note 209

BOTTOM.
Sport largely replaced large-scale sheep farming
in Morvern in the early 1900s (George Dalgleish,
Ardtornish Estate head gamekeeper, c. 1914.)

TOP.
Loch Doirenamairt and the cliffs of Aoineadh Mor (Inniemore) **see note 32**

MIDDLE.
Lochaline House Mor, built by John Sinclair (1821–5) and demolished 1998. From a sketch. **see note 54**

BOTTOM.
The 'White Glen' once known as the 'Garden of Morvern', from where some forty families were forcibly cleared by Patrick Sellar at 'one stroke of a pen' to make way for a sheep-walk. The large boulder bottom left is 'Sellar's Stone', where, according to local tradition, Patrick Sellar sheltered for a night with his sheep flocks on his way to Morvern from Sutherland in 1838. **see note 186**

TOP.
Thomas Valentine Smith (1825–1906) with his wife and Hugh Cameron (groom) at Ardtornish Tower c. 1890

MIDDLE.
Old Fiunary Manse, built in 1780 and replaced about 1860 by the present building. From a sketch by Robina Catherine Macleod, sister of Norman Macleod 'Caraidh nan Gaidheal' c. 1830s. **see note 44**

BOTTOM.
The remains of the medieval church, Kiel graveyard showing (left) the two headstones to the children of Flory Cameron.
see notes 234 and 235

TOP LEFT.
Rev Dr John Macleod (1801–1882),
'High Priest' of Morvern

TOP RIGHT.
Rev Norman Macleod (1745–1824), the
first of the Macleod of Fiunary family,
who came to Morvern in 1775

LEFT.
Patrick Sellar of Ardtornish (1780–1851)
who, along with a number of other new
proprietors with no traditional links with
Morvern, was responsible for removing
several hundred people from their smallholdings after 1819. **see note 186**

TOP.
Lochaline Viallage c. 1900.
see note 183

ABOVE.
Kiel Church, 15th-century
cross and Session-House.
see notes 209 and 210

RIGHT.
Fingal's Hill or Dun Fiunary
with the glebe and the
Sound of Mull. From an
engraving by the author,
Rev Dr Norman Macleod
(1812–1872). **see note 48**

TOP.
The Cameron of Glendessary table-tombs, Kiel graveyard. **see note 262**

LEFT.
A brass Highland ring-brooch from HMS *Dartmouth*, a naval frigate wrecked on Eilean Rubha a Ridrie, in 1690. Reproduced by kind permission of Dr Colin Martin. **see note 220**

BELOW.
The Macleod of Fiunary burial aisle in Kiel graveyard, Morvern. **see note 284**

TOP.
Laudale House, built c. 1730, the last
traditional laird's house in Morvern.
Destroyed 2001.

RIGHT.
The ruins of 13th-century Ardtornish
Castle. **see note 276**

BELOW.
The deserted settlement of
Beinn Iadain. **see note 170**

their own peculiar voices and tastes would permit: and thus his musical calling did not at all interfere with his weekday profession.

It is impossible to describe the many wants which he supplied and the blessings which he conferred. There were few marriages of any parochial importance at which he was not an honoured guest. In times of sickness, sorrow, or death, he was sure to be present with his subdued manner, tender sympathy, and Christian counsel. If anyone wanted advice on a matter which did not seem of sufficient gravity to consult about at the Manse, 'the Master' was called in. If a trustee was wanted, by a dying man, who would deal kindly and honestly with his widow and children, 'the Master' was sure to be nominated. He knew every one in 'the Parish', and all their belongings, as minutely as a man on the turf knows the horses and their pedigree. He was a true friend of the inmates of the Manse, and the minister trusted him as he did no other man. When the minister was dying the Schoolmaster watched him by night, and tended him as an old disciple would have done one of the prophets, and left him not until with prayer he closed his eyes.

His emoluments for all this labour were not extravagant. Let us calculate. He had £15 as schoolmaster; £5 in school fees; £7 as postmaster; £1 as session clerk; £1 as leader of church psalmody; £5 as catechist; £34 in all, with house and garden. He had indeed a small farm, or bit of ground with two or three cows, a few sheep, and a few acres for potatoes and oats or barley, but for all this he paid rent. So the emoluments were not large. The house was a thatched cottage with what the Scotch call a but and ben; the but being half kitchen, half bedroom, with a peat fire on the floor, the ben having also a bed, but being dignified by a grate. Between them was a small bed-closet separated from the passage by a wicker partition. All the floors were clay. Above was a garret or loft reached by a ladder, and containing amidst a dim light a series of beds and shakes-down like a barrack. In this home father, mother, and a family of four sons and three daughters were accommodated. The girls learned at home – in addition to 'the three Rs' learned at school – to sew and spin, card wool, and sing songs; while the boys, after preparing their Virgil or arithmetic sums for next day, went in the evening to fish, to work in the garden, or on the farm, to drive home the cattle, to cut peats for fuel or stack them, to reap ferns and house them for bedding the cattle in winter, or make 'composts' for the fields, and procure moss and other unmentionable etceteras.

When darkness came they gathered round the fire, while some made baskets, repaired the horses' harness or their own shoes, or made fishing lines and 'busked' hooks; others would discourse sweet music from the trump, and all in their turn tell stories to pass the time pleasantly. The grinding of meal for porridge or *fuarag* was a common occupation. This *fuarag* was a mixture made up of meal freshly ground from corn that had been well toasted and dried before the fire, and then whipped up with thick cream – a dainty dish to set before a king! The difficulty in making it good was the getting of corn freshly toasted and meal freshly ground. It was prepared by means of a quern which at that time was in almost every house.[239] The quern consisted of two round flat stones of about a foot in diameter, and an inch or so thick, corresponding to the grinding stones in a mill. The lower stone was fixed, and the upper being fitted into it by a circular groove, was made to revolve rapidly upon it, while the corn was poured through a hole in the upper stone to be ground between the two. It was worked thus. A clean white sheet was spread over the bed in the kitchen. The mill was placed in the centre. One end of a stick was then inserted into a hole in the upper stone to turn it round, while the other end of the stick, to give it a purchase and keep it steady, was fixed in the twist of a rope, stretched diagonally from one bedpost to another. The miller sat in the bed, with a leg on each side of the quern, and seizing the stick, rapidly turned the stone, while the parched corn was poured in. When ground it was taken away and cleaned of all husks. The dry new meal being whipped up with rich cream the fuarag was ready, and then – lucky the boy who got it! I cannot forget the mill or its product, having had the privilege of often sharing in the labours of the one, and enjoying the luxury of the other.

Our Schoolmaster could not indeed give entertainments worthy of a great educational institute, nor did he live in the indulgence of any delicacies greater than the one I have dwelt upon, if, indeed, there was any greater then in existence. There was for breakfast the never-failing porridge and milk – and such milk! – with oat cakes and barley scones for those who preferred them, or liked them as a top-dressing. On Sundays, there were tea and eggs. The dinner never wanted noble potatoes, with their white powdery waistcoats, revealing themselves under the brown jackets. At that time they had not fallen into the 'sear and yellow leaf', but retained all their pristine youth and loveliness, as when they rejoiced the heart of some Peruvian Inca in the land of their nativity.

With such dainties, whether served up 'each like a star that dwelt apart', or mashed with milk, or fresh butter, into a homogeneous mass, what signified the accompaniments? Who will inquire anxiously about them? There may have been sometimes salt herring, sometimes other kinds of sea-fish — lythe, rock-cod, mackerel, or saithe — but oftener the unapproachable milk alone! At times a fat hen, and bit of pork, or blackfaced mutton, would mar the simplicity of the dinner. When these came, in Providence, they were appreciated. But whatever the food, all who partook of it ate it heartily, digested it with amazing rapidity, and never were the worse, but always the better for it. No one had headaches, or ever heard of medicine except in sermons; and all this is more than can be said of most feasts, from those of the excellent Lord Mayor of London downwards, in all of which the potatoes and milk are shamefully ignored, while salt herring and potatoes — the most savoury of dishes — and even *fuarag*, are utterly forgotten.

Handless people, who buy everything they require, can have no idea how the Schoolmaster and his family managed to get clothes; yet they always were clothed, and comfortably, too. There was wool afforded by their own few sheep, or cheaply obtained from their neighbours, and the mother and daughters employed themselves during the long winter nights in carding and spinning it. Then Callum the weaver took in hand to weave it into tartans, of any known Celtic pattern; and Peter the tailor undertook to shape it into comely garments for father or son, while the female tailors at home had no difficulty in arranging suitable garments out of their own portion of the wool.[240]

As for shoes,[241] a hide or two of leather was purchased, and John the shoemaker, like Peter the tailor, would come to the house and live there, and tell his stories, and pour out the country news, and rejoice in the potatoes, and look balmy over the *fuarag*. Peter the tailor, when he went, left beautiful suits of clothes behind him; John the shoemaker completed the adornment by most substantial

shoes – wanting polish probably, and graceful shapes, but nevertheless strong and victorious in every battle with mud and water, and
possessing powerful thongs and shining tackets.

Thus the family were clothed – if we except the kilts of the
younger boys, which necessarily left Nature, with becoming confidence in her powers, to a large portion of the work about the
limbs. The master's suit of black was also an exception. When that
suit was purchased was a point not easily determined. It was generally understood to have been obtained when the Schoolmaster
went on his first and last journey to see George IV in Edinburgh.[242]
The suit was folded in his large green chest behind the door, and
was only visible once a year at the communion, or when some
great occasion, such as a marriage or a funeral, called it forth into
sunlight. The tartan coat and homemade woollen trousers were at
such times exchanged for black broadcloth, and the black silk neck-
cloth for a white cravat; and then the Schoolmaster, with his grave
countenance and grey whiskers, and bald head, might pass for a
professor of theology or the bishop of a diocese.

The worthy Schoolmaster is long since dead. He died, as he had
lived, in peace with God and man.[243] The official residence has
been changed to another part of 'the Parish', and, when I last saw
the once happy and contented home of the good man with whom
I had spent many happy days, the garden was obliterated, the foot-
paths covered with grass, and the desolation of many years was over
it. Verily, the place that once knew him, knew him no more.[244]

Chapter 16

THE 'FOOLS'

No one attempting to describe from personal knowledge the characteristics of Highland life can omit some mention, in memoriam, of the fools. It must indeed be admitted that the term 'fool' is ambiguous, and embraces individuals in all trades, professions, and ranks of society. But those I have in my mind were not so injurious to society, nor so stupid and disagreeable, as the large class commonly called 'fools.' Nor is the true type of 'fool' a witless idiot like the Cretin, nor a raving madman, fit only for Bedlam – but 'a pleasant fellow i' faith, with his brains somewhat in disorder.'

I do not know whether 'fools' are held in such high estimation in the Highlands as they used to be in that time which we call 'our day.' It may be that the Poor Laws have banished them to the calm and soothing retreat of the workhouse; or that the moral and intellectual education of the people by government pupils, and Queen's scholars, have rendered them incapable of being amused by any abnormal conditions of the intellect; but I am obliged to confess that I have always had a foolish weakness for 'fools' – a decided sympathy with them – and that they occupy a very fresh and pleasing portion of my reminiscences of 'the Parish.'

The Highland 'fool' was the special property of the district in which he lived. He was not considered a burthen upon the community, but a privilege to them. He wandered at his own sweet will wherever he pleased, 'ower the muir amang the heather;' along highways and bye-ways, with no let or hindrance from parish beadles, rural police, or poor-law authorities.

Every one knew the 'fool,' and liked him as a sort of protégé of the public. Every house was open to him, though he had his favourite places of call. But he was too wise to call as a fashionable formal visitor, merely to leave his card and depart if his friend was 'not at home.' The temporary absence of landlord or landlady made little difference to him. He came to pay a visit, to enjoy the society of his friends, and to remain with them for days, perhaps for weeks, and possibly for months even. He was sure to be welcomed and never churled or sent away until he chose to depart. Nay, he was often coaxed to prolong the agreeable visit, which was intended as a compliment to the family, and which the family professed to accept as such. It was, therefore, quite an event when some rare fool arrived, illustrious for his wit. His appearance was hailed by all in the establishment, from the shepherds, herds, workmen, and domestic servants, up to the heads of the family, with their happy boys and girls. The news spread rapidly from the kitchen to the drawing-room – ' "Calum", "Archy", or "Duncan" fool is come!' and all would gather round him to draw forth his peculiarities.

It must be remembered that the Highland kitchen, which was the 'fool's' stage, his court, his reception and levee room, and which was cheered at night by his brilliant conversation, was like no other similar culinary establishment, except, perhaps, that in the old Irish house. The prim model of civilised propriety, with its pure well-washed floors and whitewashed walls, its glittering pans, burnished covers, clean tidy fireside with roasting-jack, oven and hot plate, a sort of cooking drawing-room, an artistic studio for roasts and boils, was utterly unknown in the genuine Highland mansion of a former generation. The Highland kitchen had, no doubt, its cooking apparatus, its enormous pot that was hung from its iron chain amidst the reek in the great chimney, its pans embosomed in glowing peats, and whatever other instrumentality (possibility an additional peat fire on the floor) was required to prepare savoury joints, with such barn-door dainties as ducks and hens, turkeys and geese – all supplied from the farm in such quantities as would terrify the modern cook and landlady if required to provide them daily from the market. The cooking of the Highland kitchen was also a continued process, like that on a passenger steamer on a long voyage. Different classes had to be served at different periods of the day, from early dawn till night. There were, therefore, huge pots of superb potatoes 'laughing in their skins', and as huge pots of porridge poured into immense wooden dishes, with the occasional dinner luxury of Braxy – a species of mutton which need not be too minutely inquired into.[245] These supplies were disposed of by the frequenters of the kitchen, dairymaids and all sorts of maids, with shepherds, farm servants, male and female, and herds full of fun and grimace, and by a constant supply of strangers, with a beggar and probably a 'fool' at the side-table. The kitchen was thus a sort of caravanserai, in which crowds of men and women, accompanied by sheep-dogs and terriers, came and went; and into whose precincts ducks, hens, and turkeys strayed as often as they could to pick up debris. The world in the drawing-room was totally separated from this world in the kitchen. The 'gentry' in 'the room' were supposed to look down upon it as on things belonging to another sphere, governed by its own laws and customs, with which they had no wish to interfere. And thus it was that 'waifs' and 'fools' came to the kitchen and fed there, as a matter of course, having a bed in the barn at night. All passers-by got their 'bite and sup' in it readily and cheerfully. Servants' wages were nominal, and food was abundant from moor and loch, sea and land. To do justice to the establishment I ought to mention that connected with the kitchen there was generally a room called 'the Servants' Hall', where the more distinguished strangers – such as 'the post' or packman, with perhaps the tailor or shoemaker when these were necessarily resident for some weeks in the House – took their meals along with the housekeeper and more 'genteel' servants.

I have, perhaps, given the impression that these illustrious visitants, the 'fools', belonged to that parish merely in which the houses that they frequented were situated. This was not the case. The fool was quite a cosmopolitan. He wandered like a wild bird over a large tract of country, though he had favourite nests and places of refuge. His selection of these was judiciously made according to the comparative merits of the treatment which he received from his many friends. I have known some cases in which the attachment became so great between the fool and the household that a hut was built and furnished for his permanent use. From this he could wander abroad when he wished a change of air or of society. Many families had their fool – their Wamba or jester – who made himself not only amusing but useful, by running messages and doing out-of-the-way jobs requiring little wit but often strength and time.

As far as my knowledge goes, or my memory serves me, the treatment of these parish characters was most benevolent. Any teasing or annoyance which they received detracted slightly, if at all, from the sum of their happiness. It was but the friction which elicited their sparks and crackling fun; accordingly the boys round the fireside at night could not resist applying it, nor their elders from enjoying it; while the peculiar claims of the fool to be considered lord or king, admiral or general, an eight-day clock or brittle glass, were cheerfully acquiesced in. Few men with all their wits about them could lead a more free or congenial life than the Highland fool with his wit only.

One of the most distinguished fools of my acquaintance was 'Allan-nan-Con', or Allan of the Dogs. He had been drafted as a soldier, but owing to some breach of military etiquette on his part, when under inspection by Sir Ralph Abercromby,[246] he was condemned as a fool, and immediately sent home. I must admit that Allan's subsequent career fully confirmed the correctness of Sir Ralph's judgment. His peculiarity was his love of dogs. He wore a long loose greatcoat bound round his waist by a rope. The greatcoat bagged over the rope, and within its loose and warm recesses a number of pups nestled while on his journey, so that his waist always seemed to be in motion. The parent dogs, four or five in number, followed on foot, and always in a certain order of march, and any straggler or undisciplined cur not keeping his own place received sharp admonition from Allan's long pike-staff. His head-dress was a large Highland bonnet, beneath which appeared a small sharp face, with bright eyes and thin-lipped mouth full of sarcasm and humour. Allan spent his nights often among the hills. 'My house', he used to say, 'is where the sun sets.' He managed, on retiring to rest, to arrange his dogs round his body so as to receive the greatest benefit from their warmth. Their training was the great object of his life; and his pupils would have astonished any government inspector by their prompt obedience to their master's commands and their wonderful knowledge of the Gaelic language.

I remember on one occasion when Allan was about to leave 'the Manse', he put his dogs, for my amusement, through some of their drill, as he called it. They were all sleeping round the kitchen fire, the pups freed from the girdle, and wandering at liberty, when Allan said, 'Go out, one of you my children, and let me know if the day is fair or wet.' A dog instantly rose, while the others kept their places, and with erect tail went out. Returning, it placed itself by Allan's side, so that he might by passing his hand along its back discover whether it was wet or dry! 'Go', he again said, 'and tell that foolish child' – one of the pups – 'who is frolicking outside of the house, to come in.' Another dog rose, departed, and returned wagging his tail and looking up to Allan's face. 'Oh, he won't come, won't he? Then go and bring him in, and if necessary by force!' The dog again departed, but this time carried the yelping pup in his mouth, and laid it at Allan's feet. 'Now, my dear children, let us be going,' said Allan, rising as if to proceed on his journey. But at this moment two terriers began to fight – though it seemed a mimic battle – while an old sagacious-looking collie never moved from his comfortable place beside the fire. To understand this scene, though, you must know that Allan had taken offence at the excellent sheriff of the district[247] because of his having refused him some responsible situation on his property, and to revenge himself had trained his dogs to act the drama which was now in progress. Addressing the apparently sleeping dog, whom he called 'the Sheriff', he said, 'There you lie, you lazy dog, enjoying yourself when the laws are breaking by unseemly disputes and fights! But what care you if you get your meat and drink! Shame upon you, Sheriff. It seems that I even must teach you your duty. Get up this moment, sir, or I shall bring my staff down on your head, and make these wicked dogs keep the peace!' In an instant 'the Sheriff' rose and separated the combatants.

It was thus that, when any one offended Allan past all possibility of forgiveness, he immediately trained one of the dogs to illustrate his character, and taught it lessons, by which in every house he could turn his supposed enemy into ridicule. A farmer, irritated by this kind of dogmatic intolerance, ordered Allan to leave his farm. 'Leave it, forsooth!' replied Allan, with a sarcastic sneer. 'Could I possibly, sir, take it with me, be assured I would do so rather than leave it to you!'

When Allan was dying he called his dogs beside him, and told them to lie close and keep him warm, as the chill of death was coming over him. He then bade them farewell, as his 'children and best friends', and hoped they would find a master who would take care of them and teach them as he had done. The old woman in whose hut the poor fool lay comforted him by telling him how, according to the humane belief of her country, all whom God had deprived of reason were sure to go to heaven, and that he would soon be there. 'I don't know very well', said Allan, with his last breath, 'where I am going, as I never travelled far; but if it is possible, I will come back for my dogs; and, mind you,' he added, with emphasis, 'to punish the Sheriff for refusing me that situation!'

Another most entertaining fool was Donald Cameron. Donald was never more brilliant than when narrating his submarine voyages, and his adventures, as he walked along the bottom of the sea passing from island to island. He had an endless variety of stories about the wrecks which he visited in the caverns of the deep, and above all of his interviews with the fish, small and great, whom he met during his strange voyages, or journeys, rather. 'On one occasion', I remember his telling me with grave earnestness, as we sat together fishing from a rock, 'I was sadly put about, my boy, when coming from the island of Tiree. Ha! ha! ha! It makes me laugh to think of it now, though at the time it was very vexing. It was very stormy weather, and the walking was difficult, and the road long. I at last became very hungry, and looked out for some hospitable house where I could find rest and refreshment. I was fortunate enough to meet a turbot, an old acquaintance, who invited me, most kindly, to a marriage party which was that day to be in his family. The marriage was between a daughter of his own, and a well-to-do flounder. So I went with the decent fellow, and entered a fine house of shells and tangle, most beautiful to see. The dinner came, and it was all one could wish. There was plenty, I assure you, to eat and drink, for the turbot had a large fishing bank almost to himself to ply his trade on, and he was too experienced to be cheated by the hook of any fisherman, Highland or Lowland. He had also been very industrious, as indeed were all his family. So he had good means. But as we sat down to our feast, and my mouth was watering just as I had the bountiful board under my nose, who should come suddenly upon us with a rush, but a tremendous cod, that was angry because the turbot's daughter had accepted a poor thin, flat flounder, instead of his own eldest son, a fine red-rock cod. The savage, rude brute gave such a fillip with his tail against the table, that it upset; and what happened, my dear, but that the turbot, with all the guests, flounders, skate, haddock, and whiting, thinking, I suppose, that it was a sow of the ocean (a whale), rushed away in a fright; and I can tell you, calf of my heart, that when I myself saw the cod's big head and mouth and staring eyes, with his red gills going like a pair of fanners, and when I got a touch of his tail, I was glad to be off with the rest; so I took to my heels and escaped among the long tangle. Pfui! what a race of hide and seek that was! Fortunately for me, I was near the point of Ardnamurchan, where I landed in safety, and got to Donald M'Lachlan's house wet and weary. Wasn't that an adventure? And now,' concluded my friend, 'I'll put on, with your leave, a very large bait of cockles on my hook, and perhaps I may catch some of that rascally cod's descendants!'

'Barefooted Lachlan', another parish worthy, was famous as a swimmer.[248] He lived for hours in the water, and alarmed more than one boat's crew, who perceived a mysterious object – it might be the sea-serpent – a mile or two from the shore, now appearing like a large seal, and again causing the water to foam with gambols like those of a much larger animal. They cautiously drew near, and saw with wonder what seemed to be the body of a human being floating on the surface of the water. With greatest caution an oar was slowly moved towards it; but just as the supposed dead body was touched, the eyes, hitherto shut, in order to keep up the intended deception, would suddenly open, and with a loud shout and laugh, Lachlan would attempt to seize the oar, to the terror and astonishment of those who were ignorant of his fancies.

The belief in his swimming powers – which in truth were wonderful – became so exaggerated that his friends, even when out of sight of land, would not have been surprised to have been hailed and boarded by him. If any unusual appearance was seen on the surface of the water along the coast of the 'Parish', and rowers paused to consider whether it was a play of fish or a pursuing whale, it was not unlikely that one of them would at last say, as affording the most probable solution of the mystery, 'I believe myself it is Barefooted Lachlan!'

Poor Lachlan had become so accustomed to this kind of fishy existence that he attached no more value to clothes than a merman does. He looked upon them as a great practical grievance. To wear them on his aquatic excursions was at once unnecessary and incon-venient, and to be obliged, despite of tides and winds, to return from a distant swimming excursion to the spot on the shore where they had been left, was to him an intolerable bore. A tattered shirt and kilt were not worth all this trouble. In adjusting his wardrobe to meet the demands of the sea, it must be confessed that Lachlan forgot the fair demands of the land. Society at last rebelled against his judgment, and the poor-law authorities having been appealed to, were compelled to try the expensive but necessary experiment of boarding Lachlan in a pauper asylum in the Lowlands, rather than permit him to wander about unadorned as a fish out of water. When he landed at the Broomielaw, and saw all its brilliant gas lights, and beheld for the first time in his life a great street with houses which seemed palaces, he whispered with a smile to his keepers, 'Surely this is heaven! am I right?' But when he passed onward to his asylum, through the railway tunnel with its smoke and noise, he trembled with horror, declaring that now, alas! he was in the lower regions and lost forever. The swimmer did not prosper when deprived of his long freedom among the winds and waves of ocean, but died in a few days after entering the well-regulated home provided for his comfort by law. Had it not been for his primitive taste in clothes, and his want of appreciation of any better or more complete covering than his tanned skin afforded, I would have protested against confining him in a workhouse as a cruel and needless incarceration, and pleaded for him as Wordsworth did for his Cumberland beggar:

> As in the eye of Nature he has lived,
> So in the eye of Nature let him die.

While engaged in the unusual task of writing the biographies of fools, I cannot forget one who, though not belonging to 'the Parish', was better known perhaps than any other in the Western Highlands. The man I speak of was 'Gillespie Aotrom', or 'light-headed Archy', of the Isle of Skye. Archy was perhaps the most famous character of his day in that island. When I first made his acquaintance a quarter of a century ago, he was eighty years of age, and had been a notorious and much-admired fool during all that period – from the time, at least, in which he had first babbled folly at his mother's knee. Archy, though a public beggar, possessed excellent manners. He was welcomed in every house in Skye; and if the landlord had any appreciation of wit, or if he was afraid of being made the subject of some sarcastic song or witty epigram, he was sure to ask Archy into the dining-room after dinner, to enjoy his racy conversation. The fool never on such occasions betrayed the slightest sense of being patronised, but made his bow, sat down, accepted with respect, ease, and grace his glass of wine or whisky punch, and was ready to engage in any war of joke or repartee, and to sing some inimitable songs, which hit off with rare cleverness the infirmities and frailties of the leading people of the island – especially the clergy. Some of the clergy and gentry happened to be so sensitive to the power and influence of this fool's wit, which was sure to be repeated at 'kirk and market', that it was alleged they paid him blackmail in meat and money to keep him quiet, or obtain his favour.

Archy's practical jokes were as remarkable as his sayings. One of these I must narrate. An old acquaintance of mine, a minister in Skye, who possessed the kindest disposition and an irreproachable moral character, was somehow more afraid of Archy's sharp tongue and witty rhymes than most of his brethren. Archy seemed to have detected intuitively his weak point, and though extremely fond of the parson, yet often played upon his good nature with an odd mixture of fun and selfishness. On the occasion I refer to, Archy in his travels arrived on a cold night at the manse when all its inmates were snug in bed, and the parson himself was snoring loud beside his mate. A thundering knock at the door awakened him, and thrusting his white head, enveloped in a thick white nightcap, out of the window, he at once recognised the tall, well-known form of Archy. 'Is this you, Archy? Oich, oich! what do you want, my good friend, at this hour of the night?' blandly asked the old minister. 'What could a man want at such an hour, most reverend friend,' replied the rogue, with a polite bow, 'but his supper and his bed!' 'You shall have both, good Archy,' said the parson, though wishing Archy on the other side of the Coolins. Dressing himself in his home-made flannel unmentionables, and throwing a shepherd's plaid over his shoulders, he descended and admitted the fool. He then provided a sufficient supper for him in the form of a large supply of bread and cheese, with a jug of milk. During the repast Archy told his most recent gossip and merriest stories, concluding by a request for a bed. 'You shall have the best in the parish, good Archy, take my word for it!' quoth the old dumpy and most amiable minister.

The bed alluded to was the hayloft over the stable, which could
be approached by a ladder only. The minister adjusted the ladder
and begged Archy to ascend. Archy protested against the rudeness.
'You call that, do you, one of the best beds in Skye? You, a minister,
say so? On such a cold night as this, too? You dare to say this to *me*!'
The old man, all alone, became afraid of the gaunt fool as he lifted
his huge stick with energy. But had any one been able to see clearly
Archy's face, they would have easily discovered a malicious twinkle
in his eye betraying some plot which he had been concocting probably all day. 'I do declare, Archy,' said the parson, earnestly, 'that a
softer, cleaner, snugger bed exists not in Skye!' 'I am delighted', said
Archy, 'to hear it, minister, and must believe it since you say so. But
you know it is the custom in our country for a landlord to show his
guest into his sleeping apartment, isn't it? and so I expect you to go
up before me to my room, and just see if all is right and comfortable. Please ascend!'

Partly from fear and partly from a wish to get back to his own
bed as soon as possible, out of the cold of a sharp north wind, the
simple-hearted old man complied with Archy's wish. With difficulty, waddling up the ladder, he entered the hayloft. When his
white rotund body again appeared as he formally announced to his
distinguished guest how perfectly comfortable the resting place
provided for him was, the ladder, alas! had been removed, while
Archy calmly remarked, 'I am rejoiced to hear what you say! I don't
doubt a word of it. If it is so very comfortable a bedroom, though,
you will have no objection, I am sure, to spend the night in it. Good
night, then, my much-respected friend, and may you have as good a
sleep and as pleasant dreams as you wished me to enjoy.' So saying
he made a profound bow and departed with the ladder over his
shoulder. But after turning the corner and listening with fits of suppressed laughter to the minister's loud expostulations and earnest
entreaties – for never had he preached a more energetic sermon, or
one more from his heart – and when the joke afforded the full
enjoyment which was anticipated, Archy returned with the ladder,
and advising the parson never to tell fibs about his fine bedrooms
again, but to give what he had without imposing upon strangers, he
let him descend to the ground, while he himself ascended to the
place of rest in the loft.

Archy's description of the whole scene was ever afterwards one of his best stories, to the minister's great annoyance.

A friend of mine met Archy on the highway, and, wishing to draw him out, asked his opinion of several travellers as they passed. The first was a very tall man. Archy remarked that he had never seen any man before so near heaven! Of another he said that he had 'the sportsman's eye and the soldier's step', which was singularly true in its description.

A Skye laird, who was fond of trying a passage of arms with Archy, met him one day gnawing a bone. 'Shame on you, Archy!' said the laird; 'why do you gnaw a bone in that way?' 'And to what use, sir,' asked Archy in reply, 'would you have me put it?' 'I advise you', said the laird, 'to throw it in charity to the first dog you meet.' 'Is that your advice? Then I throw it to yourself!' said Archy, shying the bone at the laird's feet.

An old woman from Skye, who knew Archy well, has repeated to me the words which he never failed to use with reverence as his grace before meat. They seem to contain some allusion to the sin of the evil eye, so much feared and hated by the old Highlanders. I translate them literally:

> May my heart always bless my eyes
> And my eyes bless all they see:
> And may I always bless my neighbour
> Though my neighbours should never bless me.
> > Amen.

By this time I fear that my sedate and wise readers will conclude that a sympathy with fools comes very naturally to me. I must bow my head to the implied rebuke. It is, I know, a poor defence to make for my having indulged, however briefly, in such biographies, that the literary world has produced many longer ones of greater fools less innocent of crime, less agreeable, and less beneficial to society, than those which I have so imperfectly recorded among my reminiscences of the old Highlands.*

---

* Since writing the above, I have heard of a distinguished general officer who left the Highlands in his youth, but returned a short time ago to visit his early home. 'Will you believe me,' he said, with great seriousness and naïveté, to my informant, 'when I tell you that among the many things so long associated with my faithful

But lest any one should imagine for a moment that I treat lightly the sufferings of those deprived of God's highest gift of reason, let me say that my fools were generally strong and healthy in body, and in many cases, as I have already hinted, took a share in farm work, boating, fishing, etc., and that their treatment was most humane and benevolent. At the same time I do not forget another very different class, far lower in the scale of humanity, which, owing to many circumstances that need not be detailed here, was a very large one in the Highlands – creatures weak in body and idiotic in mind, who in spite of the tenderest affection on the part of their poor parents, were yet miserable objects for which no adequate relief existed. Such cases, indeed, occur everywhere throughout the kingdom to a greater extent than, I think, most people are aware of. Those idiots are sometimes apparently little removed above the beasts that perish, yet they nevertheless possess a Divine nature never wholly extinguished, which is capable of being developed to a degree far beyond what the most sanguine could anticipate who have not seen what wise, patient, benevolent and systematic education is capable of accomplishing. The coin with the king's image on it, though lying in the dust with the royal stamp almost obliterated, may yet be found again and marvellously cleansed and polished! I therefore hail asylums for idiot children as among the most blessed fruits of Christian civilisation. Though, strange to say, they are but commencing among us, yet I believe the day is near when they will be recognised as among the most needed, most successful, and most blessed institutions of our country.

remembrances that have passed away, and which I miss much – are – are – pray don't laugh at me when I confess it – are my old friends the fools!' I heartily sympathise with the general!

Chapter 17

STAFFA TOURISTS FORTY YEARS AGO

Until within the last forty years the West Highlands was a land of mystery to the London summer tourist. Dr Johnson had indeed penetrated those fastnesses, and returned in safety to London, not only without having been robbed, or obliged to wear a kilt and live on whisky and oatmeal porridge, but with a most flattering account of the people, and describing the clergy and gentry as polite, educated, and hospitable. Sir Joseph Banks[249] and Mr Pennant[250] had brought into notice, and admirably delineated, the marvellous Island of Staffa, not far from Inch Kenneth and Iona, both of which islands were visited by Johnson, and excited his enthusiasm – the one for its Laird, and the other for its memories of early piety. But when Scott adopted the Highlands as the subject of romantic story and song, investing its scenery, its feudal history, its chiefs, clans, old traditions, and wild superstitions with all the charm of his genius, then began a new era of centred comfort in every spot which his magic wand had touched. *The Lord of the Isles*, and the *Lady of the Lake* became the pioneers of the tourist. Good roads took the place of the old bridle paths winding among the heather. Coaches-and-four bowled through wild passes where savage clans used to meet in deadly combat. Steamers foamed on every Loch and banished the water kelpies. Telescopes were substituted for second sight. Waiters with white neckcloths and white towels received the travellers, where red deer used to sleep undisturbed. The eagles were banished from the mountains, and 'boots' reigned in the valleys.

Forty years ago steamers had not mingled their smoke with the mists of the hills, and the Highlands had not become common as Vauxhall to the Londoners. It was then a land of distance and darkness. No part of Europe is so unknown now to the fireside traveller as the Hebrides were then. With the 'Foreign Bradshaw' and 'Murray'[251] any man now can so arrange his journey as to fix the day on which he will arrive, and the hour at which he will dine in any town from the Baltic to the Mediterranean. As he sits in his club in London, he notes the minute when his train will arrive at Moscow or Milan, and almost the day when his steamer will land him at New York, and when he can reach the Prairies of the far West, or gaze on the Falls of Niagara or St Anthony.* The Hebrides are therefore now at his door. He dines one day in London, and sups the next beneath the shadow of Ben Lomond or Ben Cruachan. But at the time I speak of, the journey northward to Glasgow by coach or post-horses was tedious, tiresome, and expensive. When the Highlands proper were entered upon, at Dumbarton or Callander, then, between bad roads and peat-reeked pothouses, rude boats without comfort, and a crew innocent of English, with all the uncertainties of tides, squalls, heavy seas, and heavy rain, a tour among the islands of Scotland was far more hazardous than one now to India or America.

The continent of Europe was then still more difficult of access, and during the wars of Napoleon was well-nigh inaccessible. Accordingly such persons as loved adventure and had time and money at their command, and who, above all, could obtain good letters of introduction, selected a Highland journey, with Staffa as its grand termination.

Alas! for the hospitable Highland mansion which happened to be situated at a convenient resting-place for the tourist *en route* to some spot of interest! There was then prevalent among southern tourists a sort of romantic idea of the unlimited extent of Highland hospitality, and of the means at its command. It was no unusual occurrence for the traveller to land at any hour of the day or night which winds, tides, or boatmen might determine; to walk up to the house of the Highland gentleman; to get a dinner, supper, and all,

---

* Even while we write, the following paragraph appears in a London paper:

> Think of an excursion party which is to start from Plymouth on board a luxuriously appointed steamer, and which is to visit Lisbon, Gibraltar, Naples, Palermo, Malta, Athens, Constantinople, Balaklava, Sidon, Alexandria, Algiers, and Tangiers, before returning to the port of departure! All this is to be accomplished in two months. The time of putting in at each new port and the length of stay to be made there, are set out in the advertisement as specifically and formally as the arrivals and the stations on a railway timetable. Every luxury, we learn, is to be provided for the travelling company, and they are not supposed to be under any expense while on shore, as the steamer is to be their floating hotel all the time.

plentiful and comfortable; to retire to bed, without a thought where the family had packed themselves (so that the travelling party might have accommodation); and finally to obtain next day, or, if it rained, days after, carts, horses, boats, men with baskets of provisions, crammed with roast fowls, cold lamb (salt never forgot), cold salmon, grouse, milk, brandy, sherry, and bottles of whisky. The potato digging, the hay cutting, or the reaping of crops might be put a stop to; what of that? They are so hospitable in the Highlands! And then these summer visitants bade farewell with shaking of hands, and waving of handkerchiefs, and with the usual stereotyped hope expressed that, 'should they ever come to England and visit Land's End, how glad, etc.' But the reception was nevertheless all put down to a *habit* of the country, a thing called Highland hospitality, something like speaking Gaelic, smoking tobacco, or wearing the kilt.

And I am compelled to acknowledge that the families who thus received and entertained strangers never looked on their doing so in that 'light of common day' in which I cannot help placing these transactions. 'What *can* the travellers do?' I remember well the lady of one of those hospitable houses saying when a large party of strangers had departed after a stay of several days. 'There are no inns where they can put up, but those wretched holes. And then the travellers are so nice! It is truly delightful to meet with such well-bred, intelligent ladies and gentlemen – I would put myself to much more trouble to enjoy their society.' And the young ladies of the family would chime in and declare that they had never met sweeter girls than those Smiths, especially Caroline, and that they were so vexed when they went away – and as for the young men of the party— !' Here all the ladies were unanimous. The host was equally friendly – 'I don't grudge my wine a bit', he would say to Mr Smith. 'I never met a better educated, scholarly man, nor one better informed.' This is really a true picture of the feelings at the time with which those English travellers were received; for very few penetrated those recesses except the higher classes or 'well to-do gentry', who had time and money at their disposal, and who had sufficient culture to love scenery for its own sake, to appreciate the manners of the country, and cheerfully to accommodate themselves to its inconveniences.

One may be surprised to know how comforts were extempor-
ised in those out-of-the-way places. The process was a very simple
one. Large stores of groceries, and all the materials required for
every after-dinner luxury except the dessert, were obtained
periodically from Greenock or Glasgow. Bread was the chief
difficulty, as baking wheaten bread, strange to say, was an art never
practised by Highland families. But they had all sorts of delicious
hot scones made of flour, or barley-meal, in addition to crisp
oatmeal cakes, while a loaf was brought from Oban by Her
Majesty's Post once or twice a week. Every other kind of food was
abundant. As a Highland farmer once remarked, in pointing to his
plentiful board, 'We growed all that on our own selves!'

As the tourist voyages through the Sound of Mull he can hardly
fail to notice Aros Castle − unless he be reading, as some do, amidst
the noblest scenery, a green or yellow-backed shilling novel. Aros
was the landing place in those old days for parties going to visit
Staffa. A narrow isthmus of two or three miles of road here
connects the Sound with an inland arm of the sea, on the other side
of Mull, which leads out past Inch Kenneth and Ulva to the islands
of Staffa and Iona. When these famous localities had to be
approached by boats from Oban, it was necessary to take the safe
and sheltered passage of the Sound, rather than to run the risk,
whether from dead calm or wild storm, of attempting to sail
outside of Mull with a bare rock only as the termination of the
voyage.

And here I am reminded − for all gossips like Mrs Quickly are
ever tempted to digress in the telling of their story − of the 'tricks
upon travellers' which those Highland boatmen were sometimes
tempted to perpetrate. Between Oban and Mull there are several
bad 'tideways' which, in certain combinations of wind and tide, are
apt to produce a heavy sea of a most dangerous kind to all except
very skilled boatmen, sometimes putting even their skill to the
severest test. One of the pilots of those famous wherries was nick-
named 'Daring Calum', on account of the almost reckless boldness
with which he undertook to steer his boat on the wildest days,
when others, more prudent, would not venture to cross the stormy
ferry to Mull. One of the fierce tideways on this passage was called
'the dirks', from the figure of the waves which rose on every side,

tossing their sharp heads in the sky. On one occasion when Calum was piloting a Staffa party through this wild and foaming tide, the spray of the waves flew over the bow and wet the passengers. A rival of Calum on board remarked to a companion, loud enough to be heard by Calum, 'Bad steering that!' 'Bad steering!' echoed Calum, with an angry growl. 'There is no man living could carry a boat so dry through that wild sea; and if you think you can do it, come and take the helm and try it!' The rival pilot thus challenged took the helm, and ordering the boat to be put about – after passing all the danger! – once more crossed the roaring tideway, which had thus necessarily to be crossed a third time before the boat could resume her voyage in the right direction! The poor passengers were of course ignorant of the cause of their prolonged misery amidst the salt sea foam. Nemesis at last overtook poor Calum, for though he proved his superiority as a steersman on the occasion referred to, and survived his triumph thirty years, he was drowned at last.

Choosing the comparative safety of the inner passage, the travellers landed at Aros, crossed to the opposite side, and there took a boat – with four stout rowers, or a sail, in case of wind – for Staffa, which was thus reached in five or six hours.

The first time we visited the famous island was by this route; and though we have gone to it by steamer several times since then, yet the impression made by the first visit remains, and can never more be obliterated – neither, alas! can the fear be renewed. We had time and quiet to enjoy the scene, without the screaming of steam whistles or the impatient wrath of steam engines, threatening to burst unless passengers rush on board at the fixed hour.

It was a glorious summer morning. We started about daybreak, with four Highland boatmen, capital rowers, capital singers of boat songs, and crack men when sail had to be carried, and when

> The wind blew loud, and the lift grew dark,
> And gurly grew the sea.

We swept along the shore, and had full time to see and enjoy all the glories of the beach, its huge boulders, its deep black water shadowed by the beetling cliffs – with all the magnificent outline of bold rugged headlands, fantastic rocks, and ever-varying 'giant snouted' crags, with echoing caves, and secluded bays – until we at last glided into the great ocean, with its skyline broken by the Treshnish isles, the Dutchman's cap, and the more distant Tiree. A long glassy swell heaved in from the Atlantic; flocks of all kinds of birds swam and dived, and screamed around us. At length came Staffa in solemn silence, revealing its own stately grandeur of pillared cave and precipice. Alone and undisturbed we listened to the music of the ocean in that marvellous temple not built with hands. There were no human beings there but the boatmen, and they seemed as natural to the island as the limpets on its rocks, or the brown tangle which waved among the waters that laved its sides. To see Staffa thus was like visiting a great cathedral for worship; to see it with a steamboat company is like visiting the same cathedral desecrated by a public meeting!

But to return to Staffa tourists before steamboat days. There were four 'Hospitable Houses' situated in this Mull transit, where persons with letters of introduction always put up. One was Mr Maxwell's, 'the factor' or 'chamberlain' for the Duke of Argyle, his house being close to the old Castle of Aros.[252] The other, about a mile off, was Mr Stewart's, the kind-hearted proprietor of Achadashenaig – a title which no Englishman ever pretended to pronounce correctly.[253] On the other side of Mull, and beneath Benmore, was Colonel Campbell's, of Knock – himself a brave and distinguished old officer;[254] and then, six miles nearer Staffa, was the most frequented of all, Ulva House, the residence of Mr M'Donald, the laird of Staffa – the very impersonation of Highland hospitality.[255]

There was one small inn on the Sound, 'the Shore House', which received all extras, including the servants of those who were accommodated at Aros, and the neighbouring house of Acha—etc. When the travelling season commenced, the telescopes of these houses were busy in reconnoitring the white sails of boats coming from Oban. There were three well-known 'wherries', the *Iona*, *Staffa*, and *Fingal*, whose rig was familiar from afar. 'I think that is a Staffa party!' was a remark which roused the household, and caused a group to gather round the telescope, as the distant white speck was observed advancing towards the bay. By-and-by a flag was discovered fluttering from the peak. It was the sign of a party; but, coming to which house? Aros, Acha—etc., or the inn? – or to cross the isthmus to Knock or Ulva? It was necessary to prepare for a possible invasion! The larder of Aros was therefore examined in case, bedrooms were put in order; innocent chickens, geese, ducks, or turkey poults killed; and preparations for every comfort set a-going. Mutton, lamb, fish, or game, were always ready. But the destination of the party could not possibly be discovered until at the door of Aros, which was nearest the point where all landed. Suddenly a group is seen approaching the door, near the old castle: paterfamilias and his wife leading, sons, daughters, and servants following, with the luggage borne on the shoulders of four boatmen. Then the official rap at the door. Nancy, the girl, is dressed in her best, and 'looks both neat and comely'. Host and hostess, backed by the young ladies of the family, are prepared with bow and curtsey, smile and welcome, to read the letter from the Duke of Argyle recommending Sir John This, or my friend Lord That, to the kind attention of his Grace's viceroy; and soon all are settled down in comfort to rest for a few days ere they begin the voyage to Staffa under their host's direction.

A pleasing remembrance of many of these visitors remained for life in the memories of their hosts, and in cases not a few, the visitors retained a grateful and equally long remembrance of their Highland friends. I remember well how the 'factor' at Aros, who lived opposite the old manse – and with whom, as my maternal grandfather, I spent a part of my happy holidays for many a year – used to enumerate the names of those who had impressed him by their manners, their knowledge, their scholarship, or their wit. He was himself an excellent classic (to my grief when I wished to enjoy an idle holiday), and the visit of an Oxford or Cambridge man was always a delight to him. He had stories of many then beginning their travels, whose names have since become famous in the world. But he frankly confessed that Tom Sheridan,[257] who accompanied the Lord Lorne of the day,[258] was out of sight the pleasantest fellow he had ever met with. The visit was memorable from the number of bottles of old port which were consumed, and the late hours which for a series of nights were spent amidst songs and shouts of laughter. The factor declared that he could not have survived another week of Tom, whose stories and witticisms became a large literary property to him in after years, and were often told after dinner to his guests.

When Walter Scott was expected to visit Mull, an intense anxiety was felt as to which of the houses would have the privilege of entertaining him.[259] Scott was then known as the poet, not as the novelist, and was touring it in the Highlands with his young and most engaging wife. The factor, who was an enthusiast in ballad poetry, was sorely grieved when he saw the party pass his door on their way to Ulva House. But on Scott's return the factor had the happiness of having him under his roof for an evening. 'Ha!' exclaimed Scott, on their meeting, 'what puts a Maxwell and a Scott in this part of the world? We should meet, lad, on the Border!' That evening was also memorable in the history of Staffa parties.

I must not omit to record in passing the lines written by Scott, in the album of Ulva, on the Laird of Staffa – or 'Staffa', as he was always called:

> Staffa! king of all good fellows,
> Well betide thy hills and valleys;
> Lakes and inlets, steeps and shallows
> Mountains which the grey mist covers.
> Where the chieftain spirit hovers,
> Pausing as its pinions quiver,
> Stretched to quit this land for ever
> May all kind influence rest above thee,
> On all thou lov'st, and all who love thee!
> For warmer heart twixt this and Jaffa,
> Beats not than in the breast of Staffa!

I quote from memory. But whoever possesses now that Ulva album must be able to select from its pages some memorial lines which would have some interest.*

---

* (See also note 260.) The Ettrick Shepherd also left a memento in the album, but one less complimentary to the island than Scott's.

> I've roamed 'mong the peaks and the headlands of Mull,
> Her fields are neglected, uncultured, and weedy.
> Her bosom is dark, and her heaven is dull,
> Her sons may be brave, but they're horribly greedy.

An indignant native thus replies –

> O Shepherd at Ettrick, why sorely complain,
> Tho' the boatmen were greedy of grog?
> The beauties of Staffa by this you proclaim
> Were but pearls thrown away on a Hogg.

Occasionally some rare specimens of the Cockney make their appearance in those parts. One instance of the credulity of the species may be mentioned, although to believe it seems to demand an almost equal amount of credulity in the reader. A London citizen presented himself at Aros. On entering the room where the family were assembled he paused, and looked with an expression of wonder around him; then, apologising for his intrusion, he begged permission to return with his travelling companion, just for five minutes, to see the house. The landlady of 'The Shore House', the small inn where the astonished visitor 'put up', heard him say to his friend as he addressed him in breathless haste, 'I say, Dick, you must come with me instantly. I have got permission to bring you. We are quite mistaken about the people here, I assure you – confoundedly mistaken! You will not believe me until you see it with your own eyes, but I was in a regular well-built gentleman's house, with carpets, furniture, a pianoforte, actually, and the girls dressed in nice white gowns!' It is a fact that these same travellers had brought red cloth, beads, and several articles of cutlery, to barter with the natives! They seemed to have consulted Cook's voyages as the only reliable book for informing them how to deal with savages.★

I have often to crave the reader's indulgence for inflicting my 'auld lang syne' gossip on him. But these old travelling days belong to a past never to return; and those old kind-hearted hosts who made the tour easy and agreeable to many a happy family, and to many an invalid in search of health, have all passed away, and have left no representatives in their once hospitable homes. I like to record their names even in the most evanescent form.

★ This reminiscence suggests an illustration of another kind of credulity which occurred in a Highland steamer a few years ago, and which is perhaps worth telling. A quiet man, very busy discussing a plentiful breakfast while passing Jura, was much bored by a London citizen, who asked questions without end on the most commonplace and uninteresting points connected with his journey. Just as our quiet friend was engaged upon some fresh herring, the citizen consulted him to explain the cause of the whirlpool which he was told was near Jura. 'The whirlpool', replied his tormented informer, 'is a great mystery. Even Sir Walter Scott was puzzled by it. Some people account for it by the arrangement of the rocks under water, some by the meeting of the tides, and others by the shoals of herrings. But I have heard scientific men affirm that it is chiefly owing to the suction of the hills called the Paps of Jura, and if you go on deck you may perhaps observe the phenomenon now; and I strongly advise you to go.' 'Really!' said the astonished citizen. 'Ah – very odd – but – but, I don't see, at this moment, how what you say is possible. But I shall go on deck, and tell you the result of my observations.' 'Do, and please don't leave till I join you.' 'Thank you very much. I shall remain till you come.'

Chapter 18

THE CUSTOMS OF NEW YEAR'S EVE
AND MORNING

AS NARRATED BY A HIGHLAND PIPER*

According to promise, I will give you a true account of the manner in which we used to part with the old year, and welcome the new, during my younger days in the family of Glendessary.[261] The last night of the year was, as you know, called *oidhche Challuinn* (the night of *Calluinn)*. They tell me that this word signifies noise, or rattling; and that the Highlanders so designated this night† from the noisy mirth with which they celebrated it.

Well, my father was piper to Glendessary, as was his father before him, and every son of mine has, as soon as weaned, taken to the pipe-chanter just as naturally as the young kid takes to scrambling up the rocks. It was the habit of this family to gather for *Calluinn* night (New Year's Eve) all the tenantry on their lands, young and old, especially all the foster-fathers, mothers, brothers, and sisters, and according to wont, *Evan Ban maor* (Fair-haired Evan the ground-officer), went round amongst them a few days before the time. 'It is the wish of the family', says he, 'that we should observe the *Calluinn* as of old, and see, my lads, that you have your *Camain*

---

* This chapter is translated from the first Gaelic magazine ever published, which was conducted by my father, the late Dr MacLeod of Glasgow.[262] The account of these Highland customs, though bearing the signature of 'Findlay the Piper,' was written by himself, and is now offered, along with a few illustrative notes, as a Reminiscence of 'the Parish,' and also as a characteristic specimen of the narratives of the Highland peasantry.

† The term *Calluinn*. The derivation of this word has sorely puzzled Celtic antiquarians, and it is enough to show the straits to which they are reduced, to mention that some derive it from *Kalends,* and others from the name of the goddess Kalydon, said to have been worshipped by some tribes of Slavonians on the shores of the Baltic. We consider the explanation given by the piper full as good as either

(shinties, or clubs) right and ready for New Year's Day.' The piper set off in his full Highland garb about the height of the evening (as the sun was beginning to decline). We reached the great house; and can I expect that my heart will ever be as light and joyous as it was on that night? The young ladies of the family met us with bows of ribbon for the chanter of the pipe. The piper played a round on the green before the door, as the men gathered.

The time of *Calluinn* came, when someone had to carry the dry cow hide on his back and run round the house, and every one that

---

of these. Let it be remembered. however, that the corresponding term *Hagmana,* used of old in England (possibly still in some parts of it), or *Hogmanay,* universally used in Scotland, is of equally uncertain origin – some deriving it from the Greek '*Hagia mene*', sacred month, while others resolve it into the French, '*Homene est ne*', the man is born, referring of course to our Saviour's nativity. And we may remark, without going into antiquarian dissertation, that with the view of discovering the derivation of the word *Yule,* used in England and Scotland, almost every language from Hebrew to Danish has been questioned and tortured all to little purpose.

The Gaelic term *Calluinn,* then, is not alone in the mystery of its origin. The *Cainneal,* or *Coinneal,* used to denote the first day of the year, has also exercised the ingenuity of linguists. Its simplest solution is, however, probably the nearest to the truth. It literally signifies candle, and in all likelihood refers to the illuminations customary at that joyous season.

Nalluig, or *Nollaig,* the Gaelic term for Christmas, is evidently of the same origin with the French *Noël,* derived from *Natalis.*

We need say nothing about the Highlanders observing the season of the New Year as a festive, and a joyous one. Almost all nations, Pagan and Christian, have done so, visiting their friends, feasting on the best, and giving a liberal supply to their cattle as well. The piper giving a sheaf of corn to his cows reminds one of Burns' well-known lines to his old mare Maggie, on New Year's Day.

The expressing of their joy through rhymes was also common to other nations as well as to the Highlanders. Abundant specimens both of French and English verses used on occasions are to be found in our older books, nor are we aware that the Gaelic rhymes deserve any special mention. We have heard many which were mere doggerel – others, again, through which a vein of satirical humour ran, well fitted to rebuke any churlish tendency in those who were addressed; but the great majority of them, like the English ones, expressed kindly wishes towards the households visited, while they all craved a good *Calluinn* for the rhyming visitors.

The carrying about of the hide, beating on it with sticks, and surrounding the house three times, going always in the direction of the sun, or *Deas-iul,* is, at least in modern times, peculiar to the Highlanders. Till very recently it was generally observed, and is, we believe, in remote localities still practised. Some writers imagine that the thus walking around the house, clothed in the skins of a slaughtered animal, has reference to sacrificial and propitiatory rites. We learn,

could, tried to get a stroke at it with his stick. 'Who will carry the hide this year?' says Evan Ban. 'Who but Para Mor?' (Big Patrick) says one. 'Who but Broad John?' says another. 'Out with the hide Para Mor,' says Evan Ban, 'and you Broad John, stand by his shoulder in case he may stumble.' Para Mor drew the hide about his head, taking a twist of the tail firmly around his fist. '*Cothrom na Féinné*'* (i.e. fair play as among the Fingalians, or Fingalian justice), exclaimed he, as he drew near the door of the house where the Laird *(Fear a' bhaile,* the man of the place) was standing with his

---

however, from *Brand's Popular Antiquities*, edited by Ellis, that this is a remnant of the wild and fantastic orgies of the old Roman Saturnalia, where men often disguised themselves in the skins of wild beasts, and abandoned themselves to the wildest enjoyments. Early Christian writers state that many of their flocks followed after these heathenish customs, saying expressly — '*vestiuntur pellibus pecudum*' — 'they are clothed in the skins of cattle'.

We read of slight traces of this strange transformation being discernible in Yorkshire till a comparatively recent date, but like many other old customs it found beyond the Grampian mountains a more lasting abode than anywhere else.

One other observance we mention, which we believe was peculiar to the Highlands. The *Caisein uchd,* or the piece of skin covering the breast bone of sheep or cow — more especially the former, with its short curly wool — was kept as carefully as was the hide; and on New Year's Eve, after being well singed in the fire, was applied to the nose of everyone within the house, visitor or dweller. Thereafter it was carried to the byre, and the olfactories of the cattle also regaled with its fragrance. All we can say of this practice is that it was observed with the view of conferring some benefit on man and beast. Pennant mentions that the cattle in the North Highlands were, on the evening in question, made to smell burnt juniper.

We gather from the *Old Statistical Account* that in some parts of the Highlands *Hogmanay* is called *oidhche dar na Coille* — i.e. 'The night of the fecundation of the trees', and that according to the direction of the wind on this night the character of the following season might be predicted. The fresh wind promised fish, and milk. The South, warmth, and general fruitfulness. The North, cold and shivering — literally, skinning. And the East wind even as in the land of Pharaoh — the withering of the fruit.

For the principal statements in the foregoing long note, see *Brand's Popular Antiquities*.

* Fingalian Justice, or Fair Play. — We will not enter on the controversy as to whether 'Fingal fought', or 'Ossian sang'. We must remark, however, that expressions like the above, referring to the belief in the existence of a band called Féinne or Fingalians, renowned for dauntless valour, high-souled honour, and unfailing constancy, are in daily use among the Highlanders from West to East, from North to South.

We may add that the names of the principal heroes, and the scenes of their exploits, are familiar as household words among young and old.

Caman (shinty) in his hand. '*Calluinn* here!' says he, giving the first
rattle to the hide. Para Mor set off, but, swift of foot as he was, the
men of the Glen kept at his heel, and you would think that every
flail in the country was at work on the one threshing-floor, as every
mother's son of them struck and rattled at him, shouting, 'a *Calluinn*
here! The *Calluinn* of the yellow sack of hide! Strike ye the skin! A
Calluinn here!' Three times they went *Deas-iul* (in a southerly direction, according to the course of the sun) around the house. 'Blow
up, piper,' *(Seid suas)* said Evan Ban, 'and when the company are in
order, let them assemble in the Rent-room.' My father played 'Failt'
a' Phrionnsa' (the Prince's Welcome); for though there was not in
the kingdom a man more leal and loyal to the family which then sat
upon the throne, yet he loved to listen to this tune; and often have
I seen him shedding tears on hearing that thrilling music which had
stirred his forefathers to deeds of manliness on these renowned
battlefields, where alas! they lost their men and their estates.

We went into the chamber where the family and the neighbouring gentry were assembled. He himself, the graceful president
of the feast, stood in the midst, and his mild, winsome lady by his
side. The lovely young branches of the family were around them,
though, woe's me! few of them are alive today. The Laird (good
man) of Corrie was standing at the door to guard against anyone
slipping in without saying his *Calluinn* rhyme, and John Ban, of the
casks (the butler), beside him with a bottle in his hand. Everyone
had a rhyme that night except Lowland John and a young con-
ceited fellow from the Glen, who had been for a year or two in
Glasgow, and affected to have forgotten his native tongue, as well as
the customs of his native land. John Ban dealt round the drink, and
the bread and cheese, piled up plenteously, were distributed freely.

After a short time the songs began. He himself gave us an iorram
(boat song), and well could he do it. Many a sweet song, lay, and
ditty was sung, as well as those which were historical and com-
memorative. The fox-hunter gave us 'Dan a' choin ghlais' (the song
of the grey dog), and Angus of the Satires repeated a tale of the
Fingalians. After the songs the dancing began, very different from
the slow, soft, silken steps of the present day. First came in a smart
dame, dressed like a housekeeper, with a bunch of keys jingling by
her side; strong, sturdy and active she looked. The women sang *Port*

á Beul (i.e. a tune from the mouth), selecting 'Cailleach an Dudain' (the old wife of the milldust), and it was she who capered and turned, and sprang nimbly. After this they danced the *Dubh-Luidneach* (Black Sluggard). But the best fun was when the 'Goat Dance', 'Weave the Gown' (*Figh an Gùn*), and the Thorny Croft (*Croit am Droighin*) were danced.*

The time of parting at length came. The gentry gave us the welcome of the New Year with cordiality and kindliness, and we set off to our homes. 'My lads,' says he to himself, 'be valiant on the field tomorrow. The sea-board men (*Leththir*, i.e. half-land) boast that they are to beat us Glenmen at the Shinty match this year.' Thus we passed the last night of the year at Glendessary, and neither I, nor my father, ever saw a quarrel, or heard an improper word at such a gathering. It is since the gentry have ceased thus to mingle freely with the people that disgusting drunkenness has become common, in these black tippling-houses, which prove the highway to almost every vice. The people of each estate were as one family – the knot of kindness tying every heart together, and the friendly eye of the superiors was over us all.

I might here give many useful advices to our lairds; but they do not understand Gaelic, and they would not take the counsel of the piper, so I must hasten to tell you about our way of passing the first day of the new year.

---

* Songs and dances. – We have preserved these names in the hope that someone more learned than we in Highland antiquities may explain them. The singing called *Port á Beul,* a tune from the mouth, we have ourselves heard, and heard with high pleasure. In the absence of musical instruments, persons trained to it imitate dancing-music with the voice, and when they sing in parts the imitation is remarkably happy. We have seen a company dancing for hours to this primitive music.

As to the dances, there are some of them that we can give no account of. A poor remnant of the 'Sword Dance' is still preserved among us, and may often be witnessed on the stage, sometimes on the decks of steamers, and even on the streets of our large towns, burlesqued by idle vagabonds who assuredly disgrace 'the garb of Old Gaul', by exhibiting it in such contemptible performances. We learn from Brand that among the Northern nations, and of old in England, the Sword Dance was practised on the most public and solemn occasions, and in a way that put the skill, the strength, and the nerve of the performers to a very severe test.

We know that in one other of those mentioned in our text – the Thorny Croft – there was much pantomimic acting, as well as very dolorous recitative. A farmer,

On this New Year's morn the sun was late of showing his countenance; and after he came in sight his appearance was pale and drowsy. The mist was resting lazily on the hillside; the crane was rising slowly from the meadow; the belling of the stag was heard on the mountain;[263] the black-cock was in the birch-wood, dressing his feathers, while his sonsie mate – the grey-hen – was slowly walking before him.

After I had saluted my family, and implored the blessing of the Highest on their heads, I prepared the Christmas sheep (*Caora Nallaig*), gave a sheaf of corn to the cattle, as was customary, and was getting myself in order, when in walked Para Mor, and my gossip Angus Og (Young Angus). They gave me the welcome of the New Year. I returned it with equal heartiness. Then Para Mor produced a bottle from his pocket. 'A black-cock,' says he, 'whose gurgling voice (crowing, *Celticè, gogall*) is more musical than any roar (*raan*) that ever came out of the chanter of the pipe.' We toasted to one another, and then Mary, my wife, set before us a small drop of the genuine Ferintosh, which she had stored up long ago for great occasions in the big chest.[264]

It was my duty to gather the people together this morning with the sound of the pipe. So we set off, going from farm to farm up the Glen, making the son of the cave of the rock (i.e. echo) answer to my music. I played '*A Mhnathan a' Ghlinne so*',★ and if the pipe had been dry that day it had ample means of quenching its thirst!

whose lot it was to be located on ground covered with thorns and briers, gives a woeful account of the hardship of his fate – with the view, we believe, of exciting compassion of some fair spectator – and we believe there was a considerable amount of dramatic acting in all of them.

The *Dubh-Luidneach* – Black-Sluggard, or black clumsy one – we may observe, is the name by which the natives of Lochaber still designate the yacht in which Argyle sailed away on the day of the battle of Inverlochy – leaving his men to the fury of Montrose and the MacDonalds. Of the dance so called we can give no account.

★ The tune '*A Mhnathan a' Ghlinne so*,' etc.

This still popular pipe tune, known, we believe, as Breadalbane's March, is said to have been composed on the following occasion: The father of John Glas, i.e. Grey John, of Breadalbane, to whom such frequent reference is made in the case of the disputed succession at present, was married to a daughter of the Earl of Caithness. The promised dowry was not paid to him, and he, apparently content with his wife herself as his portion, lived and died in peace with the Lindairs. His son, John Glas,

The company continually increased in numbers until we came down by the other side of the Glen to the ground-officer's house, where it was appointed for us to get our morning meal. The lady had sent a three-year-old wedder to his house. We had a roebuck from the corrie of Yew-trees; fish from the pool of whitings; and such quantities of cheese, butter, and solid oatcake, sent by the neighbours round about, as would suffice for as many more – though we were fifty men in number, besides women and children. Grace was said by Lachlan of the Questions (*Lachum ceistear*), the Bible reader. Evan Ban well sustained the hospitable character of the house which he represented. We had an ample and a cheerful feast.

Breakfast over, I set off and played the tune of the 'Glasmheur', while Red Ewen, the old soldier, was marshalling the men. We reached *Gualanancarn* (the shoulder of the cairns), where the gentry were to meet us and before we knew where we were, who placed himself at our head but our own young Donald, the heir of the family! He had reached home that very morning, having hastened on without sleep, or rest, all the way from Dun-Edin (Edinburgh). Dear heart! he was the graceful sapling. I could not, for awhile, blow a breath into the pipe. 'Play up, Finlay,' says Para Mor. 'What sadness has seized you?' 'Sadness!' said I; 'very far is it from me.' The people of the sea-board then came in view, and Alastair Roy of the Bay at their head. When the two companies observed each other, they raised a loud shout of mutual rejoicing. We reached the field, and many were the salutations between friends and acquaintances exchanged there.

The sun at length shone forth brightly and cheerfully. On the eminences around the field were the matrons, the maidens, and the children of the district, high and low, all assembled to witness the *Camanachd* (shinty match).[265] The goal at each end of the large field was pointed out, and the two leaders began to divide and choose

---

however, was of a different mind. Collecting a hardy band of Campbells from the age of thirty-five to that of fifty, he made a secret and sudden raid on the land of the Sinclairs, gathered as much spoil as would cover the amount of his mother's tocher, utterly defeated the Caithness men, who were unprepared for such an invasion, and, as he was leaving their territory, early in the morning, he summoned the poor women to arise, telling them that their cattle had been lifted, and their husbands wounded.

each his men. 'I claim you!' *(Buailidh mi ort,* literally, 'I will strike on thee'), says young Donald. 'I permit you' *(Leigidh mi leat),* says Alastair Roy of the Boy. 'If so,' says young Donald, 'then Donald Ban, of Culloden, is mine.' This was by far the oldest man present, and you would think his two eyes would start from his head with delight as he stepped proudly forth, at being the first chosen.

When the men were divided into two companies – forty on each side – and refreshments set at each goal, Alastair Roy flung his shinty high up in the air. '*Bas, no Cas,* Donald of the Glen,' said he (i.e. Head, or Handle). 'Handle, which will defy your handling till nightfall!' replies Donald. Alastair gained the throw (toss) and was about to strike the ball immediately, when the other exclaimed, 'A truce *(Deis-dè)*; let the rules of the game be first proclaimed, so that there may be fairness, good-fellowship, and friendship observed among us as was wont among our forefathers.' On this, Evan Ban stepped forth and proclaimed the laws, which forbade all quarrelling, swearing, drunkenness, and coarseness, all striking, tripping, or unfairness of any kind; and charged them to contend in a manful, but friendly spirit, without malice or grudge, as those from whom they were descended had been wont to do.

Alastair Roy, as he was entitled to do, gave the first stroke to the ball, and the contest began in earnest; but I have not language to describe it! The sea-board men gained the first game. But it was their only game. Young Donald and his men stripped to their work, and you would think the day of *Blar na Lèine* (Battle of the Shirts)* had come again. Broad John gave a tremendous blow, which sent the ball far beyond the goal. We thus gained the day, and we raised the shout of victory; but all was kindness and good feeling among us.

---

* (See also note 266.) *Blar na Léine* – Battle of the Shirts. This was a very fierce clan battle recorded in history, and of which tradition preserves a very vivid remembrance. MacDonald, of Moidart, married one of the Frasers, of Lovat. The son and heir, Ronald, was brought up at Lovat, or Beaufort Castle, and was known to his Clansmen as Raonull Gallda, or Ronald the Lowlander. At his father's death, he came to take possession; but to the utter disgust of the people, he forbad the killing of ox or sheep for the inaugurative feast, saying that poultry would be quite enough. He was at once dubbed Ronald of the Hens, expelled from the country with ignominy, and a natural brother, John of Moidart, was chosen as chief in his unworthy stead. The Frasers were far too powerful to allow such an affront to pass. They speedily mustered, and, to 'make assurance doubly sure,' asked, and obtained

In the midst of our congratulations Para Mor shouted out, 'Shame on ye, young men! Don't you see these nice girls shivering with cold. Where are the dancers? Play up the reel of Tulloch-gorum, Finlay.' The dancing began, and the sun was bending low towards the Western Ocean before we parted. There was many a shin and many a cheek of the colour of the *Blae-berries* (i.e. black and blue) that day, but there was neither hate nor grumbling about these matters.

We returned to the house of nobleness, as on the preceding evening. Many a torch was on that night beaming brightly in the hall of hospitality, though dark and lonely is its state today. We passed the night amid music and enjoyment, and parted not until the breaking of the dawn guided us to our own homes.

And now you have some account of the manner in which your ancestors were in the habit of passing New Year's Eve and New Year's Morn – *Calluinn* and *Cainneal* – in days not long gone by.

I know that people will not now believe me, yet I maintain that many good results followed from this friendly mingling of gentles and commons. Our superiors were at that time acquainted with our language and our ways. The highest of them was not ashamed to address us by name, in our native tongue, at kirk or market. There was kindness, friendship, and fosterage between us; and while they were apples on the top-most bough, we were all the fruit of the same tree. We felt ourselves united to them, and in honouring and

the aid of some friendly clans in the direction of Strathspey. They invaded Moidart with a force which it was vain for the MacDonalds to resist. They therefore betook themselves to the most inaccessible fastnesses, and made no show of opposition. But whenever the invading host departed, the Moidart men followed carefully in their track for the southern end of Loch Lochy; the auxiliaries from the east struck off by the Badenoch road, judging their friends quite secure at such a distance from the land of Moidart. At the north end of Loch Lochy, however, quite close to where the Caledonian Canal enters that Loch, the Moidart men made a fierce onslaught on the Frasers, now left alone. Both parties, it is said, stripped to the waist, and on the '*lucus a non lucendo*' principle, the battle was called the Battle of the Shirt. Both 'Ronald of the Hens' and his father were slain, and the Frasers were defeated with great slaughter. History carries us thus far; but we see in a ballad published by Mrs Ogilvie on the subject, that eighty of the Fraser widows were considerate enough to bear each a posthumous son, and these not only restored the weakened clan, but, as a matter of course inflicted dread vengeance on the men of Moidart.

defending them we respected and benefited ourselves. But, except in the case of the one family under whom I now am,

> All this has passed as a dream,
> Or the breaking of the bubble on the top of the wave.

Our superiors dwell not among us; they know not our language, and seek not to converse with us. Pipers are no more, and even their servants many of our Lairds scorn to take from among their own men. They must have their *Flunkies* from the Lowlands – spindle-shanked *shaughling* creatures, with their short breeches and white stockings, without pith or courage enough to rescue the young heir of the family from the beak of the turkey-cock! Not so were thy men, Donald of the Glen, on the day when 'thy king landed in Moidart!'[267]

Chapter 19

THE EMIGRANT SHIP*

Returning from Iona on the loveliest summer evening which I ever beheld, we reached a safe and sheltered bay at the north end of the Island of Mull.

I never saw a harbour so well defended from the violence of winds and waves.[269] A long narrow island encircled it seawards, spreading its friendly wings over every vessel that comes to seek its covert from the storms of ocean, or to await under its shelter for favourable weather to double the great headland beyond. On the right hand where we entered, the land rises up steep and abrupt from the shore. We sailed so close to the rocks that the branches of the trees were bending over us. The fragrance of the birch was wafted on the breeze of summer, and a thousand little birds, with their sweet notes, were singing to us from amid the branches, bidding us welcome as we glided smoothly and gently past them.

A glorious view presented itself to me wherever I turned my eye. I saw the lofty mountains of Ardnamurchan clothed in green to their very summits; Sunnard,[270] with its beautifully outlined hills and knolls; the coast of Morven stretching away from us, rejoicing in the warmth of the summer evening.

When we neared the anchorage there was nothing to be seen but masts of ships, with their flags floating lazily in the gentle breeze – nor to be heard, except the sound of oars, and the murmur of brooks and streams, which, falling over many a rock, were pouring into the wide bay, now opening up before us. From side to side of the shore, on the one hand, there runs a street of white houses; and immediately behind them there rises up a steep and high bank, where the hazel, the rowan, and the ash grow luxuriantly, and so very close to the houses that the branches seem to bend over their tops. At the summit of this lofty bank the other portion of the small

* (See also note 268.) From the Gaelic of the late Rev. Dr MacLeod, of St. Columba's, Glasgow.

town is seen between you and the sky, presenting a view striking for its beauty and singularity.

The bay, however, presented the most interesting sight. There were in it scores of vessels of different sizes; many a small boat with its painted green oars; the gay *birlinn* with its snow-white sails, and the warship with its lofty masts and royal flag flying.

But in the midst of them all I marked one ship which was to me of surpassing interest. Many little boats were pressing towards her, and I noticed that she was preparing to unmoor. There was one man in our boat who had joined us at the back of Mull, and who had not during the whole day once raised his head, but who now was scanning this great ship with the keenest anxiety.

'Do you know', I asked, 'what this ship is?'

'Alas!' said he, ''tis I who do know her. Grieved am I to say that there are too many of my acquaintances in her. In her are my brothers, and many of my dearest friends, departing on a long, mournful voyage for North America. And sad is it that I have not what would enable me to accompany them.'

We pulled towards the vessel; for I confess I felt strongly desirous of seeing these warm-hearted men who, on this very day, were to bid a last farewell to the Highlands, in search of a country where they might find a permanent home for themselves and their families.

It is impossible for me to convey to anyone who was not present a true idea of the scene which presented itself on going on board. Never will it fade from my memory. They were here young and old – from the infant to the patriarch. It was most overwhelming to witness the deep grief, the trouble of spirit, the anguish and brokenness of heart which deeply furrowed the countenances of the greater number of these men, here assembled from many an island and distant portion of the Hebrides.

I was, above all, struck with the appearance of one man, aged and blind, who was sitting apart, with three or four young boys clustered around him, each striving which could press most closely to his breast. His old arms were stretched over them, his head was bent towards them, his grey locks and their brown curly hair mingling, while his tears, in a heavy shower, were falling on them. Sitting at his feet was a respectably dressed woman, sobbing in the anguish of bitter grief; and I understood that a man who was walking backwards and forwards, with short steps and folded hands, was her husband. His eye was restless and unsettled, and his troubled countenance told that his mind was far from peace. I drew near to the old man, and in gentle language asked him if he, in the evening of his days, was about to leave his native land.

'Is it I, going over the ocean?' said he. 'No! On no journey will I go, until the great journey begins which awaits us all; and when that comes, who will bear my head to the burial? You are gone; you are gone; today I am left alone, blind and aged, without brother, or son, or support.

'Today is the day of my desolation, God forgive me! Thou, Mary, my only child, with my fair and lovely grandchildren, art about to leave me! I will return tonight to the old glen: but it is a strange hand that will lead me. You, my beloved children, will not come out to meet the old man. I will no more hear the prattle of your tongues by the riverside, and no more shall I cry, as I used to do, though I saw not the danger, 'Keep back from the stream!' When I hear the barking of the dogs, no more will my heart leap upwards, saying, 'My children are coming.' Who now will guide me to the shelter of the rock, or read to me the holy book? And tomorrow night, when the sun sinks in the west, where will you be, children of my love? or who will raise the evening hymn with me?'

'Oh, father,' said his daughter, creeping close to him, 'do not break my heart!'

'Art thou here, Mary?' said he. 'Where is thy hand? Come nearer to me, my delight of all the women in the world. Sweet to me is thy voice. Thou art parting with me. I do not blame thee, neither do I complain. Thou hast my full sanction. Thou hast the blessing of thy God. As was thy mother before thee, be thou dutiful. As for me, I will not long stand. Today I am stripped of my lovely branches and light is the breeze which will lay low my old head. But while I live, God will uphold me! He was ever with me in every trial, and He will not now forsake me. Blind though I be, yet blessed be His name! He enables me to see at His own right hand my best Friend, and in His countenance I can see gentleness and love. At this very moment He gives me strength. His promises come home to my heart. Other trees may wither; but the 'Tree of Life' fades not. Are you all near me?

'Listen,' said he, 'we are now about to part. You are going to a land far away; and probably before you reach it I shall be in the lofty land where the sun ever shines, and where, I trust, we shall all meet again; and where there shall be no partings, nor removals. No. Remember the God of your fathers, and fall not away from any one good habit which you have learned. Evening and morning bend the knee. Evening and morning raise the hymn, as we were wont to do. And you, my little children, who were as eyes and as a staff unto me – you, who I thought would place the sod over me – must I part with you? God be my helper!'

I could not remain longer. The little boat which was to bear the old man to the shore had come to the side of the ship. Those who were waiting on him informed him of this. I fled; I could not witness the miserable separation.

In another part of the vessel there was a company of men, whom I understood from their dress and language to belong to the Northern Islands. They were keenly and anxiously watching a boat which was coming round the point, urged alike by sails and oars. Whenever they saw her making for the ship, they shouted out: 'It is he himself! Blessings on his head!'

There was one person among them who seemed more influential than the others. When he observed this boat, he went to the captain of the ship, and I observed that the sailors who were aloft among the masts and spars were ordered to descend, and that the preparations for immediate sailing were suspended. The boat approached. An aged, noble-looking man who was sitting in the stern rose up, and, although his head was white as the snow, he ascended the side of the ship with a firm, vigorous step, dispensing with any assistance.

The captain saluted him with the utmost respect. He looked around him, and, quickly noticing the beloved group who had been watching for him, he walked towards them. 'God be with you!' he said to them, as they all rose up, bonnet in hand, to do him reverence. He sat down among them. For a while he leaned his head on the staff which was in his hand, and I observed that great tears were rolling down his face – one of the most pleasant faces I had ever looked on. They all grouped around him, and some of the children sat at his feet.

There was something in the appearance of this patriarchal man which could not fail to draw one towards him. Such goodness and gentleness surrounded him that the most timid would be encouraged to approach him; and, at the same time, such lofty command in his eye and brow as would cause the boldest to quail before him.

'You have come,' said they, 'according to your promise; you never neglected us in the day of our need. Tonight we are to become wanderers over the face of the ocean, and before the sun will rise over those hills we shall be forever out of their sight. We are objects of pity today – day of our ruin!'

'Let me not hear such language,' said the minister. 'Be manly; this is not the time for you to yield. Place your confidence in God: for it is not without His knowledge that you go on this journey. It is through His providence that all things are brought to pass, but you speak as if you were to travel beyond the bounds of the kingdom of the Almighty, and to go whither His Fatherly care could not extend unto you. Alas! is this all your faith?'

That is all true, answered they; 'but the sea – the great wide ocean?'

'The sea!' said he. 'Why should it cast down or disquiet you? Is not God present on the great ocean as on the land; under the guidance of His wisdom and the protection of His power, are you not as safe on the wide ocean as you ever were in the most sheltered glen? Does not the God who made the ocean go forth on its proud waves? Not one of them will rise against you without His knowledge. It is He who stills the raging of the sea. He goeth forth over the ocean in the chariots of the wind as surely as He is in the heavens above. Oh, ye of little faith, wherefore do ye doubt?'

'We are leaving our native land,' said they.

'You are indeed leaving the place of your birth,' he replied, 'the island where you were nourished and reared. You are certainly going on a long journey, and it need not be concealed that there are hardships awaiting you, but these do not come unexpectedly on you: you may be prepared to meet them. And as to leaving our country, the children of men have no permanent hold of any country under the sun. We are all strangers and pilgrims, and it is not in this world that God gives any of us that home from which there is no departure.'

'That is undoubtedly true,' said they; 'but we go as 'sheep without a shepherd'. Without a guide to consult in our perplexities. Oh, if you had been going with us!'

'Silence!' said he. 'Let me not hear such language. Are you going farther from God than you were before? Is it not the same Lord that opened your eyelids today and raised you from the slumber of the night, who rules on the other side of the world? Who stood by Abraham when he left his country and his kindred? Who showed himself to Jacob when he left his father's house, and slept in the open field? Be ashamed of yourselves for your want of trust. Did you say you were as 'sheep without a shepherd'? Is there any, even the youngest of your children, who cannot repeat these words: 'The Lord's my shepherd, I'll not want?' Has not the Great Shepherd of the sheep said: 'Fear not; for I am with thee. Be not dismayed: for I am thy God'? Has He not said: 'When thou passest through the waters I will be with thee; and through the rivers, they shall not overflow thee'?

'There are not, perhaps, houses of worship so accessible where you are going, as they were in your native land; nor are ministers of religion so numerous. But remember you the day of the Lord. Assemble yourselves under the shelter of the rock, or under the shade of the tree. Raise up together the songs of Zion, remembering that the gracious presence of God is not confined to any one place; that, by those who sincerely seek Him in the name of Christ, He is to be found on the peak of the highest mountain, in the strath of the deepest glen, or in the innermost shade of the forest, as well as in the midst of the great city, or in the most costly temple ever reared by man's hands. You are all able to read the holy word. Had it been otherwise, heavy indeed would be my heart, and very sad the parting. I know you have some Bibles with you: but you will today accept from me, each a new Bible, one that is easily carried and handled; and You will not value them the less that your names are written in them by the hand which sprinkled the water of baptism on the most of you – which has often since been raised up to Heaven in prayers for you, and which will continue to be raised for you with good hope through Christ until death shall disable it.

'And you, my little children, the precious lambs of my flock, now about to leave me. I have brought for you also some slight memorials of my great love to you. May God bless you!'

'Oh,' said they, 'how thankful are we that we have seen you once more, and that we have again heard your voice!'

The people of the ship were now generally gathering round this group, and even the sailors, though some of them did not understand his language, perceived that it was in matters pertaining to the soul he was engaged. There was so much earnestness warmth and kindliness in his appearance and voice, that they stood reverently still; and I saw several of them hiding the tears which rolled down those cheeks that had been hardened by many a storm.

The reverend man uncovered his head, and stood up. Everyone perceived his purpose. Some kneeled down, and those who stood cast their eyes downwards, when in a clear strong voice he said, 'Let us pray for the blessing of God.' Hard indeed would be the heart which would not melt, and little to be envied the spirit which would not become solemnised, while the earnest, warm-hearted prayer was being offered up by this good man, who was himself raised above the world. Many a poor, faint-hearted one was encouraged. His words fell like the dew of the evening, and the weak, drooping branches were strengthened and refreshed.

While they were on their knees, I heard heavy sighings and sobbings, which they strove hard to smother. But when they rose up I saw through the mist of the bitter tears which they were now wiping off, the signs of fresh hope beaming from their eyes.

He now opened the Book of Psalms, and the most mournful, the most affecting in every way, yet at the same time the most joyful sacred song which I ever heard was raised by them all. The solemn sound reached every ship and boat in the harbour. Every oar rested. There was a perfect silence; a holy calm as they sang together a part of the 42nd Psalm.

> O! why art thou cast down, my soul?
>   Why, thus with grief opprest
> Art thou disquieted in me?
>   In God still hope and rest
> For yet I know I shall him praise
>   Who graciously to me
> The health is of my countenance,
>   Yea, mine own God is he.

Chapter 20

THE STORY OF MARY OF UNNIMORE[271]

AS TOLD BY HERSELF*

That was the day of the sadness to many – the day on which Mac Cailein† (Argyle) parted with the estate of his ancestors in the place where I was reared.

The people of Unnimore thought that flitting would not come upon them while they lived. As long as they paid the rent, and that was not difficult to do, anxiety did not come near them; and a lease they asked not. It was there that the friendly neighbourhood was, though now only one smoke is to be seen from the house of the Saxon shepherd.

When we got the 'summons to quit', we thought it was only for getting an increase of rent, and this we willingly offered to give; but permission to stay we got not. The small cattle‡ were sold, and at length it became necessary to part with the one cow. When shall I forget the plaintive wailing of the children deprived of the milk which was no more for them. When shall I forget the last sight I got of my pretty cluster of goats bleating on the lip of the rock, as if inviting me to milk them? But it was not allowed me to put a cuach (pail) under them.

The day of 'flitting' came. The officers of the law came along with it, and the shelter of a house even for one night more was not to be got. It was necessary to depart. The hissing of the fire on the

---

* (See also note 272.) From the Gaelic of the late Dr MacLeod, of St Columba's, Glasgow.

† Mac Cailein. Sir Walter Scott, and after him Macaulay, writes Argyle's patronymic as Mac Callum, a mistake which sounds very offensive to a Celtic ear. Colin – Celtic, *Cailein* – was the founder of Argyle.

‡ Cows forming the chief property of the Highlanders, known as *ni*, 'substance', or 'wealth', and furnishing epithets expressive of strong affection, the sheep were thought to be highly honoured by being styled 'small cows', or 'small cattle'; and here we are reminded, of Isaiah xliii. 23 – 'the small cattle of thy burnt-offering'.

flag of the hearth as they were drowning it, reached my heart. We could not get even a bothy in the country; therefore we had nothing for it but to face the land of strangers (Lowlands). The aged woman, the mother of my husband, was then alive, weak, and lame. James carried her on his back in a creel, I followed him with little John, an infant at my breast, and thou who art no more, Donald beloved, a little toddler, walking with thy sister by my side. Our neighbours carried the little furniture that remained to us, and showed every kindness which tender friendship could show.

On the day of our leaving Unnimore I thought my heart would rend. I would feel right if my tears would flow; but no relief thus did I find. We sat for a time on 'Knock-nan-Carn' (Hill of Cairns),[273] to take the last look at the place where we had been brought up. The houses were being already stripped. The bleat of the 'big sheep'* was on the mountain. The whistle of the Lowland shepherd and the bark of his dogs were on the brae. We were sorrowful, but thanks to Him who strengthened us, no imprecation or evil wish was heard from one of us. 'There is no fear of us,' says James. 'The world is wide, and God will sustain us. I am here carrying my mother, and thou, Mary, with my young children, art walking with me on this sorrowful 'flitting'; yet we are as happy, and possibly as great objects of envy, as the owner of this estate who has driven us to the wandering.'

What have you of it, but that we reached Glasgow, and through the letter of the saintly man who is now no more, my beloved minister (little did I think that I would not again behold his noble countenance), we got into a cotton work. Here James got good steady earning,† as did also the children when they grew up. We

* The small cattle (*meanbh-chro*), the indigenous breed of sheep, small in size, most delicate in flesh, and fine in wool, like the Shetland kind, housed every night, and milked every day, were favourites with the people; but the large sheep that ranged the mountain and the strath alike, and which have led to so many unhappy clearances, are to the common Celt objects of utter detestation. The 'tooth of the big sheep' is 'the root of all evil' in his estimation, and the 'good time coming' is always associated with the extirpation of this accursed breed. We knew a minister who preached in Skye – a native not of the Highlands, however, but of the Lowlands – within the last thirty years; and who, wishing to present a very attractive picture of heaven, assured his hearers that 'there would be no big sheep there'.
† Earning is the Gaelic equivalent of employment. I suppose it may be inferred from

were comfortable, and I hope that we were grateful. The old woman was still living, her intellect and memory as good as ever they had been. She knew so much of old Highland lore that it was a relief to James, when he came home weary from the work, to sit down and converse with her.

We were able to do much justice (give a good opportunity) to the children. They read English and Gaelic equally well, and nothing did the old woman ever see that she valued like listening to thee, Donald beloved, reading the Bible and other good books; and it is thou who could do that distinctly and sedately.

It pleased God to call the old woman away, and she fell into the quiet sleep of death, bequeathing her soul to the blessed Saviour who went to death for her. We missed her greatly. Instead of being thankful for the time that it had pleased God to spare her, we lamented for her beyond measure. God chastised us. My beautiful, splendid boy took the infectious fever, which was at the time in the great city, and shortly after his father and his sister took it. It is He alone who enabled me to stand that has knowledge of what I endured at the time. Let men never say that there is not kindness in the Lowlanders. It is I who did not find them destitute of pity. Though the fear of the fever kept away the greater number of my acquaintance, God raised up friends who sustained me. A neighbour's wife, with whom I was but slightly acquainted, took the lassie from me, and I sent John to a friend's house to avoid the fever. My husband (the man)* and Donald were taken to the infirmary at the head of the town, and it was permitted to myself to follow them. Cheerless and heavy was my step after the carriage that conveyed them. I thought it could not be more sorrowful, though I were following them to the churchyard; but, oh! far asunder, as I have since felt, are the two things.

I heard so many stories of this nursing-house, that horror was on me for it; but it is I who did not need. They were placed in a

---

this that the Highlander was often employed without remuneration; and, beyond question, 'remunerative work' would readily solve the difficulty as to the maintenance of the population of the Highlands.

* The husband, styled in Scotch the 'good-man,' is in Gaelic styled simply *the man*, and, possibly, *the* man – the man, *par excellence, is* the most complimentary title that can be given.

chamber which might suffice for a king, and a physician and a sick nurse were as kind to them as if they had been their dearest on the face of the world. Fifteen days after they went in – on the morning of the Communion day – that pang entered my heart which has not left, and never will leave it. From that time the world was lost for me much of its gladness. Thou didst change (die) Donald, son of my love, who never said to father or mother, 'It is ill.' But why should I complain? He who called him to himself had more right to him. We must be resigned.

Donald departed: but thanks to the benign Father, all did not depart. James recovered, and eight weeks after he had gone in we returned again to our home; but, oh! it was on that home that the change had come. Donald was not. It was he who used to read to us in the evening at the time of going to rest. I noticed the sad cloud that was on the countenance of my husband as he said:

'Wife, where is the Bible? Bring it to myself tonight.'

'Come here, John,' said I, 'and take the Bible.'

'Oh! it is not right?' said James. 'Thank God that you are spared!'

James had no strength for work. He was feeble and without courage. We had nothing but what John brought in from day to day; so that it was necessity to me to sell, little by little, what we could best spare of the furniture, hoping that better days would come. At length the rent was to be paid and nothing to meet it. James went out with Donald's watch, and the name of my darling cut on the back of it. He returned after paying the rent, and laid himself down on the bed without a word out of his head. But, as God brought it round, who came in that very evening but the minister, and that was the visit of blessedness to us. He held much discourse with us. He offered up a prayer which dropped on our hearts. Our courage rose greatly. His language was like dew of the evening on tender plants which were withering.

The health of James was improving, and he obtained some kind of night work during the year. But on a night of those nights at the beginning of winter five years ago, John came in and great grief was on his countenance, as if he had been weeping.

'What is the matter, my love?' I said.

'There is not much,' he said. 'Perhaps another place may open, though the work in which I am has stopped. The work-people have risen against the masters, demanding a heightening of wages, and threaten to burn the works if they will not yield. They have drawn out a writing, and they threaten evil to everyone who will not put his hand to it.'

James was stretched on the bed, but as soon as he heard this, he raised his head and said:

'I hope, John, that thou hast not put thy hand to that bad paper.'

'Is it I, father?' said the poor lad. 'Truly I have not put, and will not put.'

'Thou never wilt, my brave boy. Be faithful and true, as were the men from whom thou hast come. Stand thou by thy king and the laws of thy country, and let there be to thee no companionship with those who seek to lawlessness. We have what will suffice us tonight, and put the Sabbath past. When Monday comes God will open another door. 'God comes in want, and there is no want when He comes.' Let us go to rest. Bring over the books, John, and let us give praise to God. Tonight let us sing the 146th Psalm, and raise the tune together. Oft have I sung it in the great assembly, with many of those who are not now on the face of the world, and I never heard it that it did not give relief to my heart.' We went to church on the next day, and heard teaching that helped us to forget this poor world.

'Blessed', said James, as we returned home, 'is the day of the Sabbath; it is God himself hath set it apart.'

At the beginning of the week two men, whom we knew, came from the cotton-mill, asking James and my son to stand out with them, saying there was no good for them to continue separate; speaking much against the tyranny and covetousness of the great merchants, and very much about king and kingdom which I could not understand.

'Leave me,' says James. 'There is no use in your speaking further. I will not stand out, neither will I do injury to the kind man who has given me employment ever since I came to the place, and whom I found truly steadfast in every distress. Leave me; the blood of rebelliousness is not in my veins.'

They told him it was in their power to help him – that they had money from England to aid those who would stand out with them, and as a proof of this they offered to leave a crown-piece with him.

'No,' said James. 'Not a penny of your money shall be left in this house – there is a curse along with it. I will not stand with you; no more will my son. I have only him. I saw his brother, my good and faithful son, borne to the grave without the power of my being under his head, and it was a hard trial; but I would choose to see him who is alive laid by his brother's side before seeing him in the midst of those who seek to bring confusion and bloodshed on the country. Take away your money. There is not a coin tonight in my house. I have not a single (red*) penny on the face of the world; but on the day that I rise with you may I be without shelter, for the night. Go,' said he; 'but I beseech you give up your folly; it will not prosper with you.'

They gave a loud laugh, and went away ridiculing his language.

Day after day was passing, and employment was not to be found. Everything that could be sold was gone, except the two beds and a few small articles which were not worth the disposing of. James lost his cheerfulness entirely. He would not go over the door; but kept rocking himself by the fireside, without a syllable from his head. We had new Bibles, which had belonged to Donald. I noticed my husband taking them now and then out from the place in which they were locked, and after gazing on them he would shed tears, start back with a heavy sigh, and replace them in the very spot where they had been.

'You will not sell these, father, while I am alive,' said John.

Truly, my son, I would not wish to part with them, if I were at all able to keep them.'

That very evening John went out, and as he did not return at the time of our usual going to rest, we were under great anxiety (many pangs†) for him. When he came, there was a kind of flush in his cheek, and a raised look in his countenance, which caused us to wonder and to fear.

'Father,' said he, 'forgive me; and thou, mother of my love, do not thou condemn me. You shall not sell the Bibles of Donald, nor yet the bed on which you are lying. There is what will help you.'

---

* A red penny, i.e. a copper penny, the lowest coin contrasted with the *white* penny – the silver shilling. White money is the common expression for silver coin generally.
† *Iomaguin*, literally, 'many pangs', or 'shooting pains', translated by 'anxiety', is a most expressive word; better than even the Greek, which refers to being taken to pieces.

He took out ten gold coins, and he placed them on the table. His father started with horror, and had there not been a support to his back he would have been clean over on the floor.

'What is this that thou hast done, my son? What hast thou done? Has God let thee completely off His hand?* What, I say, has befallen thee (has risen to thee)?'

'Nothing,' said he, 'but that I have joined the army. Tonight I am a soldier belonging to Red King George;† and I trust I shall not bring shame on my ancestors or on my country.'

James raised his eyes, and the blood which had forsaken his cheek returned.

'John, come near me. It might have been worse, my brave boy, much worse.'

'Oh, it is good that it is not worse; but wherefore did you not tell us what was in your intention?'

'It is not customary with youth', said he, 'to consult with their parents before they take the gold, and good is it to the king that it is thus. I have enlisted with Allan of Errach‡ (with the man of Errach), and he promised to come tomorrow, I to make my excuse.'

On the morrow Allan Mòr (Great Allan) came, and when he understood who we were, he assisted us liberally. What is there to say but that he did not lose sight of John when he was under him? He advanced him step by step in the army. He is now on his way home with a pension from his king and country, which will keep him easy for life. He is quit of soldiering any more, and we look for his return home in the course of a month. James is now in good health. He has got an easy place from the humane men, who did not forsake him. My daughter is married to a prudent, industrious lad from the Highlands, and now, thanks to the gracious One who sustained us, the voice of joy is to be heard among us. Hardship did meet us: but God blessed it for our good. He stood by us in every difficulty. Often does James, in the communing of the evening, go

---

* i.e. abandoned thee. The idea of being borne on the arm of the Almighty is a fine one.

† Referring to the 'Red Army,' as the Highlanders always call the regular army.

‡ (See also note 274.) Allan mòr of Errach, who raised the 79th Regiment, was one of the most popular Highland officers in the army. He was knighted for his gallantry, and has left descendants in very influential positions.

over everything that has befallen us, tracing as he best can the steps of the Lord's providence towards the good of our souls. 'It is good for me that I have been afflicted,' is his language, and of every cause of gladness the least is not that, according to every account, John remembers his God and loves his Saviour. He never parted with his brother's Bible. Often has it accompanied him on the day of battle, and his pillow at night in a far distant land.

He has been writing to us that this very Bible has been blessed for good to several of his fellow soldiers to whom he used to read it. And now have we not cause to be thankful? Oh, let people never lose their hope in God. Let neither hardships nor poverty compel them to break His law, nor to neglect His ordinances. The higher the tempest strikes (the louder the tempest rages), the closer may they flee to the shadow of the Great Rock, in the weary land. Thou, Lord, hast said, and true are all Thy words, 'Because he hath set his love upon me, therefore will I deliver him. I will set him on high, because he hath known my name'; and it is we who have experienced that 'Faithful is He who hath promised.'

Chapter 21

THE COMMUNION SUNDAY

On a beautiful Sunday in July I once again sat down at the foot of the old Iona-cross in the churchyard of 'the Parish'.[275] It was a day of perfect summer glory. Never did the familiar landscape appear more lovely to the eye or more soothing and sanctifying to the spirit. The Sound of Mull lay like a sea of glass, without even a breath of fitful air from the hills to ruffle its surface. White sails met their own shadows on the water; becalmed vessels mingled with grey islets, rocky shores, and dark bays, diminishing in bulk from the large brigs and schooners at my feet, to the snow-white specks which dotted the blue of the sea and hills of Lorn. The precipice of Unnimore, streaked with waterfalls, rose in the clear air above the old keep of Ardtornish.[276] The more distant castled promontory of Duart seemed to meet Lismore. Aros Castle,[277] with its ample bay, closed the view in the opposite direction to the west; while over all the landscape a Sabbath stillness reigned, like an invisible mantle of love let down from the cloudless heaven over the weary world below.

It was a Communion Sunday in 'the Parish'.

Few of the people had as yet arrived, and the churchyard was as silent as its graves. But soon the roads and paths leading to the church from the distant glens and nearer hamlets began to stir with the assembling worshippers. A few boats were seen crossing the Sound, crowded with people coming to spend a day of holy peace. Shepherds in their plaids; old men and old women, with the young of the third generation accompanying them, arrived in groups. Some had left home hours ago. Old John Cameron, with fourscore-years-and ten to carry', had walked from Kinloch[278], ten miles across the pathless hills. Other patriarchs, with staff in hand, had come greater distances. Old women were dressed in their clean white 'mutches', with black ribands bound round their heads; and some of the more gentle-born had rags of old decency – a black silk scarf, fastened with an old silver brooch, or a primitive-shaped bonnet – adornments never taken out of the large wooden chest since they were made, half a century ago, except on such occasions as the present, or on the occasion of a family marriage feast, or a funeral, when a bit of decayed crape was added. And old men were there who had seen better days, and had been 'gentlemen tacksmen' in the 'good old times', when the Duke of Argyle was laird. Now their clothes are threadbare; the old blue coat with metal buttons is almost bleached; the oddly shaped hat and silk neckerchief, both black once, are very brown indeed; and the leather gloves, though rarely on, are yet worn out, and cannot stand further mending. But these are gentlemen nevertheless in every thought and feeling. And some respectable farmers from 'the low country', who occupy the lands of these old tacksmen, travelled in their gigs. Besides these, there were one or two of the local gentry, and the assisting clergymen.

How quiet and reverent all the people look, as, with steps unheard on the greensward, they collect in groups and greet each other with so much warmth and cordiality! Many a hearty shake of the hand is given; and many a respectful bow, from old grey heads uncovered, is received and returned by their beloved pastor, who moves about, conversing with them all.

No one can discover any other expression than that of the strictest decorum and sober thoughtfulness, among the hundreds who are here assembling for worship.

It has been the fashion, indeed, of some people who know nothing about Scotland or her Church, to use Burns as an authority for calling such meetings 'holy fairs'. What they may have been in the days of the poet, or how much he may himself have contributed to profane them, I know not. But neither in Ayrshire nor anywhere else have I ever been doomed to behold so irreverent and wicked a spectacle as he portrays. The question was indeed asked by a comparative stranger, on the Communion Sunday I am describing, whether the fact of so many people coming from such great distances might not be a temptation to some to indulge overmuch when 'taking refreshments'. The reply by one who knew them well was, 'No, sir, not one man will go home in a state unbecoming a Christian.'

The sentiment of gratitude was, naturally enough, often repeated:

'Oh! thank God for such a fine day!' For weather is an element which necessarily enters into every calculation of times and seasons in the Highlands. If the day is stormy, the old and infirm cannot come up to this annual feast, nor can brother clergymen voyage from distant island parishes to assist at it. Why, in the time of the old minister, he had to send a man on horseback over moors, and across stormy arms of the sea, for sixty miles, to get the wheaten bread used at the Communion! And for this reason, while the Communion is dispensed in smaller parishes and in towns every six months and sometimes every quarter, it has hitherto been only celebrated once a year in most Highland parishes. At such seasons, however, every man and woman who is able to appear partakes of the holy feast. No wonder, therefore, the people are grateful for their lovely summer day!

The previous Thursday had been, as usual, set apart for a day of fasting and prayer. Then the officiating clergy preached specially upon the Communion, and on the character required in those who intended to partake of it; and then young persons, after instruction and examination, were for the first time formally admitted (as at confirmation in the Episcopal Church) into full membership.

The old bell, which it is said was once at Iona,[279] began to ring over the silent fields, and the small church was soon filled with worshippers. The service in the church today was in English, and a wooden Pulpit, or 'tent', as it is called (I remember when it was made of boat sails), was, according to custom, erected near the old arch in the churchyard, where service was conducted in Gaelic. Thus the people were divided, and, while some entered the church, many more gathered round the tent, and seated themselves on the graves or on the old ruin.

The Communion service of the Church of Scotland is a very simple one, and may be briefly described. It is celebrated in the church, of course, after the service and prayers are ended. In most cases a long, narrow table, like a bench, covered with white cloth, occupies the whole length of the church, and the communicants are seated on each side of it. Sometimes, in addition to this, the ordinary seats are similarly covered. The presiding minister, after reading an account of the institution from the Gospels and Epistles, and giving a few words of suitable instruction, offers up what is called the consecration prayer, thus setting apart the bread and wine before him as symbols of the body and blood of Jesus. After this he takes the bread, and, breaking it, gives it to the communicants near him, saying, 'This is my body broken for you, eat ye all of it.' He afterwards hands to them the cup, saying, 'This cup is the New Testament in my blood, shed for the remission of the sins of many, drink ye all of it; for as oft as ye eat this bread and drink this cup, ye do show forth the Lord's death until He come again.' The bread and wine are then passed from the communicants to each other, assisted by the elders who are in attendance. In solemn silence the Lord is remembered, and by every true communicant is received as the living bread, the life of their souls, even as they receive into their bodies the bread and wine. During the silence of communion every head is bowed down, and many an eye and heart are filled, as the thoughts of Jesus at such a time mingle with those departed ones, with whom they enjoy, in and through Him, the communion of saints. Then follows an exhortation by the minister to faith and love and renewed obedience; and then the 103rd Psalm is generally sung, and while singing it the worshippers retire from the table, which is soon filled with other communicants; and this is repeated several times, until the whole service is ended with prayer and praise.

Let no one thoughtlessly condemn these simple services because they are different in form from those he has been accustomed to. Each nation and church has its own peculiar customs, originating generally in circumstances which once made them natural, reasonable, or perhaps necessary. Although these originating causes have passed away, yet the peculiar forms remain, and become familiar to the people, and venerable, almost holy, from linking the past with the present. Acquaintance with other branches of the Christian Church; a knowledge of living men, and the spirit with which the truly good serve God according to the custom of their fathers; a dealing, too, with the realities of human life and Christian experience, rather than with the ideal of what might, could, would, or should be, will tend to make us charitable in our judgments of those who receive good and express their love to God through outward forms very different from our own. Let us thank God when men see and are guided by true light, whatever may be the form or setting of the lens by which it is transmitted. Let us endeavour to penetrate beneath the variable, the temporary, and accidental, to the unchangeable, the eternal, and necessary; and then we shall bless God when, among 'different communions' and 'different sacraments', we can discover earnest believing souls, who have communion with the same living Saviour, who receive with faith and love the same precious sacrifice to be their life. I have myself, with great thankfulness, been privileged to receive the sacrament from the hands of priests and bishops 'in the rural churches and hoary cathedrals of England, and to join in different parts of the world, east and west, with brethren of different names, but all having the same faith in the One Name, 'of whom the whole family in heaven and earth is named'. I am sure the 'communion' of spirit was the same in all.

Close behind the churchyard wall I noticed a stone which marked the grave of an old devoted Wesleyan minister. It had been his wish to be buried here, beside a child whom he had greatly loved. 'In memory', so runs the inscription, 'of Robert Harrison, missionary of the Lord, who died 29th January, 1832.[280] I have sinned; I have repented; I have believed, I love; and I rest in the hope that by the grace of God I shall rise and reign with my Redeemer throughout eternity.' Beyond the churchyard are a few old trees surrounding a field where, according to tradition, once stood the 'palace' of Bishop Maclean.[281] The Bishop himself lies under the old archway, near the grave of Flora Cameron.[282] Now, I felt assured that could Wesleyan missionary and Episcopalian bishop have returned to earth, they would neither of them have refused to have remembered Jesus with these Presbyterian worshippers, nor would they have said 'this is no true Sacrament'.

When the service in the church was ended, I again sat down beside the old cross. The most of the congregation had assembled around the tent in the churchyard near me. The officiating minister was engaged in prayer, in the midst of the living and the dead. Suddenly the sound of psalms rose from among the tombs. It was the thanksgiving and parting hymn of praise:

> Salvation and immortal praise
> To our victorious King,
> Let heaven and earth, and rocks and seas,
> With glad hosannas ring!
> To Father, Son, and Holy Ghost,

> The God whom we adore,
> Be glory as it was and is,
> And shall be evermore![283]

So sang those humble peasants, ere they parted to their distant homes – some to meet again in communion here, some to meet at a nobler feast above. So sang they that noble hymn, among the graves of their kindred, with whose voices theirs had often mingled on the same spot, and with whose spirits they still united in remembering and praising the living Saviour.

Some, perhaps, there are who would have despised or pitied that hymn of praise because sung with so little art. But a hymn was once sung long ago, on an evening after the first Lord's Supper, by a few lowly men in an upper chamber of Jerusalem, and the listening angels never heard such music ascending to the ears of God from this jarring and discordant world! The humble Lord who sang that hymn, and who led that chorus of fishermen, will not despise the praises of peasant saints; nor will the angels think the songs of the loving heart out of harmony with the noblest chords struck from their own golden harps, or the noblest anthems sung in God's temple in the sky.

As the congregation dispersed, and the shades of evening began to fall, I went to visit the spot where the many members of the old Manse repose.[284] A new grave was there, which had that week been opened. In it was laid the wife of the parish minister.[285] This was the last of many a sad procession which he had followed from the old Manse to that burying-place since boyhood, and of all it was the most grievous to be borne. But of that sweet one so suddenly taken away, or of the bitter sorrow left behind, I dare not here speak.

These 'reminiscences' began with death, and with death they end.

As I stood today among the graves of the Manse family, and sat in the little garden which its firstborn cultivated as a child nearly eighty years ago, and as at midnight I now write these lines where so many beloved faces pass before me, which made other years a continual benediction, I cannot conclude my reminiscences of this dear old parish, which I leave at early dawn, without expressing my deep gratitude to Almighty God for his gift of those who once here lived, but who now live for evermore with Christ – enjoying an eternal Communion Sunday.

NOTES

ABBREVIATIONS USED

Caraid nan Gaidheal	Clerk, the Rev. A., 1899 ed.
Clan Gillean	MacLean Sinclair, *The Clan Gillean*, 1899
Cregeen, 1963	Cregeen, Eric, 'Inhabitants of the Argyll Estate, 1779', *SRS*, 1963
Cregeen, 1964	Cregeen, Eric, 'Argyll Estate Instructions, 1771–1805', *SHS*, 1964
Cregeen, 1969	Cregeen, Eric, *The Tacksmen & their Successors*, Scottish Studies, 1969, vol. 13, pt 2
Currie	Currie, Jo, *Mull*, 2000
Donaldson, 1920	Donaldson, M.E.M., *Wanderings In the Western Highlands and Islands*, 1920.
Donaldson, 1926	Donaldson, M.E.M., *Further Wanderings, Mainly in Argyll*, 1926
Fassiefern	Clerk, The Rev A., *Memoir of Col. John Cameron*, 1858
Fasti	Scott, Hew, *Fasti Ecclesiae Scoticanae*, rev. ed., 1915–
Fergusson	Fergusson, Sir James, *Argyll in the '45*, 1951
Gaelic Companion	Thomson, Derrick, ed., *The Companion to Gaelic Scotland*, 1983
Gaskell	Gaskell, Philip, *Morvern Transformed*, 1968
Highland Ponies	MacDonald, John, *Highland Ponies and some Reminiscences of Highlandmen*, 1937
Inveraray	Inveraray Castle Papers
Jamieson	*Jamieson's Dictionary of the Scottish Language*, 1912
MacLeod D.	MacLeod, Donald, *Memoir of Norman MacLeod*, 1876
MacLeod, J. N.	MacLeod, John, N., *Memorials of the Rev. Norman MacLeod*, 1898
Macphail	Highland Papers, *SHS*, 1914
MacTavish	Minutes of the Synod of Argyll 1639–61, *SHS*, 1943–44
Maxwell	MacLeod, Sir Hamish, *Memoirs of the Maxwells of Cattadale*, 2001
Memorials	MacLeod, J. N., *Memorials of the Rev Norman MacLeod of St Columba's*, 1898
'North Argyll'	Cameron, Alastair
NSA	The *New Statistical Account of Scotland*, 1843 (Morvern), MacLeod, J.
OSA	The *Old Statistical Account of Scotland*, 1794 (Morvern), MacLeod, N.
OT	The *Oban Times*
PSAS	*Proceedings of the Society of Antiquities of Scotland*
Rankine	Rankine, John, *The Law of Land-Ownership in Scotland*, 1909
RCAHMS	The Royal Commission on the Ancient and Historical Monuments of Scotland, Argyll Inventories, 1971–92
SHS	Scottish History Society
SRS	Scottish Record Society
SWHIHR	Society of West Highland and Islands Historical Research
TGSI	*Transactions of the Gaelic Society of Inverness*
Thornber, *Kiel*	Thornber, Iain, *From Time to Eternity – a History of Kiel Graveyard, Morvern*, forthcoming.
Watson	Watson, W.J., *History of the Celtic Place-Names of Scotland*, 1926

NOTES

1. Ferguson, Ronald, *George MacLeod*, 1990.
2. Scott, J. F., *The Parish of Morvern*, Scottish Geographical Magazine, LXX, 1956.
3. *The Tertiary and Post-Tertiary Geology of Mull, Lochaline and Oban*, Memoirs of the Geological Survey, Scotland, 1924.
4. PSAS 106 (1974–75).
5. PSAS 72 (1937–38).
6. RCAHMS, Argyll, 3.
7. *ibid.*
8. Watson.
9. McDonald, Andrew, *The Kingdom of the Isles*, 1997.
10. Fergusson.
11. Gaskell.
12. Sellar, E. M., *Recollections and Impressions*, 1907.
13. *TGSI*, vol. 53, 1985.
14. *Caraid nan Gaidheal.*
15. *The Scots Magazine*, August 1966.
16. Ferguson, 1990.
17. MacLeod, J. N.
18. Duff, David (ed.), *Queen Victoria's Highland Journals*, 1983.
19. The Scots Magazine, ibid
20. *Good Words*, 1882; MacLean, William Campbell, *Memories of a Long Life,* 1895.
21. *Good Words*, 1882.
22. *OT,* June 1882.
23. *The Scotsman*, 3 June 1882.
24. Morvern Kirk Session Minutes Book (1882–1929), Scottish Record Office (Ref CH2/775/1).
25. *Low country sheep-farmers, redolent of wool:* the craze for keeping large flocks of sheep made landowners, after 1820, bring in Lowland tenants and shepherds. Ignorant of the Highlander's culture and love of the past, they were responsible for the diminution of the Gaelic language and the destruction of many archaeological monuments. Examples of the latter are to be found at Fiunary and Acharn, where great quantities of stone from an Iron Age hill-fort and several Bronze Age burial cairns were removed for the construction of sheep fanks and walled enclosures.
26. *Who does not believe in Ossian?* an ironic reference to the authenticity of James MacPherson's eighteenth-century 'translations' of the poems

of Ossian in which 'Woody Morvern' featured so prominently. MacLeod's views on the matter have not been recorded but doubtless he met many of MacPherson's supporters who had beat a path to the Ossianic homeland in search of proof, if any was required, of the existence of the Fingalian race. One such visitor was Thomas Ford Hill, a literary Englishman who travelled extensively in the Highlands with the object of collecting original Ossianic material. He stayed at Drimnin with the Laird, Allan MacLean, and recorded:

> The songs relating to the Feinn and their chieftain Fingal are wholly confined to Argyllshire and the Western Highlands ... in that district almost everyone is acquainted with them; and all whose station in life enables them to be acquainted with the subject are zealous asserters of the authenticity of the Ossian of Mr MacPherson. Yet it is remarkable that I never could meet with Mr MacPherson's work in any part of the Highlands; and many of the defenders confessed that they had never seen it. The only book I met with which had any intimate connection with it, was Mr Hole's poetic version of Fingal, which I saw in the house of Mr MacLean of Drimnin, in Morven.

(*OT* 30 August 1913; MacPherson, James, *The Poems of Ossian*, 1785.)

27. The Parish of Morvern measures approximately 142 square miles and contains some 85,369 acres (*NSA*).

28. Clearly MacLeod is describing, firstly, the most southern part of the Morvern Peninsula from Rudha an Ridirie to the mouth of Loch Aline, including the line of basaltic cliffs which rise precipitously behind Inniemore and Ardtornish Point with its ruined castle. Secondly, he is referring to the more gentle basalt slopes between Lochaline and Drimnin. The 'white waterfalls', known locally as 'the Morvern Witches', caught the attention of the Hon. Mrs Murray of Kensington when she visited Ardtornish Bay in July 1800:

> This bay is nearly surrounded by tremendous high cliffs, and in times of hard rain, innumerable streams from the mountains behind, reach the summit of them, and there form a grand cascade, falling in one semicircular sheet from the top of the cliffs to the sea. I should have been well pleased to have seen the cliffs of Ardtorinish [sic] in a streaming state, the wind blowing strongly from the west; for then I should have had the gratification of beholding the phenomenon of the wind on the cascade, the water in which at such times is whirled back over the mountains in spray, by the violence of the west wind, so that not a drop reaches the sea.

(Murray, the Hon. Mrs of Kensington, *A Companion and Useful Guide*

to the Beauties in the Western Highlands of Scotland and in the Hebrides,
vol. 2, 1803.)

29. *We must ascend to the top of* —: Sithean na Raplaich, (the Noisy Knoll)
– a long basalt ridge with a disappointing summit 1,806 feet above sea
level.

30. *the shielings of Corrie Borrodale:* Corrie Borrodale lies some two miles
NN-E of Fiunary Manse and contains the remains of about fifty
circular and sub-rectangular stone-walled huts of various sizes. The
majority are single-chambered but a few have two apartments with
opposing doorways. The site, at NGR NM 628501, is approximately
900 feet above sea-level and was most likely shared by the tenants of
the two neighbouring farms of Salachan and Fiunary until about the
turn of the eighteenth and nineteenth centuries. The movement of
womenfolk, children and stock to the shielings traditionally began on
May Day, the Celtic festival of Beltane, and ended in August (Love,
John, *Rum, A Landscape without figures*, Edinburgh, 2001).

31. *Before sheep-farming was introduced generally into the Highlands:* it is
generally believed that the first great sheep flocks, known in Gaelic as
na caoraich mora, literally, 'the big sheep', appeared in the Highlands
about 1760. By 1794 there were 14,000 sheep in Morvern and
29,000 by 1843 (*OSA, NSA: Sar Ghaidheal,* Essays in Memory of
Rory Mackay, Inverness, n.d.).

32. *A chain of small lakes…round whose green shores a prosperous tenantry once
lived:* Lochs Teacuis, Doirenamairt, Arienas and Aline, forming part of
the Aoineadh Mor (Inniemore) Valley, described as an 'abyss of
poetry':

> *Morvern and morn and spring and solitude,*
> *In front is not the scene magnificent.*
> *Beauty nowhere owes to ocean*
> *A lovelier haunt than this. Glen Unimore,*
> *A name is its wild sweetness to our ear,*
> *Fitly denoting a dream world of peace.*

(Wilson, John, 'Christopher North' (1785–1854), Professor of Moral
Philosophy, Edinburgh University, in Sands, the Hon. Lord,
Kinlochmoidart's Dirk, 1931.)
For the history of the settlement of Inniemore and its clearance see
Chapter 21.

33. *Bentealagh:* Ben Talaidh (2,496 ft).

34. *A low isthmus:* the narrow neck of land lying between Salen and Loch
na Keal almost divides Mull in two.

35. *the Slate Isles:* Easdale, Belnahua, Seil and Luing in the Firth of Lorn

produced slate from about 1745-1911. Unlike the better known Ballachulish slate, the Easdale slate was blue-black in colour and contained large quantities of iron pyrites, which weakened it and made it less desirable for roofing (RCAHMS, 2; Withall, Mary, *The Islands that Roofed the World*, 2001).

36. *the shepherds of Etive Glen:* Buchaille Etive Mor (3,120 ft) and Buchaille Etive Beg (3,029 ft) – 'the Big and Little Shepherds of Glen Etive' – two mountain crags towering over the upper reaches of Glen Etive where it opens out onto Rannoch Moor.

37. *Corrie Borrodale, Corrie Lundie and Ess Stangadale:* Corrie Borrodale (note 30) and the adjoining Corrie Lundie, above and to the north of the manse of Fiunary, are recorded as being the places where two Norwegian leaders were killed by Somerled and his men following a local battle in the early twelfth century.

According to various sources, including the author's uncle, the Rev. John MacLeod, Somerled, the Irish Celt who founded the Lordship of the Isles, and his father, Ghiolla Brighde, came from Ireland to Morvern, where they lived for some time in a cave – which still exists – near Glensanda on the shores of Loch Linnhe. While they were there Somerled was approached by local people, who asked him if he would lead them against the occupying Norse forces. Undecided, he told them he would make his mind up after a fishing expedition to the Gearr Abhainn – the River Aline. If he was successful he would become their leader. The outcome was that he landed a fresh-run salmon – hence the reason, it is said, that there is a salmon in the MacDonald coat of arms to this day.

Somerled's decisive battle with the Norwegians, which led to their expulsion from the western sea-board, was fought in Morvern near Achagavel at the head of the Black Glen, at a place called *Tor na Cabair* (the hillock of the sticks), so named as most of the fighting appears to have been done with wooden staves. The Norwegians scattered into Ardgour, Sunart and Morvern, and in the days which followed many isolated skirmishes took place. One such fleeing party was overtaken crossing the ford over the River Shiel, where the leader was killed. As he was called Thorkill, the ford was named *Ath Tharracaill*, now better known as Acharacle.

Three other Norse chiefs, Borrodail, Lundie and Stangadail, retreated into Morvern in a bid to reach their longships at anchor in the Sound of Mull. Borrodail and Lundie were overtaken and killed in the corries referred to. Stangadail managed to find his way into Sleibhte Corrie and down the side of the Barr River. He tried to cross above a waterfall and forced his horse to jump; but the distance was too great. The beast shied and only its forelegs touched the opposite bank, with the result that both rider and mount were swept into the pool and drowned. The place is still called *Eas Stangadail*, 'Stangadail's waterfall', and on a clear day when the water is very low the marks of the horse's hooves are said to be seen on the rocks where he struck the Drumbuie side of the river bank.

An interesting early record of the incident has come to light through Edward Lhuyd, second keeper of the Ashmolean Museum, Oxford, who, during the period 1697–1701, made a grand tour of the Celtic-speaking countries gathering important Gaelic documents. In his travels Lhuyd met the Rev. John Beaton (*c.*1640–1715), Episcopalian minister of Killninian, Mull and the last member of that famous medical family whose ancestors were physicians to the Lords of the Isles. Beaton showed him a fourteenth-century manuscript containing the following. 'The mark of the two hooves of the horse of Stangadel, the great King of the Norsemen, is on a rock in the waterfall of Stangadel, in Morvern, since the time when he fought with Somhairle Mac Gile Brighde Mac Gille Domhnain.' (Campbell, J. L., and Thomson, D., *Edward Lhuyd in the Scottish Highlands 1699–1700*, Oxford, 1963; *NSA*.)

38. *The Manse:* The earliest reference to a manse at Fiunary found by the editor is 1651 and is contained in a report of the Synod of Argyll's Committee on the Plantation of Churches 1650–51, recommending the erection of a new church, manse and glebe on lands at Fiunary to replace the two medieval places of worship at Cill Choluimchille (Kiel) and Killintag (near Killundine), which had given their names to two separate parishes within Morvern. Although these parishes were cojoined about that time, no church seems to have been built at Fiunary. That there was a manse there in the seventeenth century is suggested by the witnessing of an agreement by Hector Maclaine, minister of Morvern (?1639–79) and later bishop of Argyll, between Sir Allan MacLean of Duart and John and Hew MacLean of Ardgour on 8 March 1671. Ten years earlier the same Hector Maclaine complained to the Privy Council that he had been twice robbed and burnt out of his house, but whether this was at Fiunary or Kiel, where he was also tacksman, is not known.

The derivation of the Gaelic place-name Fiunary, sometimes written by the MacLeod family as 'Fuinary', is generally Fionn Airigh – 'the white, or fair, shieling'. However, the Rev. Norman MacLeod, the writer's grandfather and a much respected Gaelic scholar and lexicographer, gives Fionn-airigh, 'Fingal's (or Fionn's) shieling'.

In support of the Fingalian connection there is a family tale that not long after Rev. Norman MacLeod came to Morvern in 1775 he went to Inveraray and complained to his patron, John, fifth Duke of Argyll, that his stipend was too small, and asked if something could be done to augment it. If the story is true the Duke could speak Gaelic as fluently as the minister himself, as the conversation went as follows.

> 'Living in so retired a place your expenses cannot be great,' said the Duke, 'and besides, even if your stipend is small you have a good glebe.' 'As to the glebe your Grace,' the minister replied, 'what can you say about it, but that, as its name itself implies, it is a small shieling once occupied by Fingal.' 'My dear man,' retorted the Duke, 'consider how strong an argument that is that you should be contented with it; for you know the old saying that Fionn was a wise man, and knew what he was about so well that he never resided anywhere milk and fish at least were not to be had in abundance.'

The minister, thus hoist with his own petard, could only smile over his unfortunate reference; the story goes that the Duke was so pleased by his own clever retort that he agreed to the minister's request.

However, in an order to his estate factor in Morvern dated May 1776, the Duke wrote:

> Let me know the amount of his [the minister of Morvern's] stipends, the rent of the farm, and what is the real value of it, that I may see whether any augmentation should be laid upon it. (MacTavish; MacPhail; *OT*, 9 June 1883; Cregeen, 1963.)

39. *A small farmer or 'gentleman tacksman'*: Donald MacLeod (1700–81), tacksman and blacksmith of Swordale, near Dunvegan, Isle of Skye, whose wife was Ann Campbell, the daughter of Kenneth and Margaret Campbell of Scalpay, Harris. A tacksman was a superior tenant, or gentleman farmer, usually having a lease, or tack, of one or more farms, and generally resident.

40. *the then Laird of MacLeod*: Major-General Norman MacLeod (1754–1801), twenty-third chief of the Clan MacLeod and MP for Inverness-shire.

41. *The gentleman tacksman's eldest son*: Norman MacLeod, born at Swordale, Skye in 1745. Educated at King's College, Aberdeen and Edinburgh, where he graduated on 30 March 1767. For some years tutor to Norman MacLeod, twenty-third chief and schoolmaster of Duirinish. Licensed to preach by the Presbytery of Skye, 21 April 1771; presented by John, fifth Duke of Argyll, to the Parish of Morvern, his first and only charge, in August 1775 and ordained on

23 November in the same year. (*Maxwell*; *Fasti*; tombstone and plaque, Kiel, Morvern.)

42. *He was accompanied from Skye by a servant-lad . . . little Rory:* Roderick MacLeod, married to Catherine MacPhee, commemorated on a headstone at Kiel erected by their grandson Roderick MacLeod, Greenock. There was a tradition in Morvern until recently that 'young Rory' was an illegitimate son of Rev. Norman MacLeod which might account for the reason why he appears to have been included among the MacLeod family in the 1779 Argyll Estate census. (*OT*, 17 May 1902; 25 May 1902; 26 February 1916; Thornber, *Kiel*; Cregeen 1963.)

43. *'the big house':* generally the estate owner's principal dwelling or mansion-house. As the owner of Fiunary in 1775 was the non-resident Duke of Argyll, his factor and principal tacksman, Angus Gregorson, would have been looked on as the 'laird' and his handsome mansion at Ardtornish (demolished 1907) considered as the 'big house'.

44. *the old manse was nevertheless respectable:* the manse to which Norman MacLeod came in 1775 was rebuilt five years later for the sum of £375. A sketch (see plate section) shows it to have been a plain, two-storey building, with single storey wings on both north and south gables, with a central door masked by a projecting gabled porch with a side entrance. Replaced *c.* 1860 by the present structure. (Gaskell; *The Scots Pictorial*, 3 December 1898; *OSA*.)

45. *bounded on one side by a 'burn':* Amhainn Shalachain – the River Salachan which rises on the slopes of MacLeod's 'Righi of Argyll' and flows through Corrie Borrodale on its way to the sea.

46. *small grey islets:* Eileanan Glasa – the Grey Isles, a group of three small islands lying in the Sound of Mull halfway between Fiunary and Salen. The wreck site of the *Rondo*, a 2,362-ton steel steamship, which struck the Dearg Sgeir in January 1935 and sank, bow first, in the deep water to the east of the island.

47. *The Duke of Argyll's walk:* when George, sixth Duke of Argyll, broke up and sold his Morvern estate in 1819, in order to reserve his feudal superiority, as was customary, he retained a small piece of ground on each of the newly-formed smaller estates. This would appear to have been the Fiunary portion. Others bearing the Argyll title are to be found at Savary, Drimnin, Killundine, Acharn and Laudale. (*OT*, 3 November 1977.)

48. *Fingal's Hill:* a small defensive enclosure, or fort, occupying the summit of Dun Fiunary, probably dating to the Iron Age period (*c.* 600 BC – *c.* AD 400). The site, which lies some 300 yards WN-W of the Manse, once had a defensive wall round it. This was removed by

workmen for the construction of nearby farm-buildings and enclosures before MacLeod's arrival. (RCAHMS 3; *OSA*.)

49. *the minister soon took to himself a wife:* Norman MacLeod married on 22 July 1777 Jean, daughter of John Morison, tacksman of Achnaha, Morvern, whose wife was Jessie Campbell, grand-daughter of the Rev. William Morison (*c.* 1690–1735), minister of Tiree, and Elizabeth Cameron of Glendessary, whose family used to live in Morvern.

50. *and his wife bore him sixteen children:* Ann (1778–83), Janet (1780–83), Donald (1782–87), Norman D.D. (1783–1862), Ann (1785–1875), Margaret (1787–1826), Grace (1789–1826), Archie (1790–91), Elizabeth (1791–1854), Jean (1793–1875) (married John Maxwell of Aros), Mary (1794–?), Janet (1796–?), Donald (1798–1822), Catherine (1799, b. May, d. August), John (1801-82) (succeeded his father as minister of Morvern), and Archie (1805–?). John N. MacLeod (son of Norman, 1783–1862) records that his grandfather had seventeen of a family – further proof, perhaps, that Roderick, or 'Rory', was indeed a member of the MacLeod family. (*Fasti*; MacLeod, J. N.)

51. *A small farm was added to the glebe:* Fiunary Farm, consisting of 275 acres of arable and 847 acres of pasture, traditionally let by the Duke of Argyll to the Morvern ministers at a concessionary rental. Norman MacLeod's rent is not known but it was probably fifteen guineas, which was what had been paid by his predecessor. The glebe amounted to about sixty acres. (Gaskell; *Instructions from The Duke of Argyll to Donald Campbell, factor in Mull and Morvern,* October 1753, Inveraray Castle Papers, unpublished; *NSA*; MacLean, William Campbell, *Memories of a Long Life,* 1895.)

52. *Old Rory, with his wife and family was located near the shore:* Old Rory's house, or 'Thatched Cottage' as it was known latterly on account of its being the last inhabited dwelling in Morvern to have a thatched roof, lies immediately below the Manse and a few yards above a small sheltered inlet of the Sound of Mull. It was abandoned in 1960 and rebuilt in 1979 by the present owner and his family, who sailed to Morvern from Canada in a twenty-five-foot yacht and who continue to maintain Fiunary's links with the sea through traditional boat-building and dispensing hospitality to way- and seafarers. Rory married Catherine MacDiarmid from Kilmore, Argyll, by whom he had at least four sons including Alexander, who was born in 1809 and succeeded him as church officer, and Samuel, born 18 November 1813, educated at Morvern School and Glasgow University, licensed by the Presbytery of Mull and ordained at Acharacle, Argyll, 30 July 1840. In 1842 he was translated to Logierait, Perthshire, where he

died 18 February 1872. (*Fasti*; *OT*, 27 July 1775; 1851 Census; tombstone at Kiel.)

53. *a poor decayed gentlewoman . . . Mrs Stewart . . . a tenth cousin of the minister's wife:* probably a Stewart of Ardsheal, Appin, to whom Jean Morison was related by marriage.

54. *the manse was the grand centre:* a similar picture of life in a large Morvern household in the nineteenth century is painted by Agnes King in her memoirs of her grandfather, John Sinclair, who lived next door to the MacLeods at Lochaline House. (Gaskell: see also *Memories of a Long Life*, 1895, in which the author, William Campbell MacLean, Professor of Military Medicine, Honorary Surgeon to Queen Victoria and brother-in-law of the Rev. John MacLeod, 'The High Priest of Morvern', describes boyhood visits to the Manse of Fiunary in the 1820s.)

55. *cruise of oil:* properly cruisie, a type of lamp common throughout the western world from early times, made of iron and suspended from the wall or ceiling. Some had a double pan to catch the drips and a ratchet arm to regulate the flow of oil to the wick. The fuel was usually fish oil, sometimes from boiled saithe's liver, and the wick was made of the pith of rushes dried by the fire and then plaited. *Cruisgein* were in use in the Outer Hebrides until about 1940. (Sinclair, Colin, *The Thatched Houses of the Old Highlands*, 1953; Shaw, Margaret Fay, *Folksongs and Folklore of South Uist*, 1955.)

56. *breaking a fiddle:* influenced by the belated introduction of fundamental Calvinism into the Highlands the Rev. Roderick MacLeod (1794–1868), *Maighstear Ruaraidh,* minister of the Established Church of Bracadale and subsequently the Free Church of Snizort in Skye, set fire to a pile of bagpipes and fiddles as big as a house on the shores of Loch Eishart, with the remark:

> Better is the little fire that warms in the day of peace than the great fire that consumes on the day of wrath.

About the same time a lay-preacher on Eigg stopped Donald MacKay from playing his fiddle, reputed to be a Stradivarius. Although the old man as a youth had sold ten young bullocks to buy it, he was forced to part with it for ten shillings. (MacLean, Calum, *The Highlands*, Inverness, 1975; MacLeod, Rev. Dr Roderick, *The Bishop of Skye*, *TGSI*, vol. LIII, 1985.)

57. *a letter written by the minister in his old age:* i.e. Rev. Norman MacLeod (1745–1824), written about 1813.

58. *his first-born son:* Norman (1783–1862), minister of St Columba's, Glasgow, 'Caraid nan Gaidheal' – Friend of the Highlander.

59. *your sister Anne and [brother] Archy:* Anne died 1783 aged five years, Archie, born 1790, died the following year. A daughter born 1805 was also called 'Archie' but she too died while still an infant.

60. *your wee son:* this was the author himself, son of Norman MacLeod and Agnes Maxwell, born 3 June 1812.

61. *I had cause more than once to repent:* the author is clearly referring to the loss of some of his children, six at least of whom had died by the time this letter was written.

62. *James, as we shall call the tutor:* as yet unidentified, but almost certainly a future minister, as they usually were.

63. *Tom Campbell the poet:* Thomas Campbell (1777–1844), author of *Lord Ullin's Daughter, Lochiel's Warning, Ye Mariners of England, the Battle of the Baltic* and many other well-known poems. Tutor in the family of Captain Alexander Campbell at Sunipol in Mull in 1795, and also apparently in Morvern. Gaskell disputes this but the reference here and in Agnes King's *Memoirs* would seem to prove the matter beyond all reasonable doubt. (Currie; Gaskell.)

64. *game-laws being then unknown:* the Game (Scotland) Act came into force on 17 July 1832, making it unlawful for any person to enter, during the daylight hours, any land in search or pursuit of game, red deer, roe, woodcock, snipe, quail, landrails, wild duck or rabbits, without the proprietor's permission. The fine, on being summarily convicted before a Justice of the Peace, was a maximum of £2 and forfeiture of the carcass. Five or more persons having their faces blackened for the purpose of disguise and found guilty of taking any of the above could be fined up to £5 plus expenses. (Rankine.)

65. *as watched from those green islands:* probably Eilean Rudha an Ridire in Inniemore Bay, eight miles S-E of Fiunary, where there is shelter and fresh water and excellent fishing on the flood tide.

66. *the minister's boat was about eighteen feet keel:* eighteen feet in length with a single mast, for'rad jib and main-sail. The old stone jetty which the Morvern minister used and the *Roe's* shelter, or noost, can still be seen cut into the bank a little way above the high water mark in front of Old Rory's cottage.

67. *'gurly grew the sea':* a quotation from Sir Patrick Spens:

> They hadna sail'd upon the sea
> A day but barely three
> Till loud and boisterous grew the wind,
> And gurly grew the sea.

'Gurly' comes from an old Scottish word meaning to growl, as applied to the wind. (William Allingham (ed.), *The Ballad Book*, 1872; *Jamieson*)

68. *wild cats and otters:* the killing of wild cats and otters was once
     common practice in the Highlands and Islands but is now strictly
     illegal. Both were prized for their skin, which was used for sporran-
     making and lining the inside of targes (shields). According to a tenth-
     century Welsh manuscript, otter skins were valued at the same price
     as an ox, a deer and a fox and eight times as dear as the skin of sheep
     or goat. The true wild cat was once relatively numerous in Morvern
     but is now scarce. A record exists of no less than 198 of them being
     killed in Glengarry, Inverness-shire, between Whitsunday 1837 and
     Whitsunday 1840. These animals, with their broad foreheads and
     ringed tails, are believed to be the lineal descendents of the Pleistocene
     cats. (Forbes, Alexander, *Gaelic Names of Beasts, Birds and Fishes*, 1905;
     Ellice, Edward, *Placenames of Glengarry and Glenquoich*, 1931.)
69. *fumart:* an old Scottish word for a polecat. (*Jamieson.*)
70. *Clachoran:* this is a printer's error for *Clach Dobhran* – the otter's rock –
     a huge rock on the shore between the manse and Caisteal nan Con,
     Killundine. In her book, *Further Wanderings, mainly in Argyll, 1926*, Miss
     M.E.M. Donaldson, the well-known writer and folklorist, who was
     unfortunately not a Gaelic speaker, erroneously associated it with St
     Oran. (Information given to the editor by the late David Cameron
     Bonuvullin, Drimnin, 1906–1976.)
71. *the minister, accompanied by Cuilag:* from the description it would
     appear the minister travelled north, probably to the Knoydart Penin-
     sula in West Inverness-shire, crossing the lochs Sunart, Shiel, Ailort,
     Morar and Nevis. How his dog managed to make its way home to
     Fiunary round the head of these long waterways was indeed
     remarkable.
72. *the first death which occurred amongst the manse boys:* Donald died 1797
     aged 15.
73. *a small stipend:* the minister of Morvern's stipend in 1799 was £80 a
     year, with the glebe as well as Fiunary farm leased from the Duke of
     Argyll at a low rent. (MacLeod, J. N.)
74. *the following extract from the college life of the eldest son:* Norman
     (1783–1862) entered Glasgow University in November 1799.
75. *Sandy M'Intyre with two horses:* Sandy Macintyre has not been iden-
     tified. Macintyre was not a common surname in Morvern then or
     since. Only two families appear in the 1779 *Argyll Estate Census* living
     at Fernish and Ardtornish. Later there were Macintyres at Tearnait
     and Kinlochaline and a gravestone at Kiel records the death of
     Donald Macintyre, schoolmaster of Morvern, who died 25 January
     1881, aged 72. (Thornber, *Kiel.*)
76. *the ferry of Auchnacraig:* also known as 'Grass Point'. Situated at the

mouth of Loch Don, this was the main ferry terminal for Mull and an important route for transporting black cattle from the islands throughout the eighteenth and nineteenth centuries. In 1771 the ferry and the inn were leased by the Duke of Argyll, whose Mull tenants were obliged by their leases to use the ferry, to John Gregorson, who acquired 'the exclusive privilege of ferrying cattell and passengers from Torosay to the continent of Lorn'. His brother Angus, who succeeded him and his monopoly of the ferry, became tacksman of Ardtornish and later proprietor of Acharn in Morvern. (Cregeen, 1963; Gaskell.)

77. *our old host:* by 1799 the tack of Achnacraig, including the inn, had passed to Dugald MacLachlan, a member of an influential local family who later bought land in Mull and Morvern. An interesting description of both MacLachlan and his inn was recorded by an English travel writer, who stayed at Achnacraig in 1800 during a visit to Mull. (Murray, ibid.)

78. *the 'Gobhain Sassenach':* at the turn of the century there were two blacksmiths in Oban who were not local. John Addison, who joined the Oban Masonic Lodge in December 1793, and John Swan, who appears in the local militia list for 1804. Either may have been English. Perhaps if the 'drunken wit and poet' had composed Gaelic songs, his name would have been recorded in the annals of the district. (Information from Mr Murdo MacDonald, Archivist, Argyll & Bute District Council.)

79. *Tynuilt:* Taynuilt.

80. *Port Sonachan:* there was an inn and ferry at Portsonachan on the south shores of Loch Awe for hundreds of years. Rob Roy Mac-Gregor was reputed to have used the ferry; so too did the messenger carrying the news from Ardnamurchan to Inveraray in 1745 that Charles Edward Stewart had landed in Moidart. A local family, the MacPhedrans, held the ferry rights by charter for generations, providing they carried free of charge the Argyll family and their servants, soldiers, foreigners, the lame and the blind. The ferry service was discontinued in 1953 after five and a half centuries of recorded history. (*History of South Lochaweside,* Anon; Weyndling, Walter, *Ferry Tales of Argyll and the Isles,* 1996.)

81. *we walked to the manse (Arrochar) occupied by an old college friend of my father's:* the Rev. John Gillespie, presented to the Parish of Arrochar by Sir James Colquhoun of Luss in 1781, where he remained until his death on 28 August 1816.

82. *little did I expect that I should ever possess a cottage there* (Gareloch): 'Fiunary', his father's house at Shandon.

83. *we reached the house of my grand-uncle:* Neil Campbell, Greenock, son of John Campbell of Barnicarry.

84. *on the evening of the 1st of May:* the dates of the four 'old' Scottish University sessions were fixed to allow students, mostly from the country, to be at home to help with the harvest and other seasonal activities. (Information from Mr R.A.C. Balfour.)

85. *Argyle bowling-green;* Argyll's Bowling Green is the name still given to a range of rugged mountains lying between Loch Goil and Loch Long in the Cowal Peninsula.

86. *at the hotel at Oban:* There were only two hotels, or inns, in Oban during the time of Norman MacLeod's visit. One was called *Tigh clach a' Gheodha,* 'house of the creek stone', which stood to the south of the present North Bridge that spans the Black Lynn stream. It had been tenanted by a Duncan Campbell, whose wife Anna composed some robust anti-Jacobite verse and who later lived for a time at Barr, in Morvern. Dr Johnson and James Boswell passed a night in this inn on 22 October 1773 during their journey from Mull to Inveraray, which Johnson later referred to in his journal as 'tolerable'. This old inn was demolished in 1870, but the site on which it stood was marked by a plaque stating that Johnson and Boswell had stayed in it. The other inn stood on the site of the present Bridgend Bar. (Scott, James E. *Kilbride in Lorn, TGSI,* vol. XLVII, 1971–72; Shedden, Hugh, *The Story of Lorn, its Isles and Oban,* 1938; SWHIHR, *Notes & Queries,* No. XV11, 1982.)

87. *young MacLean of Coll:* Hugh MacLean (1782–1861), eldest son of Alexander, fifteenth MacLean of Coll and Catherine Cameron of Glendessary, to whom young Norman MacLeod was related through his great-grandmother Elizabeth Cameron of Glendessary. Hugh MacLean was married twice. He served for a time in one of the Guard Regiments and became a Lieutenant Colonel. He purchased Ben More Estate in Mull and had a property near Tobermory but fell into debt and was forced to sell in 1856. As the proprietor of the Island of Rum he was responsible in 1826 and 1828 for the worst clearances in the history of the West Highlands. Through his kinsman, Lachlan MacLean, tenant of the island, and his brother-in-law, Alexander Hunter, an Edinburgh lawyer, 350 people were herded into three 'coffin ships', the *Harmony,* the *Highland Laddie* and the *St Lawrence,* for an uncomfortable and confined thirty-seven-day voyage to Nova Scotia. He died at his daughter's house in London. (*Clan Gillean*; Love, ibid.)

88. *soon after my return I joined the 'Volunteers':* following the passing of the Militia Act in 1802, a company of Volunteers, the equivalent of the

Home Guard in the Second World War, was established in every parish in Argyll. There were eight companies in Mull and Morvern, commanded by James Maxwell of Aros, the Duke of Argyll's Chamberlain for Mull and Morvern, whose daughter Agnes was to become Norman's wife. The Morvern Company, which was entirely voluntary, met at 8 a.m. in front of Kiel Church for drill probably once a month. The wages were 9s. 5d. a day for the captain, 5s. 8d. for the lieutenant, 4s. 8d. for the ensign, 1s. 6d. for the sergeants, 1s. 2d. for the corporals and 1s. each for the privates. Norman MacLeod attained the rank of corporal (*Caraid nan Gaidheal*, MacLeod J. N.; Love, ibid.)

89. *I still have in my possession the names of 110 officers:* the list has not survived but another, or part of the original, giving the names of 98 officers was reproduced by Norman MacLeod's son in *Norman MacLeod of St Columba's*. The list is given on p. 256.

90. *my cousin Neil Campbell:* related to Norman through his grandmother, Jessie Campbell, daughter of John Campbell of Barnicarry whose father had been the Duke of Argyll's factor on Tiree, *c.* 1745. (Cregeen 1964.)

91. *M'Millan . . . a medical student from Lochaber:* not yet identified.

92. *Van Dieman's Land:* Tasmania. The voyage of discovery referred to may have been that led by Lieutenant John Murray (1799–1803) in the *Lady Nelson*. This expedition established that Tasmania was detached from the Australian mainland and also discovered Port Phillip.

93. *old 'Barnicarry':* John Campbell, non-resident tacksman of Gortendonuil, Tiree. 1785. (Cregeen, 1969.)

94. *a dead 'subject' for the medical students:* i.e. a corpse for dissection.

95. *A poor student of the name of M'Gregor, from Lismore:* not identified, nor has a gravestone been found for him on Lismore.

96. *The manse girls were many:* (in the order they were born) Ann, Janet, Ann, Margaret, Grace, Elizabeth, Jane, Mary, Janet, Catherine and 'Archie'. Of these only five reached maturity.

97. *Fort William:* the fort, from which the town takes its name, was built by General Monck, Oliver Cromwell's commander, in 1654 to keep in check the wild Highland clans, especially the Camerons. It was originally called Inverlochy, because Inverlochy was the nearest settlement to it with a place-name, until in 1690 when it became Fort William in honour of King William of Orange. The fort was garrisoned by regular soldiers until the beginning of the Crimean War in 1854 and thereafter by a small detachment of the Staffordshire Volunteers who were employed by the local excisemen to suppress smuggling in the area.

Fort Augustus: originally called Kilcumein, the church of St Cumein,
the fortified settlement was renamed Fort Augustus by General Wade,
the renowned Highland road and military engineer, in about 1729 in
honour of the youthful Prince William Augustus, Duke of Cumberland, who was later to gain so much notoriety in the area following
the Battle of Culloden. The fort ceased to be garrisoned after 1819
but remained in government hands until 1867, when it passed to
Lord Lovat, who leased it to the English congregation of Benedictine
monks. (Blundell, Odo, *Kilcumein and Fort Augustus*, 1914; *Glen-Albyn,
Tales and Truths of the Central Highlands*, The Abbey Press, Fort
Augustus, n.d.)

98. *'No more we'll see such deeds again':* from 'Sound the Pibroch', taken
from an old Gaelic air and rewritten by Mrs Norman MacLeod (née
Jean Morison), who was a descendant of Roderick Morison
(*c.* 1656–1713/14), the famous 'Clarsair Dall' – the Bind Harper,
Gaelic Scotland's last minstrel. (*Gaelic Companion*.)

99. *thus it came to pass that none of them, save one, ever married:* Jean, who
married John Argyll Maxwell in 1835 when she was forty-two years
old.

100. *Castle Duart:* thirteenth-century Duart Castle, dominating the
southern approaches to the Sound of Mull, is the hereditary
stronghold of the MacLeans. It became a ruin after 1748 but was fully
restored in 1911–12 by Col. Sir Fitzroy MacLean, twenty-sixth chief
of the Clan MacLean. (RCAHMS, 3.)

101. *and returned to the manse of —:* Fiunary.

102. *out of the trenches at Ticonderoga:* 'Ticonderoga' was the local Indian
name given to the eighteenth-century French-held Fort Carillon,
situated on a point of land between Lake George and Lake
Champlain on the Canadian-American border. An attack on 7 July
1758 by British-American forces under the command of Lord
Abercrombie was unsuccessful, and accounted for 647 dead or
wounded officers and men of the Black Watch, out of a thousand in
action. Among the officers killed was Duncan Campbell of Inverawe
whose death was prophesised before he left Argyll two years before.
(*The Scots Magazine*, July 1973.)

103. *that journey could only be done on horseback:* if the governess and her
groom did not take the route to Inveraray through Mull and Oban,
which her master followed when he accompanied his son to Glasgow
College in 1799, then they must have travelled through Morvern and
Ardgour to Appin via the Corran and Ballachulish ferries. From there
they would have travelled south to Creagan, taking the ferry over
Loch Creran to Barcaldine. Thereafter their route would have been

through Glen Salach to Bonawe, a ferry to Taynuilt, through Glen
Nant to Taychreggan, and another ferry to Portsonachan. From there
they probably rode to Ardbrecknish and struck east over the hill pass
to Taynafead and then down Glen Aray to the town of Inveraray. A
journey of over eighty miles.

104. *'Old Archy'* . . . *a servant in the family of the pastor's father-in-law:* Old
Archie's identity is unknown but he was obviously employed by John
Morison, tacksman of Achnaha.

105. *Dr Macculloch's Tour:* John MacCulloch (1773–1835), surgeon, geolo-
gist, traveller and correspondent of Sir Walter Scott, made a series of
annual journeys through the Highlands and Islands between the years
1811–21 resulting in a four-volume work entitled *The Highlands and
Western Islands of Scotland,* which he published in 1824. There is a
slight hint of pique in the author's remark, probably because he felt
MacCulloch was not as complimentary about Morvern as he ought
to have been:

> That part of Morvern which bounds the Sound of Mull is now as
> familiar as Cheapside; but very few indeed, if any, have explored the
> wilds of this barren region.

Neither, he implies, would they want to, for a trip by sea to the
romantic castles celebrated in Sir Walter Scott's poems would be
exploration enough.

106. *Dr Johnson's: A Journey to the Western Islands of Scotland* (in 1773) was
published in London in 1775. Unfortunately neither Dr Samuel
Johnson nor his colleague James Boswell set foot in Morvern.

107. *but the minister of whom I write:* his grandfather, Norman MacLeod
(1745-1824) of Morvern.

108. *shelty:* the term correctly applies to a Shetland pony but it was often
given to any small pony in the Highlands and Islands. (For more
interesting information on the different breeds and their history see
Highland Ponies, ibid)

109. *Mr M'Queen in Skye:* the Rev. Donald MacQueen (1719–85),
minister of Kilmuir, Skye and son of the Rev. Archibald MacQueen,
minister of Snizort. Possibly the best known and most distinguished
minister in the Highlands and Islands at the time. He favourably
impressed both Thomas Pennant and Dr Johnson on their visits to
Skye. A Gaelic eulogy in his memory survives in which his attentive
personality, his social qualities, his mental attainments and accom-
plishments are enlarged upon by his daughter Jane who married the
Rev. Roderick MacLeod, 'the fiddle-burner' of note 58. Licensed by
the Presbytery of Skye 4 June 1737, ordained 9 May 1740, and died

on Raasay 1 February 1785. (Information from Mr R.A.C. Balfour, Inverness.)

110. *Mr Maclean of Coll:* the Rev. Hector MacLean MA (1696–1775) married Janet, daughter of Hector MacLean, tacksman of Knock, Morvern. Describing his visit to Coll in 1773, Dr Samuel Johnson wrote:

> We called on Mr Hector MacLean, the minister of Coll, whom we found in a hut, that is, a house of only one floor, but with windows and chimney, and not inelegantly furnished. Mr M has the reputation for great learning; he is seventy-seven years old, but not infirm, with a look of venerable dignity excelling what I remember in any other man. His conversation was not unsuitable to his appearance. I lost some of his goodwill by treating a heretical writer with more regard than, in his opinion, a heretic could deserve. I honoured his orthodoxy, and did not much censure his asperity. A man who has settled his opinions does not love to have the tranquillity of his conviction disturbed; and at seventy-seven it is time to be in earnest. He has no public edifice for the exercise of his ministry, and can officiate to no greater number than a room can contain; and the room of a hut is not very large. This is all the opportunity of worship that is now granted to the inhabitants of the islands, some of whom must travel thither perhaps ten miles. Two chapels were erected by their ancestors, of which I saw the skeletons, which now stand faithful witnesses of the triumph of the Reformation. (*Fasti*.)

111. *whose name was MacLeod:* the Rev. Neil MacLeod MA (1729–80), minister of Kilfinichen and Kilvicheoan, Mull, from 1756 until his death. He was a brother of Donald MacLeod, tacksman of Swordale, and therefore the writer's great-grand-uncle. During his travels through Mull Dr Johnson visited the manse of Kilfinichan and afterwards remarked that the Rev. Neil MacLeod was

> the clearest-headed man he had met with in the Western Isles.... And whose elegance of conversation and strength of judgement would make him conspicuous in places of greater celebrity.

Both his son and grandson were distinguished clergymen in the USA. (*Fasti*; MacLeod J. N.; MacLeod family tree given to the editor by Sir John Norman Maxwell MacLeod of Fiunary, Bt 1952– a great-grandson of the author).

112. *He had the good fortune to meet the famous traveller at Dunvegan Castle:* Norman MacLeod's meeting with Dr Samuel Johnson occurred in

September 1773 while he was tutor to Norman, twenty-third Chief of the Clan MacLeod. (Wellwood, John, *Norman MacLeod*, Famous Scots Series, 1897.)

113. *Many of his parishioners had been out in the '45:* some 400–500 men from Morvern took part in the Jacobite Rising. These were largely Camerons, led by Miss Jean Cameron of Glendessary, who was present at the raising of the Prince's standard at Glenfinnan; a detachment of MacLachlans from Laudale; and about 200 MacLeans from Drimnin, Kingairloch and Ardgour, commanded by Charles MacLean of Drimnin. After the battle of Falkirk the MacLeans and the MacLachlans combined to make one unit, out of which less than 40 returned. (Fergusson; Seton, Sir Bruce Gordon and Arnot, Jean Gordon, *The Prisoners of the '45*, SHS, 1928; Forbes, Robert, *The Lyon in Mourning*, SHS, 1975.)

114. *the minister himself was a keen 'Hanoverian':* the very reason the Duke of Argyll presented Norman MacLeod to Morvern where, even in 1775, many of the principal tacksmen and heritors were still loyal to King James.

115. *the predecessor of our minister:* Norman MacLeod's immediate predecessor was the Rev. Alexander MacTavish, minister of Morvern (1753–75), whose family had once been standard-bearers to the MacLeans of Kingairloch. The minister referred to in this instance was in fact the Rev. Daniel MacNeil (1684–1724), minister of Morvern from 1705–24. The laird who told MacNeil he would shoot him in the pulpit if he continued to pray for the Hanoverian King was the fervent Jacobite Allan Cameron of Glendessary, whose daughter Margaret later married the minister. (*Fasti; OT*, September 1919; Thornber, *Kiel*.)

116. *no fewer than thirty persons expelled (from the parish) for theft:* the year was 1786 (*OSA*).

117. *a court of law established in the neighbourhood:* Tobermory, Isle of Mull, where a Sheriff Court was established in 1818.

118. *a salary of £40, which was afterwards raised to £80:* According to Norman MacLeod (1745–1824), the Morvern stipend in 1775 was £58.11s.0d (plus £5 in lieu of the manse and outbuildings which were obviously in a poor state of repair) and an additional £5 towards the provision of communion elements (*OSA*).

119. *'There are two churches so-called':* the quotation is from Norman MacLeod's contribution to the *Old Statistical Account*. The two buildings referred to were Cill Choluimchille, where there was a church which was replaced in 1799, and Fernish, built in 1780 and in use until the building of the present place of worship in 1892.

120. *metrical translations of the Psalms in Irish:* in 1835 the author's father was commissioned by the General Assembly of the Presbyterian Church of Ireland to provide a metrical version of the Psalms in Irish Gaelic in which he was assisted by an Irish scholar called Thaddeus Connellan. Despite the difficulty of the language they made good progress until they came to the fourth verse of the 23rd Psalm, 'Thy rod and Thy staff, they comfort me', where they could think of no suitable Gaelic rendering for the word 'staff'. Time passed but they were no nearer a solution and retired for the night. Suddenly, in the early hours of the morning, MacLeod was wakened by his colleague knocking at his door shouting, 'I have it now, I have it now – "Shillelah."' But as 'Shillelah' was not usually associated with comfort, the proposal was rejected! (Smith, Sydney, *Donald MacLeod of Glasgow*, 1926.)

121. *what could one or two schools avail in so extensive a parish?:* in 1794 there was a parish school in Morvern attended by nearly fifty scholars, including six girls, and another paid for by the Society in Scotland for Propagating Christian Knowledge (SSPCK), who also contributed £6 a year for a 'spinning mistress'. In addition seven or eight 'gentlemen tacksmen' kept private teachers for their families, 'as they can have no access to the public schools, on account of the distance'. The overtly Presbyterian SSPCK was founded in Edinburgh in 1709 to promote Christian knowledge, especially in the remoter corners of the Highlands and Islands. Its teachers, however, were not allowed to teach either Latin or Gaelic in case it encouraged Roman Catholicism. This often resulted in children who did not understand English being instructed by teachers who did not know Gaelic. A school was established at Portabhata, Drimnin, by The Society for the Support of Gaelic Schools (funded by the SSPCK), where the teacher in 1826 was Peter Maclachlan. Writing to the Society in 1825 the Rev. John MacLeod, the author's grand-uncle, reported that:

> No sooner ... was the school at Portavata opened...than your teacher, on entering the humble edifice appropriated for his use, upwards of fifty children appeared before him, untutored and untaught – unacquainted even with the alphabet.

(*Fifteenth Annual Report of the Society for the Support of Gaelic Schools, Edinburgh*, 1826, *OSA*; Love, ibid.)

122. *there was not a road in the parish:* or, as Norman MacLeod dryly wrote in 1794, 'as to the roads of this parish little can said'. By 1843 the situation was no better, causing his son to remark, 'There are no roads. The only approximation to a road is along the Sound of Mull and of

this line there are not above five continuous miles on which even a cart can be driven with safety. The interior is pathless.' Morvern had to wait until 1864 before it had a proper road linking it with the outside world. (*OSA; NSA;* Gaskell.)

123. *'John Macdonald in the Black Glen is dying':* there is no indication from this reference that John MacDonald was a 'real person'. Indeed, given the circumstances, it would have been out of keeping for MacLeod to have provided a surname. Although there were a number of MacDonald families living in Morvern in the early part of the nineteenth century, none appear in the few records there are extant for the three main settlements in the Black Glen, which were Crosben, Lurga and Achagavel.

124. *and reaches the manse about five in the morning:* from this description it is fairly obvious that on his return from the Black Glen, MacLeod was summoned to a house at Aonach Beag (Inniebeg) or Aoinidh Mor (Inniemore). Leaving either of these settlements he would have climbed up the steep path through Bealach na Sgairn towards Sithean na Raplaich where he became lost in the mist. Instead of turning down into Savary Glen and home to Fiunary, he appears to have travelled in a NW direction before turning back down into Inniemore. From there he and the shepherd probably walked along the shores of Loch Teacuis to Barr, or more likely Dorlin, where there was a ferryman who would have taken him home by 'a circuitous route'.

125. *Corrie Borrodale;* see note 30.

126. *I have had playmates, I have had companions:* Lamb, Charles (1775–1834), 'The Old Familiar Faces'.

127. *a son of the manse, his youngest, was, to his joy, appointed to be his assistant and successor:* John MacLeod (1801–82). Licensed by the Presbytery of Mull on 5 November 1823.

128. *I cannot forget the last occasion on which 'the old man eloquent' appeared in the pulpit:* the author would have been about twelve the last time he heard his grandfather preach in Morvern.

129. *soon afterwards he died:* Norman MacLeod died at Fiunary Manse on 5 March 1824 in his eightieth year and the forty-ninth of his ministry and was buried at Kiel, Morvern. (*Thornber,* Kiel.)

130. *the widow did not long survive her husband:* Jean Morison died 6 December 1827, and was buried at Kiel, Morvern. (Thornber, *Kiel*).

131. *her last years were spent in peace in the old manse, occupied then and now by her youngest son:* John (1801–82).
    her first-born in his lowland manse far away: Norman (1783–1862), minister of Campsie, Stirlingshire at the time of his mother's death.

John was not in fact her first-born child but the first to survive childhood.

132. *Next day Rory was dead. Old Jenny, the hen wife, rapidly followed:* neither death has been recorded but the dates can be established through the author's reference to Norman's youngest son John's visit to Canada in 1845, twenty years after their death, although his reckoning would appear to be a year out.

133. *nearly forty years after the old minister had passed away:* about 1860.

134. *the minister:* (John 1801–82).

135. *'astonished to discover that every property in the parish had changed its owner . . . since I had succeeded my father':* soon after George, sixth Duke of Argyll, succeeded his father in 1806 he was forced to place his Morvern properties on the market creating a massive land-grabbing exercise. For the first time in its recorded history every single property in Morvern changed hands between 1813 and 1838. (Gaskell.)

136. *'And look . . . at those who are in this boat':* John (1801–82), minister of Morvern; Norman (1783–1862), minister of St Columba's; Norman (1812–72), minister of the Barony (author of this book); possibly Donald (1831–1916), minister of The Park, Glasgow; and John (1840–98), minister of Govan.

137. *the son of 'old Rory':* Alexander MacLeod died at Fiunary 9 May 1881 aged 72. (Thornber, *Kiel*).

138. *Professor Wilson:* see note 10.

139. *He had married in early life the daughter of one of the most honourable of the earth:* the author's mother, Agnes, daughter of James Maxwell (1758–1829), Argyll's Chamberlain for Mull and Morvern from 1787 to 1829.

140. *her father's house was opposite the old manse:* James Maxwell lived at Aros near Salen, Isle of Mull, in the house now called Aros Mains.

141. *the old parish:* Morvern.

142. *he had for more than twenty-five years ministered to an immense congregation of Highlanders in Glasgow:* Norman MacLeod (1783–1862) was minister of St Columba's in Glasgow and preached in Gaelic there. (*Caraid nan Gaidheal.*)

143. *many of whom were from the old parish:* by 1862 many Morvern people had been evicted from their land and had made their way to Glasgow and other Lowland cities and towns in search of employment. (*OT.* 3 March, 1883.)

144. *emigration:* the population of Morvern peaked at 2,137 in 1831, then steadily declined throughout the whole of the nineteenth century, during which something like 3,250 people left the parish. Gaskell

maintains that no more than 750 people were forcefully evicted from the whole of Morvern, but subsequent research suggests the figure was probably much higher. A note appended to the 1841 Morvern Census returns states:

> There is a decrease in the population of this Parish of nearly 400 since the last census of 1831 was taken. This partly arises from attaching a few farms remote from the Parish Church to the quod [sic] sacra Parish of Strontian; but more especially, from local changes by which so many of the small tenants and cottars were dispossessed to make way for extensive sheep walks and thus led to the entire removal of a number of families by emigration and otherwise... a dozen families have emigrated from the Parish to N.S.Wales and New Zealand in [the] course of the last few years.

145. *the decay of the 'kelp' trade:* the manufacture of kelp (*Laminaria digitata*) – an alkaline ash produced by the burning of seaweed and used in the making of glass, soap and linen – began in earnest in Scotland around 1756, when the usual supply of barilla, a cheaper form of kelp from Spain, was cut off by the Seven Years War. The price rose from £2 a ton to a maximum of £22 in 1810 and, although it fell to £10 a ton by 1822, the boom had changed the whole economic structure of the Highlands and Islands, with devastating results. Despite its long coastline Morvern was never a major producer of kelp with only about 70 tons a year being manufactured. (Murray, W. H., *The Islands of Western Scotland, the Inner and Outer Hebrides,* 1973; *OSA*; *Remarks on the Highlands and Islands of Scotland, the Highland Relief Board,* 1838.)

146. *before the poor law was introduced:* the Poor Law Act, passed in 1845, required proprietors and tenants to provide for the paupers in their parishes at a rate according to the annual value of their lands and leases. Prior to the Act, and following the Disruption of the Church of Scotland in 1843, the care of the poor had been in the hands of the Parochial Boards. Following the potato famines of the mid-nineteenth century the proprietors and tenants complained they were having difficulty in paying the poor rate and in the absence of any relief they began to extend the sheep walks and clear the arable ground of people. The number of poor in Morvern in 1794 was between forty and fifty, each of whom received £8 a year from the Kirk Session. (Rankine; Gaskell; *OSA*).

147. *the Fund for the Relief of Highland Destitution:* a charitable organisation established for organising relief through the free distribution of meal during the distress of the 1830s and 1840s, in which the Rev. Norman MacLeod (1783–1862) played a prominent part. The meal

for Morvern was landed from boats at the old stone jetty below
Fiunary manse and stored in a nearby building now called Fiunary
Cottage. (*Gaelic Companion*; information from the late Donald
Cameron Lawrie, Morvern.)

148. *dulse:* an edible red seaweed, *Rhodymenia palmate,* considered whole-
some when eaten fresh. Before tobacco became common it used to
be washed in fresh water, dried and then rolled up and chewed. It was
also used medicinally to promote perspiration in the treatment of
colds. (Cameron, John, *The Gaelic Names of Plants*, London, 1883.)

149. *Mr Campbell's tales:* John Francis Campbell (1822–85), 'Iain Og Ile', a
well-known Gaelic scholar, folklorist, lawyer and traveller, who spent
many years gathering stories of the Highlands, which he published in
a four-volume work called *Popular Tales of the West Highlands*,
1860–62. (*Gaelic Companion*; see also Mackechnie, Rev. John, ed., *The
Dewar Manuscripts*, 1963.)

150. *smoking his cutty:* a short clay pipe sometimes referred to as a 'cutty-
gun'.

151. *the first deputation from the Church of Scotland visited the Highlands and
Islands:* concerned about the lack of education in the Highlands and
Islands, the Church of Scotland formed a committee to investigate. A
deputation, including the former Moderator, George Husband Baird
(1761–1840), Principal of Edinburgh University, and the Rev.
Norman MacLeod (*Caraid nan Gaidheal*) set off in August 1827 from
Dunoon in a Revenue cruiser, the *Swift*, commanded by Captain
Henry Beatson. From there they sailed to Islay, Jura, Oban, Lorn,
Appin, Lismore, then on to Tobermory, Coll, Tiree, Canna, Rum,
Skye, North and South Uist and Barra. On Barra the venerable
Principal Baird, a man of considerable weight and dressed at the time
in a suit of black, shiny velveteen, had to be carried ashore on the
back of a local fisherman as there was no pier. Staggering under the
weight, the fisherman almost fell, prompting an onlooker to ask in
Gaelic, 'Is he too heavy?', to which the fisherman replied, 'Cha n'eil,
ach tha e co sleamhein re Ron.' ('Oh no, but he is as slippery as a
seal.') The final outcome of this deputation was the establishment of
344 new schools attended by over 22,000 pupils. (*Memorials.*)

152. *foster-brother:* a male child brought up with a child or children of a
different parent. Fosterage was an ancient Celtic custom by which the
children of important families were handed over to families of a lower
status to be nursed either for affection or payment. When a child was
sent to a new home a certain number of cattle, called *Mackalive*,
accompanied him, to which was added an equal number by the foster
parents. This small herd was given free pasturage and became the

child's property. In return for fostering the child, his father undertook to protect the foster parents. There were elaborate rules regarding fosterage. For example in ancient times foster children wore different coloured clothes and ate certain food. (Cameron, John, *Celtic Law*,1937; Burt, Edmund, *Letters from a Gentleman in the North of Scotland*, 1818; Gillies, William A., *In Famed Breadalbane*, 1938.)

153. *Ewen M'Millan:* son of a tenant of Ewen Cameron, Inverscaddle, Locheilside, foster-brother and faithful servant to his son who became Col. John Cameron of Fassiefern. Ewen died in 1840 at Callart, near Onich and was buried close to his foster-brother at Kilmallie, Fort William. (*Fassiefern.*)

154. *Col. Cameron, or Fassiefern:* a grand-nephew of Donald, nineteenth Chief of Clan Cameron, 'the Gentle Lochiel' of the 1745 Rising. John Cameron was mortally wounded while leading the 92nd (Gordon) Highlanders, in the famous charge at Quatre Bras 16 June 1815, two days before the Battle of Waterloo. More than 3,000 mourners are said to have been present when his remains were interred in Lochaber the following year. He is commemorated by a sixty-foot-high obelisk erected in 1816 at a cost of £1,400 by the officers and men of his regiment, bearing an inscription said to have been composed by Sir Walter Scott. (MacCulloch, D. B., *Romantic Lochaber,* 1971; *Fassiefern.*)

155. *Sir Walter Scott:* the verse is from Scott's 'Dance of Death'.

156. *Napier:* Napier, Major General Sir William, *A History of the War in the Peninsular*, 6 vols, 1832. The quotation is from volume 5.

157. *the parish minister . . . prayed with his eyes open:* this is a repetition of the story told in the earlier chapter dealing with the minister and his work. (See note 114.)

158. *our parish minister, on one occasion, when travelling with the Laird:* it is difficult to know which Laird the writer is referring to here as very few of the Morvern landowners were actually resident in the parish except John Gregorson who owned Ardtornish, Acharn, Liddesdale and Achagavel estates. It seems hard to believe that such a sophisticated and well-travelled man did not know the story of Joseph and his brethren!

159. *do penance in a long canvas shirt:* there is an interesting reference to this act of penance in Morvern to be found in the Minute Book of the Synod of Argyll. In May 1651, for the crime of supporting the Royalist Marquis of Montrose and his general, Alastair MacColla, 'the enemies of God, religion and covenant', John MacLean of Kinlochaline was 'appointed to stand in sack-cloth the first Sabbath in Morvairn, the second Sabbath in Tiri (Tiree) and to be received there be the minister thereof'. (*MacTavish.*)

160. *From the dim Shieling on the misty islands:* ever since its first, anonymous appearance in *Blackwood's Magazine,* September 1829, the 'Canadian Boat Song' has remained a mystery. Numerous composers have been suggested over the years, including Hugh Montgomerie, the twelfth Earl of Eglinton, Professor John Wilson in his guise of 'Christopher North', James Hogg, 'the Ettrick Shepherd', J. G. Lockart (1794–1854) and even Sir Walter Scott. Despite the literature which has been generated by the problem of its attribution the question of its authorship remains an unsolved puzzle
    (http://www.arts.uwo.ca/canpoetry/cpjrn/vol106/dowler.htm)

161. *Duncan Piper:* cannot be identified but it is obvious from the description of his master's tomb that the 'Laird' was Allan MacLean, fifth of Drimnin, an officer in the Jacobite army who led the MacLeans of Morvern and Kingairloch at Culloden. He died in 1792 aged sixty-eight and is buried in Cnoc Micheal near Drimnin House. Allan MacLean was such a popular figure that the year in which he died was a chronological landmark in the district. Those who were born in 1792 were said to have been 'born in the year Allan of Drimnin died'. Although Allan's son Charles did not sell the estate until 1797/8, it is unlikely, because of his lifestyle, that the local people would have looked on him with any real feeling, so in a way Allan was indeed the last of the line. (Donaldson 1926; *OT,* 30 August, 1913.)

162. *Glen Immeran:* Gleann nan Iomairean ('the glen of the small ridges of land') lies a mile or so north east of Killundine House overlooking the Sound of Mull. Although the author refers to its shieling huts it is obvious from the remains of at least ten dry-stone buildings and an arable enclosure that there was once a permanent settlement near the head of the glen, probably abandoned about 1810. (Gaskell.)

163. *'Old Jenny':* Jenny Cameron's family are said to have come to Inniemore from Lochaber after the Battle of Sheriffmuir in 1715. When they, and most of the other inhabitants of Inniemore, were evicted about 1823, they moved across the hill to Glen Iomairean. (Sands: information from the late Ronald Cameron, Kinlochteacuis and the late Mrs Jessie Cameron, Carradale, Kintyre.)

164. *when she came down from the glen once a year to the 'big house':* Killundine House, the home of the tacksman, as the laird was the absentee Duke of Argyll.

165. *the thickly-peopled valley on the other side:* Inniemore Valley which, if the narrative can be dated to about 1820, probably supported a population of several hundred.

166. *potatoes were not then so common among the poor:* although potatoes were

first introduced to the Hebrides from Ireland by Clanranald in the early 1700s, they were not widely cultivated until the end of the eighteenth century, although they were being raised in Morvern in 1794. (*OSA.*)

167. *the Highland hamlet nearest Glen Immeran:* Killundine.

168. *her three friends easily descended by the chimney:* a house of this period would have been low and thatched with a central smoke hole in the roof through which it would have been easy to have entered the room below. What the author does not tell us is that his grandfather was one of the party who went up to Glen Iomairean, as it had been assumed that Jenny was probably dead. (Information from the late Mrs Jessie Cameron, Carradale and formerly Killundine, Morvern, whose grandfather accompanied the minister.)

169. *a hare almost every day:* although hares were numerous in Morvern until the early 1900s there are none now. The last one seen by the editor was on Clounlaid in the White Glen in the late 1960s. They are, however, plentiful between Salen and Tobermory on the opposite side of the Sound of Mull.

170. *a widow left her home early one morning in order to reach the residence of her kinsman:* the widow's route is a tantalising one and not easily traced as there appears to be a strong element of exaggeration in the narrative. It is possible though that she started off from the village of Lochaline, passed along the shores of that sea loch, forded the Gearr Abhain below Acharn, and followed the track along the north shore of Loch Arienas to the settlement at Crossaig. From there she may have climbed up the steep slopes towards Beinn Iadain, making her way towards the settlement nestling below the steep, dark, basalt cliffs, which was her intended final destination.

171. *the eldest son of the manse:* Norman (1783–1862), father of the author.

172. *I happened to pass your church door:* St Columba's in Glasgow.

173. *The minor chiefs such as:* Campbell of Lochnell, Cameron of Lochiel, MacLean of Coll, MacLeod of MacLeod and MacLeod of Raasay. Cameron of Lochiel and MacLeod of MacLeod could hardly be described as 'minor chiefs' as they were the heads of Clans.

174. *spread the news of the chief's arrival:* perhaps the greatest example of Highland vanity was that attributed to the Macneils of Barra, whose steward, it is said, used to sound a great horn from the battlements of Kismul Castle, and proclaim out across the wild Atlantic:

Hear oh ye people, and listen oh ye nations! The great Macneil of Barra having finished his meal, the princes of the earth may dine now. (Moncreiffe, Sir Iain of that Ilk, *The Highland Clans*, London, 1967.)

175. *The Isle of Saints, where stands the old grey cross:* the Island of Iona.

176. *the tacksmen formed the most important and influential class of a society:* see Cregeen 1969).

177. *the old house of Glendessary:* Allan Cameron of Glendessary purchased Acharn in Morvern from the Duke of Argyll in 1703. He lived there in a house constructed of wickerwork between oak beams, completely covered with heather and turf outside and lined with wood within, the interior being

> divided into several compartments, and finished in a style of taste and elegance corresponding with the enlightened refinement of the occupants.

This house, and its successor, described as a small, neat, whitewashed building, having all the marks of a house built in the latter half of the eighteenth century and probably one of the first slated houses in Morvern, were demolished sometime in the nineteenth century and the stone used to build the present agricultural sheds on the same site. The avenue of lime trees on either side of the old track leading from the ford over the White Glen River to the house is reputed to have been planted by Allan Cameron about the time he purchased Acharn. (*NSA: OT*, 11 June 1910.)

178. *'The house and furniture', writes Dr Johnson:* part of Johnson's description of Lachlan MacQuarrie's house on Ulva which he visited in 1773.

179. *Writing of Sir Allan Maclaine and his daughters:* the reference is to Sir Allan's house on the Island of Inchkenneth, off the coast of Mull, where Johnson and Boswell stayed in 1773.

180. *their descendants are now among England's aristocracy:* Allan Cameron of Glendessary (*c.* 1660–1721) married his second cousin Christian, daughter of Sir Ewen Cameron of Lochiel, sixteenth chief. Their eldest daughter Catherine married Alexander MacLean of Coll and had one son and six daughters. One of these daughters, Janet, married the Hon. George Vere Hobart, second son of the Earl of Buckinghamshire. (*Clan Gillean.*)

181. *I remember the names of 61 officers:* see note 89.

182. *the poor of the parish:* see note 146.

183. *people flocked from their empty glens to occupy houses in wretched villages near the sea-shore:* e.g. Bonavullin, near Drimnin, where a terrace of ten one-roomed houses was built in 1840 to accommodate many smallholders who had been 'moved' by Christina Stewart of Glenmorvern:

> The Village of Lochaline, founded by John Sinclair, has lately been formed in the country, but, in the total absence of manufacturing or mercantile industry, we cannot look upon this as of any advantage.

Indeed, we see little other purpose it can serve, than that of affording a temporary refuge to a set of miserable paupers, and encouraging them in idleness and ignorance, and ultimately, we fear, in crime. As the fisheries have here, as elsewhere, much fallen off during the last few years, the condition of the people is very miserable with little motive or stimulus of any kind, they seem contented to live and die in a state of ignorance little, if anything, removed from that of the natives of Madagascar or New Zealand.

Dervaig on Mull was another such village. (Fullarton & Baird, *Remarks on the evils at present affecting the Highland & Islands of Scotland*, 1838; *The construction and planning of new urban settlements in Scotland in the 18th century*, Lockhart, Douglas G., Wolfenbutteler Forschungen, *Grundung und Bedeutung kleinerer Stadte im nordlichen Europa der fruhen Neuzeit*, Hanover, 1991.)

184. *the miserable pittance which is given and received with equal heartlessness:* one wonders what MacLeod would have had to say about the cost of The Highland Council's Social Work budget currently running at £45m per annum!

185. *no sound is now heard for twenty or thirty miles but the bleat of sheep or the bark of dogs:* of which Dr John Maclachlan of Rahoy (1804–74), bard and physician wrote:

> What sounds unsweet have disturbed me, marring
> The long-sought slumbers around me falling?
> The Lowland shepherd, with accent jarring,
> Directs his sheep dog with hideous bawling.
>
> The ancient customs and clans are banished,
> No more are songs on the breezes swelling,
> Our Highland nobles alas! Are vanished,
> And worthless upstarts are in their dwelling.

Gillies, H. C. *The Gaelic Songs of the Late Dr John MacLachlan, Rahoy*, 1880.

186. *tenants in a long glen:* Glen Geal, the White Glen, once known as 'the Garden of Morvern' on account of its productivity, gave a living to 300 people between Acharn Bridge and Clounlaid. All were evicted by Patrick Sellar about 1838. (*OT,* 3 March 1883; 24 April 1909.)

187. *Charles Lamb's cracklin pig:* Lamb, Charles (1775–1834), *The Essays of Elia,* a dissertation upon roast pig.

188. *Dumbarton and Falkirk 'Trysts':* 'tryst' is derived from the old word 'triste' or 'trust' and applied to a meeting-place for merchants and customers, especially cattle dealers who 'trysted' the owners of beasts

to meet them at an agreed place for the sale of their stock. The Falkirk Tryst came into being around 1716 and was held three times a year, when it accounted for the disposal of about 60,000 head of black cattle and 40,000 sheep each year. The Dumbarton Tryst was another old and important market to which most of the Morvern cattle were driven because it was nearer. Both diminished in popularity with the changing methods of agriculture and the advent of rail and steam transport. Local cattle markets and fairs were held twice a year in May and November at Knock, Acharn, Lurga, in the Black Glen and Strontian. The last market held in Morvern was on the third Monday of May, 1882. (Haldane, A. R. B., *The Drove Roads of Scotland*, Colonsay, 1995; Gaskell: *OT*, 4 June 1910.)

189. *Let Yarrow be unseen, unknown:* William Wordsworth, 'Yarrow Unvisited' (Symington, Andrew, *The Poetical Works of William Wordsworth*, 1885).

190. *'luck's penny':* a coin or small sum of money given back by the person who receives money in consequence of a bargain.

191. *yell:* barren; *crock:* an old sheep incapable of producing a lamb; *stirk:* a bullock or heifer between one and two years old; *stot:* young male cow, sometimes castrated; *tup:* a ram; *wether:* a castrated ram, *shot:* a ewe or ram rejected by a purchaser when he buys with the right of selection, usually *shott (Jamieson).*

192. It was, and often still is, customary in the Highlands to name the head of a family after his or her place of residence. Here we have *Colonsay,* who was probably a MacNeill from the Island of Colonsay in the Inner Hebrides; *Corrie,* John Cameron (1780–1856) of Corriechoillie, near Spean Bridge; *Drumdriesaig,* (Druimdrishaig, Knapdale), another MacNeill, from whom the author was descended; *Achadashenaig,* John Stewart (1790–1853) of Achadashenaig, now called Glenaros, Isle of Mull, who was also related to the author through marriage. (Information from Mr Lorne Campbell, London; 'North Argyll', *John Cameron "Corrychoillie", Our Greatest Highland Drover*, n.d.; Cregeen, 1964.)

193. *A great sheep farmer:* John Cameron of Corriechoillie, see note above.

194. *Mary Campbell:* as none of the characters named in this chapter can be found in the parish records it must be assumed they are fictitious.

195. *a very Malvina:* in MacPherson's Ossianic poems Malvine is betrothed to Oscar, son of Ossian.

196. *at the house of a tacksman, an uncle of the bride's:* the only Morison tacksman in Morvern at the time was John of Achnaha. (See note 49.)

197. *the sheriff:* John Gregorson of Ardtornish (1775–1846), Sheriff of Mull and Morvern. (Currie.)

198. *it could only have been by a certain glen:* Savary, where there was an ancient track leading across the hill to Inniemore.

199. *a small inn, which was the frontier house of the parish:* perhaps Doirlinn, where there was also a ferry over Loch Sunart to Glenborrodale, which might suggest Mary Campbell, if that was her real name, was related to one of the Campbell tacksmen of Ardnamurchan. Other possibilities are Achagavel in the Black Glen or Loch Head, Loch Sunart.

200. *'I would sooner be chained to a rock at low water, and rest there until the tide came and choked my breath':* a fairly common method of dealing with female miscreants long ago. Two notable local examples occurred at Castle Tioram, Moidart and Laudale, Loch Sunart, both involving theft. (Donaldson, 1920; 'North Argyll', *Annals and Recollections of Sunart*, n.d.)

201. *a Waterloo medal:* Although styled the 'Waterloo Medal', it was awarded to anyone who had taken part in the battles of Ligny (16 June), Quatre Bras (16 June) and Waterloo (18 June) 1815. Every soldier present at either of these battles was credited with two extra years' service. This was the first medal issued by the British Government to all soldiers present and the first campaign medal awarded to the next-of-kin of men killed in action. The Waterloo Medal also had the distinction of being the first on which the recipient's name was impressed around the edge by machine. (Gordon, L L *British Battles and Medals,* 5th ed., rev., Spinks and Son Ltd, London, 1979.)

202. *buried thirty years ago in the old churchyard:* no headstone for Donald MacLean has been found in Kiel graveyard, Morvern.

203. *tombstone, whose inscription is seldom more than a statistical table of birth and death:* often graves were marked only by a simple cairn or a single stone. There were two reasons for this. Firstly, it was only relatively few families who could afford to pay a mason to cut a headstone, and secondly, it was considered by many old Highlanders that to put a name on a grave marker would bring misfortune to the family concerned – a sentiment echoed in the inscription of a gravestone of a thirteenth-century Franciscan now in the Museum of Budapest, which reads:

> Stranger do not seek my name but when you pass say an Ave for my soul.

(Thornber, Iain, *Dail na Cille, The Field of the Church*, privately printed, 2000.)

204. *a small green island in Loch Shiel:* St Finan's Isle which takes its name

from St Finan the Leper, one of the early Celtic saints. ('North Argyll', *St Finan's Isle, Eilean Fhianain, Its Story,* 1957; Macdonald, Rev. Charles, *Moidart, Or Among the Clanranalds,* Oban, 1889.)

205. *on the green alluvial plain at the head of the loch:* Glenfinnan, where Prince Charles Edward Stuart raised his standard on 18 August 1745 signalling the beginning of the Jacobite Rising.

206. *Ben Reshabol:* Ben Resipol, 2,774 ft.

207. *the bell now we believe preserved by the Laird:* there are only two other occasions on which it is recorded that the bell of St Finan has been taken off the island. Firstly, in 1746 when a party of government troops stole it and from whom it was recovered by the sexton at Glenfinnan, and secondly, in 1911 when it was put on display at the Scottish Exhibition of National History, Art and Industry in Glasgow. (*Moidart,* above; *Scottish Exhibition of National History, Art & Industry, Palace of History, Catalogue,* 1911; Thornber, Iain, *The Bell of St Finan, The Scottish Field,* June 1975.)

208. *the only monument we remember:* a strange remark given the number of gravestones on the island which predate the time of the author's visit. (Fisher, Ian, *Early Medieval Sculpture in the West Highlands and Islands,* Edinburgh, 2001; *Moidart,* above; *St Finan's Isle,* above, and a photographic survey by the editor in the National Monuments Record of Scotland Collection, RCAHMS, Edinburgh.)

209. *the Parish churchyard:* Cill Choluim Chille (Kiel), Morvern. The site contains a fourteenth- to fifteenth-century free-standing, disc-headed cross, the remains of a medieval church, a large collection of late medieval carved stones and some 250 inscribed tombstones. (RCAHMS 3; Steer, K. A. & Bannerman, J. W. M., *Late Medieval Sculpture in the West Highlands,* 1977; Thornber, Iain, *The Carved Stones of Kiel, Morvern, Argyll,* privately printed, 2000; Thornber, *Kiel.*)

210. *a beautiful tall stone cross from Iona:* this cross was carved by craftsmen belonging to a school of carving which flourished on Iona in the fourteenth and fifteenth centuries. Other major schools were established in Kintyre, the Island of Oronsay, Loch Awe and Loch Sween, all of which ceased production at the Reformation. (Steer and Bannerman, above; Ritchie, Graham, and Harman, Mary, *Exploring Scotland's Heritage, Argyll and the Western Isles,* 1990.)

211. *the modern building is to the old one what a barn is to a church:* the 'modern' church the writer is referring to was built in 1799 and replaced an earlier church on the same site. (Gaskell.)

212. *'the Shepherds of Etive Glen':* see note 36.

213. *nor could an old saint find a better resting place:* the first church at Kiel is dedicated to St Columba − Choluim Chille, who also founded the

famous monastery on Iona in the sixth century. According to local tradition, he crossed Loch Linnhe with St Moluag from the Island of Lismore and, landing together, they climbed the Garbh Shlios. On the summit of Glas Bheinn, with its commanding views of the Morvern coastline, St Columba planted his foot on a flat rock, and, pointing to a green knoll a little way above the entrance to Loch Aline, exclaimed:

There is the place where we will build out next church.

It is said the indelible footprint of the Saint is still to be seen on the hilltop. (Donaldson 1926.)

214. *a cairn of stones is always raised on the spots where the coffin has rested:* 'funeral cairns', as they were called, are still found beside many old Highland roads. The most notable example in Morvern is at Clach na Criche, 'the boundary stone', a mile west of Fiunary, which marks the boundary of the ancient parishes of Cille Choluim Chille and Cill Fhiontain. Here numerous little cairns, half-hidden among the bracken, mark the occasions where corteges rested in the days when coffins were physically carried to their last resting place. Despite motor transport the custom lives on and funeral parties travelling from one parish to another still halt to allow each mourner to gather a stone from the shore to build a simple cairn in memory of the deceased. Further examples can be found in Moidart and Ardnamurchan along the old 'coffin routes' which lead to St Finan's Isle on Loch Shiel. (Thornber, Iain, 'The Wishing Stone', *Scotland's Magazine*, September 1975; *Dail na Cille*, ibid *Burial Customs of Mull and Morvern; OT,* 23 October, 6 November 1909.)

215. *The bagpipe is sometimes still played at funerals:* before the Disruption of 1843 a piper usually played at Highland funerals, but it was not generally approved of by the clergy, especially after the burial when refreshments were served in the customary liberal fashion. At one funeral the piper had indulged too freely and instead of playing sad laments, struck up '*Calum Crubach'*, 'Lame Calum' – a lively and cheerful dance tune! On another occasion a Morvern laird, said to have been a MacLean of Drimnin, took his piper with him to a funeral in Lochaber and upset the assembled company to such an extent that one of them stuck his dirk into the windbag to stop the music. (*Highland Ponies;* Garnet T., *Observations on a Tour through the Highlands and Part of the Western Isles of Scotland,* 1800.)

216. *a medical man greatly beloved and respected for his skill and kindness to the poor died at Fort William from fever:* Dr William Kennedy (1810–51) of Leanachan in Lochaber who contracted typhus while attending the

family of MacPhee, a notorious outlaw who lived on an island in Loch Quoich, Invergarry. After MacPhee's apprehension and imprisonment, his family moved to Fort William, where they lived in straitened circumstances. Typhus developed amongst them and being unable to help themselves, Dr Kennedy took a personal interest in their welfare which ultimately led to his contracting the disease. Dr Kennedy was buried at Kilmallie, near Corpach, and commemorated by a large public memorial in Cameron Square, Fort William, demolished in 1965 to make way for a car park. (MacCulloch, above; MacMillan, Somerled, *Bygone Lochaber,* Glasgow, 1971; information from Dr Chris Robinson, Fort William.)

217. *the ruins of the old archway:* the archway of the medieval church in the graveyard at Kiel, which leads from the main body of the building into a N transept or burial aisle. (RCAHMS, 3.)

218. *The old stone coffin, or the tomb of the Spanish Princess:* marked by a thin, broken stone, set on edge close to the medieval archway. (Donaldson, 1926)

219. *the good ship 'Florida':* although the name of the Spanish ship which lies at the bottom of Tobermory Bay has long been called the *Florida,* the *Florencion* and the *Florencia,* recent research has proved that it is in fact the *San Juan de Sicilia,* an 800-ton merchant vessel from the Adriatic port of Ragusa, now Dubrovnik. (Martin, Colin, *Scotland's Historic Shipwrecks,* 1998; McLeay, Alison, *The Tobermory Treasure, the True Story of the Fabulous Armada Galleon,* 1986.)

220. *Oliver Cromwell sent a vessel to the Highlands, commanded by a Captain Pottinger:* the vessel was HMS *Dartmouth,* commanded by Captain Edward Pottinger, wrecked on Eilean Rubha an Ridire, near Inniemore on the Sound of Mull, in 1690, with the loss of Captain Pottinger and most of his crew. The ship was rediscovered in 1973 by a group of experienced amateur divers from Bristol and has subsequently been excavated. Many interesting artefacts, including the ship's bell, a brass Highland ring-brooch, cast iron hand-grenades, still with their wooden fuse plugs and gun powder charges intact, and a pewter syringe for the treatment of diseases, have been recovered. The seabed round the *Dartmouth* is a Designated Shipwreck Site which prohibits diving on it except under licence. It is interesting to note, witchcraft aside, that the saga of the *Dartmouth's* loss and the name of her captain was still being spoken of in Morvern in the mid-nineteenth century. (Martin, *ibid.*)

221. *the harbour of all harbours:* Tobermory.

222. *the Lord of Duart:* Sir Lachlan Mor MacLean of Duart, d.1598.

223. *bicker:* a wooden dish or bowl. (*Jamieson.*)

224. *his body was carried around the old stone cross in the churchyard of Callum Cille:* the practice is still followed when a coffin is being taken from the present church to the old cemetery.

225. *St Moluag in Lismore:* St Moluag, a sixth-century missionary and contemporary of St Columba, founded a monastic site on the island of Lismore, in Loch Linnhe. He died in 592. (Carmichael, Ian, *Lismore in Alba*, Perth, 1948; *Fisher,* above; RCAHMS, 2.)

226. *the Well of Clara Viola:* still pointed out near Castle Coeffin on Lismore. For further information, see Campbell, Lord Archibald, *Records of Argyll*, 1885.

227. *Doideagan muileach:* the Mull Witches – a term still widely used in Mull.

228. *Flory Cameron:* probably Flora Cameron, aged 80, living alone in Lochaline Village in 1841. (Morvern Census, 1841.)

229. *the school was attached to the church:* the building, which stands a few feet to the east of the present church, is now a museum and houses the collection of medieval stones taken from the adjoining graveyard. It served as the parish school until about 1833, when it became the session-house and subsequently a dwelling house. (*OT,* 26 July 1913; McGregor, Alasdair, Alpin, *Somewhere in Scotland,* 1948.)

230. *the present minister of 'the Parish':* Rev. John MacLeod (1801–82).

231. *the account of his funeral, written by one present:* the writer was obviously the parish minister, possibly the Rev. Norman MacLeod (1775–1824), but more likely his son John, above.

232. *an old Gothic arch of peculiar beauty and simplicity:* see note 217.

233. *her good friend, the parish schoolmaster:* see note 236.

234. *a neat freestone slab:* still to be seen. It bears the inscription, 'Here lies the corpse of John M'Lean late tenant in Kilcolmkil who departed this life on the 26th December 1823 aged 35 years. From parental affection this stone is erected to his memory by his widowed mother Flory Cameron. May 1824.' (Thornber, *Kiel.*)

235. *another slab was provided:* it too still stands, sheltered by the old archway. Its inscription reads, 'This stone is erected in memory of Donald and Mary M'Lean by their widowed mother Flory Cameron, 1824'. (Thornber, *Kiel*)

236. *the Schoolmaster of 'the Parish':* Samuel Cameron (1785–1849), schoolmaster in Morvern from 1819 and a son of John Cameron, tenant of Knock, Morvern. Samuel Cameron married Mary MacLean, Cean- na Coille, Kingairloch, by whom he had two daughters and four sons. One of the sons, Alexander, composed a number of Gaelic songs which are now lost. (Thornber, *Kiel.*)

237. *a few letters for the sheriff:* see note 197.

238. *three or four newspapers a week old:* the newspapers of the day which may have reached Morvern were, the *Caledonian Mercury, Edinburgh Evening Courant, Inverness Journal*, and *The Inverness Courier*. The *Oban Times* did not appear until 1861.

239. *a quern:* the manufacturing of meal at home by use of these small handmills was generally discouraged, as by old feudal rights tenants and cottars were supposed to take their grain to appointed mills, for which the laird charged a rent, and where the miller would exact a certain percentage of the end product called moltair, a loan word from Latin meaning dues or a fine. There were three mills in Morvern at Bonnavoulin, Savary and Acharn, where the leads, ponds and, in the case of Bonnavoulin and Acharn, parts of the mill-stones can be found. The last working grain mill in Morvern was at Bonnavoulin and it closed in 1885. The dues paid to the miller of Acharn by the farmers of the White Glen in one year amounted to no less than forty bolls – a boll was a dry measure of varying capacity, but probably around 120 lbs in weight. (*OT*, 4 June 1910; Gauldie, Enid, *The Scottish Country Miller 1700–1900*, 1981.)

240. *weavers and tailors:* in 1794 there were thirty-four male and female weavers and fifteen tailors in Morvern. (*OSA*.)

241. *As for shoes:* in 1794 there were four brogue-makers and one shoe-maker in Morvern. (*OSA*.)

242. *his first and last journey to see George IV in Edinburgh:* August, 1822. (Prebble, John, *The King's Jaunt*, 1988.)

243. *the worthy Schoolmaster is long since dead:* Samuel Cameron died on 13 June 1849, aged 64 years, and is buried along with his wife, daughter and three sons at Kiel, Morvern. He was replaced as the parish schoolmaster by John Cameron – no relation. (Thornber, *Kiel*.)

244. *The official residence has been changed:* Samuel Cameron resided at 'Kyle', a little way above Lochaline village. He would have taught at the old school at Kiel. (Census, 1841; information from Mrs May Wilson, Lochaline.)

245. *Braxy:* mutton derived from a sheep which had died from a bacterial disease called braxy, introduced to the Highlands through the Linton breed. It was prevalent in hoggs during the autumn and generally fatal. In Northumberland it was known as 'midden-ill' and 'red' and as 'black-water' elsewhere in England. (Smith, John, *General View of the Agriculture of the County of Argyll*, 1798.)

246. *Sir Ralph Abercromby:* (1734–1801), a Member of Parliament who became a distinguished general. He served in America, the West Indies, Ireland, the Netherlands and Egypt. His daughter married Donald Cameron, twenty-second chief of Clan Cameron. (Chalmers,

Robert, *A Biographical Dictionary of Eminent Scotsmen*, 1840; Cameron, John, *The Clan Cameron,* 1894.)

247. *the excellent sheriff of the district:* see note 197.
248. *'Barefooted Lachlan':* 'Lachlann Casruisgte', as he was known in Gaelic, was born and brought up on the island of Oronsay at the mouth of Loch Sunart. He was married with a family, but when he became mentally unstable he left them and took up residence in a cave at the head of Loch Arienas. Impervious to the cold, he would swim backwards and forwards over the loch even during the winter. He confined his wanderings to Morvern. He was a very competent sailor and a great favourite with Sheriff John Gregorson of Ardtornish who often asked him to accompany him whenever he had to sail to Oban in poor weather. It was possibly Lachlan the enumerator for the 1841 census had in mind when he attached a note to the 5th Morvern District (including Acharn) which reads,

> All the persons, male and female enumerated on the page; except one insane person who never lodges in a dwelling house.

Lachlan had a brother called Charles, known as 'Captain John', who had suffered from sunstroke while sailing in foreign seas and became mentally unwell. His standard reply when asked, 'How is the Captain today'? was always, 'Ploughing the ocean, *a chiallain*' (my dear!) (*OT*, 3 May 1930; unpublished Gaelic MS by 'North Argyll' in the editor's possession.)

249. *Sir Joseph Banks:* 1743–1820, English naturalist who accompanied Captain Cook on his expedition round the world in the *Endeavour,* 1768–71. Visited Staffa in 1772 on the recommendation of Allan MacLean of Drimnin. (Pennant, Thomas, *A Tour in Scotland and Voyage to the Hebrides, 1772,* reprinted 1998. For other eighteenth century tourists see Faujas de Saint Fond *A Journey through England and Scotland to the Hebrides in 1784,* 2 vols, 1907; Murray, 1803, above.)
250. *Mr Penant:* Thomas Pennant (1726–98), traveller and naturalist. See note above.
251. *'Foreign Bradshaw'* and *'Murray'*: two well-known rail and travel guides.
252. *Mr Maxwell, the 'factor' or 'chamberlain':* see note 88.
253. *Mr Stewart, the kind hearted proprietor of Achadashenaig:* see note 192.
254. *Colonel Campbell of Knock:* Archibald Campbell of Knock (1771–1840), colonel of the 46th Regiment (South Devonshire) and son of John Campbell, tacksman of Mishnish, Mull. (Table-tomb in Knock graveyard and information from John Blachford, Poole, Dorset.)

255. *Mr M'Donald, the laird of Staffa:* Ranald Macdonald (1777–1838), son of Colin Macdonald of Boisdale, a kinsman of Flora Macdonald, the Jacobite heroine, who purchased Ulva and Staffa in 1785. Ranald lived in great Highland style and entertained many distinguished travellers at Ulva House, including Walter Scott. (Currie.)

256. *'wherries':* shallow, light boats, sharp at both ends, a type of barge.

257. *Tom Sheridan:* unidentified.

258. *the Lord Lorne of the day:* George William Campbell (1776–1839), later sixth Duke of Argyll. (*Burke's Peerage*, 1953.)

259. *When Walter Scott was expected to visit Mull:* Scott's visit to Mull took place in 1814. (Currie.)

260. *whoever possesses now that Ulva album:* its whereabouts are unknown.

261. *the first Gaelic magazine ever published, which was conducted by my father: An Teachdaire Gaelach, The Gaelic Messenger*, begun in 1830 by Norman Macelod (1783–1836).

262. *the family of Glendessary:* the Camerons of Glendessary, who took their territorial title from the place of that name on Loch Arkaig-side in Lochaber, were descended from Donald, a younger son of Allan, sixteenth chief of Clan Cameron. They first appeared in Morvern in 1671 as tenants of Sir Allan MacLean of Duart and later as proprietors of Acharn and other lands which they owned from 1703 until 1775, although there is evidence to suggest they may have remained as tenants for a number of years thereafter. Several of them are buried at Kiel, Morvern, where their graves are marked by elaborately inscribed table-tombs. Jean, daughter of Allan Cameron of Glendessary (1660–1721), left £20 for the poor of the parish. For that and other acts of kindness she and her family were long remembered as the last traditional Highland lairds in Morvern. ('North Argyll', Some stray notes on the Camerons of Glendeshary, *TGSI*, vol. xxxviii, 1937-41; Gaskell, *The Scottish Genealogist*, vol. xvii, 1971; Thornber, *Kiel*; *OSA*.

263. *the belling of the stag was heard on the mountain:* unlikely at New Year. Red deer stags breed in the autumn; the 20th of September being traditionally known as 'the day of the roaring' signalling the start of the rutting season.

264. *Ferintosh:* a brand of whisky produced on the Black Isle estate of Forbes of Culloden, which paid no duty, was sold in 1790 at 1s.8d. a quart and was so popular that it became a synonym for whisky. (Graham, Henry, G., *The Social Life of Scotland in the Eighteenth Century*, 1901.)

265. *all assembled to witness the Camanachd (shinty match):* Shinty is an ancient sport said to have been brought to the Highlands along with

Christianity over a thousand years ago by Irish missionaries. It was a popular game played all over Scotland during the seventeenth century, but slowly died out except in the West Coast, from where it was reintroduced into the Lowlands by Gaelic-speaking Highlanders forced into exile by the clearances. It was usual in the Highlands to include a game of shinty in the New or the 'Old' New Year celebrations, *Ag iomain bhall air La Callain, C'ait' eil coimeas ris 's an Eorpa.* (Playing shinty on New Year's day, where is its like in the whole of Europe?) The New Year shinty matches at Acharn were played in a field by the river called *Dail na Comair* – the confluence or meeting of two rivers. Players came from the White and the Black Glens, Arienas, Achadh na Gamhna, Inniemore and Inniebeg. The village of Inniemore alone could send thirty young men. Bagpipes were always in evidence and occasionally a dance took place on the field afterwards, for the games were patronised by girls and young women. In 1874 two teams of thirty men on each side played for three and a half hours and were reported afterwards to have been 'well fortified by John Barleycorn'. Shinty appears to have died out in Morvern sometime about the early 1880s for by 1883 a local Gaelic bard was lamenting its disappearance altogether. (*OT,* 16 January 1874 and 11 June 1910; Thornber, Iain, *The Gaelic Bards of Morvern;* MacLennan, Hugh Dan, 'Shinty: Some Facts and Fiction in the Nineteenth Century', *TGSI,* vols LIII and LIX, 1985 and 1997.)

266. *Blar na Leine:* this battle took place in 1544. The name is popularly supposed to mean the Field of the Shirts; but the Gaelic name is *Blar na Leanna,* the field of the swampy meadow. (Mackay, William, *Urquhart and Glenmoriston,* 2nd ed., 1914.)

267. *'thy king landed in Moidart':* from the classical piobaireachd, *Thainig mo Righ air Tir am Muideart* ('My King has landed in Moidart'), composed by John Macintyre, hereditary piper to Menzies of Menzies, commemorating the arrival of Prince Charles Edward Stuart in 1745.

268. *The Emigrant ship:* unfortunately the vessel's name has not yet been identified.

269. *a harbour so well defended from the violence of winds and waves:* Tobermory Bay, protected by Calve Island, provides a deep and secure natural harbour close to the north-west entrance to the Sound of Mull.

270. *Sunnard:* now Sunart.

271. *Unnimore:* known locally as Inniemore. There are two localities in Morvern sharing this place-name. One on the Sound of Mull between Rudha An Ridire and Ardtornish Point and the other south-west of Loch Arienas. The name comes from *Aoineadh Mor,* a Gaelic word meaning the big or steep promontory. The Unnimore in

MacLeod's account was the latter, a village comprising some twenty houses, a horizontal water mill, several corn-drying-kilns and enclosures occupied in 1779 by forty-five inhabitants, all Camerons. The events described by Mary, whose family were probably also Camerons, took place in 1828 when most of the occupants were evicted by Miss Christina Stewart of the Glenmorvern Estate. A few families remained until shortly after 1841 when it was finally abandoned. A century later Inniemore became part of the Forestry Commission for Scotland's Fiunary Forest and the village disappeared under trees until 1974 when it was uncovered during felling operations. Thanks largely to the publication of Mary's story in this book, which is one of the few firsthand accounts of a West Highland clearance, the site was preserved and a visitor carpark, paths and interpretive boards were provided by Forest Enterprise. (*Scotsman*, 13 June 1994; the *Herald*, 2 August 1994; the *Guardian*, 25 July 1994; *Lochaber News*, 11 June 1994; the *Independent*, 21 October, 2000.)

272. *as told by herself:* to Norman MacLeod, minister of St Columba's, Glasgow, who published it in Gaelic in *Good Words*.

273. *Knock-nan-Carn:* is the hilltop to the east of Bealach na Sgairn through which a track went from Inniemore down Savary Glen to the Sound of Mull.

274. *Allan of Errach:* Lieut-General Sir Alan Cameron of Erracht (1750–1828), who raised and became first Colonel of the 79th Regiment, (Cameron Highlanders.) It is generally believed that Alan's mother was Marsali, daughter of Charles MacLean of Drimnin who was killed leading the MacLeans at Culloden but a secondary source says she was a daughter of Donald Campbell of Scammadale, near Oban. (MacLean of Dochgarroch, Lorraine, *Indomitable Colonel*, 1986; *OT*, 3 February 1912.)

275. *I once again sat down at the foot of the old Iona-cross in the churchyard of 'the Parish':* Kiel, Morvern. See note 209.

276. *the old keep of Ardtornish:* Ardtornish Castle is thought to have been built by the MacDonalds about the second half of the thirteenth century. It is recorded that John MacDonald, first Lord of the Isles, died here in 1387. His grandson, John, fourth Lord of the Isles, immortalised Ardtornish in the annals of Scottish history by making it the venue of a meeting in October 1461 with the commissioners of King Edward IV of England to overthrow the Scottish Government. An agreement was drawn up, known as the Treaty of Westminster-Ardtornish, and endorsed,

> *Ex castello nostro Ardthornish decimo nono die mensis Octobris anno Domini millesimo quadringentesimo sexagesimo primo.*

The plot failed and John lost his lands and titles to the Crown and, ultimately, his neighbours the MacLeans of Duart. The castle was probably abandoned about 1690 when much of Morvern was taken from the MacLeans by the Campbells who removed a great deal of stone from the castle to build the nearby Ardtornish House where the Gregorsons lived. It too was dismantled in 1907. Loch Aline and Ardtornish Castle feature in Sir Walter Scott's epic poem, 'The Lord of the Isles'. Of the former he wrote,

> Lull'd were the winds on Inniemore,
> And green Loch Aline's woodland shore.

The latter he makes the scene of the marriage with the Maid of Lorn. The castle is described as being on a great steep cliff, ''twixt cloud and ocean hung', and reached by a stair hewn in the rock. (Scott, Sir Walter, 'The Lord of the Isles', 1857; Munro, J. and Munro, R. W. (eds), Acts of the Lords of the Isles, SHS, 1986.)

277. *Aros Castle:* commands a prominent position on the West Coast of the Sound of Mull. It was a 'hall-house', comprising two main storeys and an attic, all the floors being of timber, with the main 'hall', or living-room, in an upper room. It was probably built by the MacDougalls of Lorn sometime in the late thirteenth century before passing to the Lords of the Isles. Both Donald, second Lord of the Isles, and his grandson John, fourth Lord, are known to have granted charters from there during the fifteenth century. Following the forfeiture of the Lords of the Isles, Aros Castle passed to the MacLeans of Duart who, in turn, were ousted by the Campbells of Argyll. There are no records of it having been occupied after 1690, when it may have been abandoned in favour of a more comfortable and better-sheltered building below. (RCAHMS 3.)

278. *Kinloch:* Kinlochteacuis.

279. *The old bell, which it is said was once at Iona:* probably a small hand-bell, similar in size to St Finan's and made of bronze or iron. This bell, an old trunk for holding session records, 'handed down for generations', session records dating from 1847, and a small table from the old church at Kiel, feature in an inventory of church property in Morvern, dated 2 February 1917, but their whereabouts is now unknown. (Morvern Kirk Session Minutes, above.)

280. *Robert Harrison . . . missionary of the Lord:* Robert Harrison was an Englishman and a Wesleyan from Nottingham who, for unknown reasons, left his native town for Mull before coming to Morvern. Of a solitary nature, he wandered the countryside evangelising and would often appear in the remotest villages at the most unreasonable hours

and when he was least expected. On one occasion he arrived late one night at Barr on the shores of Loch Teacuis. Mrs Campbell, the tacksman's wife with whom he was to lodge, ventured to say to him,

> I am sorry I am not better prepared for entertaining you Mr Harrison; but I did not expect you today.

The pious man only answered,

> Beware, my dear friend, lest death find you thus unprepared.

Despite his aversion to drink, which was prevalent in the parish at the time, he was very popular, especially with the young and the old. His funeral at Kiel on 1 February 1832 was attended by a large number of people including several tacksmen, farmers and clergymen. (*OT*, 15 February 1908.)

281. *the 'palace' of Bishop MacLean:* Taigh na Easbaig, 'the Bishop's House', was situated about three hundred yards west of the graveyard and is now in Forestry Commission woodland. The bishop was Mr Hector MacLean (1605–87), minister of Morvern from 1639 to 1679, tacksman of Kiel and Episcopalian Bishop of Argyll from 1680 to 1687. He married Jean, daughter of the Rev. Thomas Boyd, by whom he had four sons and two daughters, but he is also said to have had a further sixteen daughters, most of whom were likely to have been of natural birth. (Thornber, Iain, *Bishop Hector MacLean of Knock*, SWHIHR, *Notes & Queries*, No.VI, March 1978.)

282. *the Bishop himself lies under the old archway:* Bishop Hector MacLean's grave is apparently marked by a recumbent slate of the Iona School of carving with a cross and shaft running down its centre and flanked by intertwined plant-scrolls. As this stone dates to the late fifteenth century it could not have been carved for him and therefore must have been appropriated by his family at a later date. The practice of reusing medieval stones for later memorials was quite common in the Highlands.

283. *the thanksgiving and parting hymn of praise:* Isaac Watts (1674–1748), hymn number 116 in the *Church Hymnary*, revised edition.

284. *I went to visit the spot where the many members of the old manse repose:* the burial aisle of the MacLeods of Fiunary is at the eastern end of Kiel graveyard. It comprises a large and now ruinous whitewashed, gable wall enclosed by iron railings surmounted by urn and ball filials. The east face contains three white marble panels inscribed:

> 1st Erected by Rev John MacLeod DD in memory of his much beloved wife Margaret MacLean who died on the 23rd day of June 1863 in the 61st year of her age. And of fondly cherished children,

Jessie Ann who died on the 23rd day of May 1849 aged 13 and Jane Mary who died on the 5th of October 1848 aged 6 years.

2nd In memory of the Rev Norman MacLeod who departed this life on the 5th day of March 1824 in the 80th year of his age and the 49th of his ministry in this Parish. A man greatly revered and beloved. Also his wife Jean Morison, daughter of John Morison, tacksman of Achnaha. She died on the 6th day of December 1827. Twelve of their children are buried here. Four others of whom one was the Rev Norman MacLeod DD, minister of St Columba's Parish, Glasgow and Dean of the Chapel Royal, are buried in Campsie Churchyard.

3rd In memory of the Rev John MacLeod DD Dean of the Chapel Royal and Dean of the Most Ancient Order of the Thistle who departed this life on the 30th of May 1882 in the 82nd year of his age and the 58th of a faithful and greatly honoured ministry in this Parish where he succeeded his father in 1824. Here also rests the Rev John MacLeod DD, minister of Govan Parish born 22nd June 1840, died 4th August 1898 and his wife Alexa Mary MacPherson, daughter of General Duncan MacPherson H.M.E.I.C.S. born 18th June 1838, died 20th May, 1910.

285. a *new grave . . . in it was laid the wife of the parish minister:* Margaret MacLean, wife of Dr John MacLeod, see above.

CENSUS OF THE INHABITANTS OF JOHN 5TH DUKE OF ARGYLL'S PROPERTY IN MORVERN, 1779

(The numbers in brackets represent the total in each family)

KILLUNDINE

Hugh Campbell (12)
Hugh Cameron, workman (7)
Donald Cameron, workman (6)
Donald Livingstone, cottar (2)
Lachlan McLachlan, workman (4)
John McIntyre, cottar (8)
John Carr, cottar (4)

FERNISH

Alexander McNiven, tenant (8)
Mrs McNeil (5)
Mrs MacKenzie (4)
Hugh MacDougall, tenant (7)
John Livingstone, tenant (4)
Gilbert McCallum, tenant (4)
Lachlan McLachlan, tenant (5)
John Campbell, workman (4)
Duncan McEachern, workman (3)
John McEachern, workman (5)
Hugh McEachern, workman (3)
Neil Livingstone, workman (5)
John Livingstone, workman (5)
Angus McPherson, cottar (2)
John Livingstone (2)
Margaret McLean, cottar and a herd (2)
Catharine McDonald, cottar and daughters (3)
Catharine McDiarmaid, cottar (1)
Ann Livingstone, cottar and sons (4)
Mary McDonald, cottar (1)
Christian McPherson, cottar (1)
Duncan McIntyre, workman (8)

MUNGASDAIL

John Beatton, tacksman (18)
Angus Robbison, workman (7)

Hugh McEachern, workman (7)
Donald Beatton, workman (6)
John McKeannalich, workman 6)
Farquhard McEachern, cottar (6)
Rory McDonald, cottar (5)
Donald McEachern, miller (6)
Kirsty McInnis, cottar (5)
Neil Beatton, cottar (5)
John Beatton, cottar and wife (2)
Mary Beatton, cottar (4)
Hugh McKay, grasskeeper (7)
Marion McEachern, cottar (1)

AULISTON

Lachlan McPherson, tenant (6)
Archibald McDougall, tenant (7)
John McColl, tenant (5)
Hugh Livingston, tenant (3)
Donald McPhee, tenant (3)
Hugh McPhee, tenant (4)
Hugh Kennedy, tenant (6)
Huigh McPhaden, tenant (3)
Duncan Livingstone, tenant (4)
John McPherson, tenant (5)
Donald McPhee, herd and wife (2)
Archibald Sinclair, herd (6)
Archibald McLachlan, cottar (4)

PORTAVATA

Donald McKay, grasskeeper (5)
Hugh Livingstone, grasskeeper (4)
Donald McLean, cottar (5)
Angus McKay, cottar (2)

BARR

Duncan Campbell, tacksman (13)
Donald McPhee, workman (9)

Hugh McLachlan, cottar (7)
Donald Livingstone, cottar (3)
Hugh Cameron, workman (5)
John Livingstone, workman (5)
Hugh McPhee, cottar (5)
Alexander McPhee, workman (8)
Donald Campbell, cottar (6)
John McMaster, cottar (7)
Catharine McKay, cottar (4)

INNIEMORE

Donald Cameron, tenant (6)
Hugh Cameron, tenant (7)
Ewen Cameron, tenant (6)
Angus Cameron, tenant (3)
Donald Cameron, tenant (4)
Alexander Cameron, herd (5)
Hugh Cameron, grasskeeper (6)
Hugh Cameron, cottar (4)
Cottar wives (4)

KINLOCHTEACUIS

Charles McLachlan, grasskeeper (5)
John McLachlan, cottar (6)
Hugh Cameron, cottar (7)
Alexander McKenzie, herd (4)
Duncan Cameron, cottar (2)
Kate Cameron and daughter cottars (2)

RAHOY

Archibald Campbell, tacksman (13)
Duncan McCalman (5)
Archibald Cameron, workman (8)
Donald Cameron, workman (7)
Donald Livingstone, workman (5)
Donald McMillan, grasskeeper (6)
Duncan Cameron, grasskeeper (6)
Effy McLachlan, cottar (2)
Catharine Livingstone, cottar (3)

GLENCRIPESDALE

Archibald McPherson, overseer (5)
Marion McPherson, cottar and daughter (2)
Donald McColl, cottar (2)
John McKenzie, cottar (2)
Angus McMillan, cottar (4)
Dugald Campbell, wood ranger (7)

LAUDALE

Alexander McCallum, herd (7)
Angus McNaughten, herd (9)
Donald McNaughtan (sic), cottar (2)
Hugh McNaughton (sic), cottar (7)
Donald McLachlan, grasskeeper (6)
John McPhee, cottar (3)

LIDDESDALE

Allan McDougall, tacksman (18)
Angus Beatton, cottar (4)
John McDougall, cottar (6)
Donald McPherson, workman (6)
Paul McPherson, workman (5)
Ann McMaster, cottar (4)
Janet McPherson, cottar (2)
Donald McCulloch, herd (6)
William Brody, cottar and wife (2)

ACHAGAVEL

John McPhee, herd (4)
Duncan McDougall, herd (8)
Coll McDonald, grasskeeper and maid (2)
Catharine McMillan, cottar (2)
John McDougall, cottar (6)
Archibald McPhee, cottar (6)
Archibald McDougall, cottar (4)

BEACH

Duncan McMillan, herd (4)
Donald McPherson, herd (7)

ARDTORNISH

Angus Grigarson (Gregorson), tacksman (16)
John McGrigor, cottar (4)
Donald McIntyre, workman (4)
Donald McKinnon, workman (4)
Hugh McKinnon, workman (5)
James McGrigor, change keeper (6)
John McEachern, herd (5)
Archibald Cameron, cottar (5)
Peggy Stewart, cottar (6)

TERNAIT

Malcolm McCallum, herd (6)
Alexander McEachern, herd (4)
Margaret McKinnon and son (2)

KIEL

John Cameron, tenant (4)
Hugh McLachlan, tenant (4)
Hugh Cameron, workman (6)
Hugh McMillan, workman (7)
John McPherson, workman (4)
Ann Cameron, cottar and daughter (2)
Duncan Cameron, cottar (6)
Donald Cameron, workman (7)
John McKinnon, cottar (4)
Flory McMaster, cottar and grand-daughter (2)
Catharine McKenzie, cottar (2)
Colin Cameron, cottar (3)

SAVARY

Mrs Campbell (3)
John Campbell, tenant (8)
Malcolm Livingstone, tenant (6)
Donald McInnish (sic), tenant (5)
Donald Livingstone, tenant (10)
Angus McInnish (sic) tenant (5)
Archibald McInnish, tenant (5)
Donald McMillan, workman (8)

Hugh Livingstone, grasskeeper (8)
Sandy McDiarmaid, workman (6)
John Cameron, cottar (4)
Neil McInnis, workman (3)
Lachlan McLean, cottar (2)
Donald McEchern, cottar (5)
Neil McLean, miller (1)
Duncan McKay, cottar (6)

FIUNARY

Mr Norman McLeod, minister (11)
Donald McPhee, workman (7)
Angus Livingstone, workman (6)
Duncan Cameron, cottar (4)

SALACHAN

John McMaster, workman (7)
Charles McLachlan, workman (5)
John Cameron, workman (5)
Archibald McLachlan, cottar (4)
Duncan McLachlan, grasskeeper (6)
Dugald McLachlan, cottar (7)
Mary McDougall, cottar (3)

LAGAN

Donald McLachlan, tacksman (22)
Hugh McLachlan, workman (3)
Lachlan McLachlan, cottar (5)
Allan Cameron, cottar (4)
Margaret McLachlan and daughter (2)

GLOSSARY
of terms used in 1779 census

Change-keeper: An inn-keeper.

Cottar: A cottage servant living on a tenant's land providing labour in lieu of rent. The term also applied to cottagers without grazing rights and land, often the aged, widows and the poor.

Grasskeeper: A herd employed in watching unfenced farm boundaries to prevent straying of animals.

Tenant: A small tenant sharing jointly in the arable land and farm grazing.

Tacksman: A superior tenant, usually having a lease of one or more farms. Generally tacksmen resided on their land and managed it with the assistance of married and unmarried servants and were seldom permitted to sub-let.

Workman: Generally a married farm servant employed by the tenant or tacksman. Usually having a share of the arable land and paying a rent of about three quarters of the grain crop.

A LIST OF PERSONS LIVING IN MORVERN IN 1841
SHOWING THEIR ABODE, AGE AND OCCUPATION

ABBREVIATIONS USED:
IND: independent means
FS: Female servant
AL: Agricultural labourer
MS: Male servant
NN: no name
numbers in brackets: individual houses
(Original spellings of Christian and surnames.)

ARDTORNISH

(1) John Gregorson, 65, IND, Mary, 35, Elizabeth, 15, Margaret, 14, Jean, 10, Angus, 9, Betsy Gregorson, 35, Hugh McDearmid, 25, student, Hugh Campbell, 15, Alexander Campbell, 14, John Gregorson, 13, Jenny McIntyre, 55, FS, Chirsty M'Phaden, 25, FS, Peggy McColl, 25, FS, Ann M'Lean, 20, FS, Ann M'Gregor, 14, FS
(2) Donald McCorquodale, 35, MS, Donald M'Lean, 15, AL, Donald M'Lean, 10, AL
(3) Colin M'Callum, 30, AL, Harriot, 25, Donald, 6, Hugh, 4, Catherine, 3, Barbara, 4 months
(4) John Cameron, 60, AL, Ann, 60, James, 25, AL, Ann, 15, Mary M'Lean, 10
(5) Malcolm Graham, 30, AL, Ann, 30, Isabella, 8
(6) Charles M'Lean, 35, AL, Peggy, 35, Euphemia, 6, Ann, 2, Jenny, 25, FS
(7) Alexander M'Gregor, 50, clerk, Ann, 40, Cathie, 9, Patrick, 7, Ann M'Lachlan, 14, FS
(8) Allan M'Lean, 35, AL, Jean, 30, Donald, 10, Hector, 4, Alexander, 60, MS, Peggy Campbell, 20, FS, Andrew M'Intyre, 20

SAMHNACHAN

(1) Finlay M'Arthur, 40, AL, Marjory, 35, John, 20, Isabella, 18, Mary, 16, Ann, 16, Hugh, 14, Catherine, 12, Peter, 9, Neil, 6
(2) Ewen Cameron, 20, AL, Mary Cameron, 60, Mary M'Lachlan, 15, FS, Ann Cameron, 55
(3) Donald Cameron, 40, AL, Margaret, 40, Mary, 15, Hugh, 15, Peter, 8, Mary, 80

SRATH SHUARDAIL

(1) John Rankin, 25, AL, Archibald, 20, Mary, 30, Sally, 25

ACHRANICH

(1) Alexander M'Nab, 20, manager, Mary, 15, Christina, 60, Emely Cameron, 25, FS Jane M'Lachlan, 20 Robert Cameron, 26, MS
(2) Hugh M'Lachlan, 25, AL, John Livingston, 25, AL, Allan M'Donald, 13, AL, John M'Millan, 15, AL, Donald M'Corquodle, 35, AL, Lazarsaus Seobbn, 40, mole-catcher
(3) Alexander M'Master, 20, hand loom weaver, Anne, 65, Catherine, 20

TEARNAIT

(1) Dugald M'Intyre, 55, AL, Kate, 50, Ann, 25, John, 15, Duncan, 14, Angus, 12, Alexander, 10, Dugald, 8
(2) Donald M'Kinnon, 80, AL, Chirsty, 70, Mary, 35, Donald M'Niven, 9

EIGNAIG

(1) Archibald McKinnon, 50, AL, Eliza, 40, Peggy, 15, Hugh, 10, Jenny, 9, Flora, 8, Elizabeth, 6, John, 4
(2) John M'Intyre, 35, AL, Kate, 35, Peggy, 10, John, 8, Allan, 6, Kate, 3, Peter, 1, Alexander M'Phail, MS

GARBH SHLIOS

(1) Angus M'Kinnon, 40, AL, Flora, 35, Betty, 15, John, 13, Donald, 11, Charles, 8, Peter, 6, Kate, 4

INNIEMORE

(1) Donald M'Phail, 30, shoemaker, Kate, 25, Peter, 3, Peggy M'Gregor, 80
(2) John M'Gregor, 30, AL, Kate, 25, Mary, 3, Peggy, 1

DUBH DHOIRE

(1) Allan M'Lachlan, 35, hand-loom weaver, Peggy, 30, John, 5, Mary, 3, Barbara, 1, Isabel, 15, FS
(2) Donald M'Donald, 45, AL, Jessie, 45, Coll, 14, Mary, 12, Anne, 10, Donald, 8, Thomas, 6, Margaret, 1, Helen, 55
(3) Hugh M'Person, 60, AL, Ann, 60, Catherine, 35
(4) Ronald M'Donald, 30, AL, Colin, 35, AL

CLAGGAN

(1) Donald M'Intyre, 30, schoolmaster, Catherine, 25, Donald, 1, Anne M'Coll, 13
(2) Hugh M'Varish, 55, AL, Catherine, 40, Duncan, 13 , Donald, 11, Mary, 9, John, 7, Jessie, 5, Niel, 1
(3) Anne M'Intyre, 60, Donald Cameron, 25, shoemaker

ACHARN

(1) John Davidson, 55, manager, Samuel, Davidson, 20, AL, Thomas Laidlow, 20, AL, Hugh M'Kay, 15, MS, Margaret Watson, 30, FS, John Munro, 35, AL, Robert Munro, 35, AL, James Campbell, 30, AL

CROSBEN

(1) Angus M'Kay, 30, AL, Isabel, 25, Donald, 3, Charles, 2, Alexander, 1 month, Alexander M'Kay, 40, mason, George Baillie, 45, AL

LURGA

(1) Hugh Cameron, 35, AL, Sarah, 30, Catherine, 1, Cirstie M'Intyre, 20, FS, Donald Cameron, 20, MS

LAUDALE

(1) Colin M'Lachlan, 40, farmer, Ewen M'Lachlan, 35, farmer, Catherine Munn, 30, FS, Sarah M'Lachlan, 30, FS, Mary Cameron, 20, FS, John M'Lean, 50, Hugh M'Dougald, 60, IND, A. L. M'Donald, 35, IND, Duncan M'Lachlan, 20, AL, John Campbell, 15, AL,
(2) Duncan Cameron, 20, MS, Richard M'Kean, 25, MS, Duncan M'Grigor, 15, MS, Allan Ferguson, 15, MS, Alexander Rankin, 11, MS, Henry M'Lachlan, 45, MS, Dougald M'Lachlan, 45, MS
(3) John Campbell, 60, AL, Mary, 60, Donald, 20, AL, Duncan Cameron, 30, tailor, Mary, 25, Catherine M'Lachlan, 15, FS, Colin M'Lachlan, 8, John M'Lachlan, 6, Barbara Campbell, 3
(4) Donald Ferguson, 45, AL, Anne, 30, Hugh, 20, Cirstie, 15, Anne, 5, John, 2, Mary M'Kenzie, 85, Catherine M'Dearmid, 65
(5) John M'Lachlan, 55, AL, Anne, 45, Anne, 20, Archibald, 15, AL, Isabel, 12, Flora, 9, Mary, 7
(6) Colin M'Phee, 65. AL, Mary, 30, Alexander M'Master, 30, AL, Julian M'Master, 30, Cirstie M'Master, 5, John M'Master, 1
(7) Mathew Morison, 50, AL, Mary, 40, Marjory, 20, Flora, 16, Margaret, 11 Angus, 9, John, 7, Mary, 5, Cirstie, 2, Catherine Turner, 15, FS

BEACH

(1) John Cameron, 30, AL, Janet, 40, Mary, 5, Flora, 3, Anne, 6 months, Donald M'Donald, 15, MS, Angus M'Innis, 20, AL, Cirstie Cameron, 30, FS
(2) Anne M'Master, 65, Sarah, 15, Sarah, 9, Mary Stewart, 9
(3) Patrick M'Intyre, 30, AL, Elisa, 30, Catherine, 6, Mary, 4, Donald, 9 months, John Cameron, 20, AL

CLOUNLAID

(1) James Douglas, 30, AL, Elisabeth, 20, William, 8 months, Donald M'Grigor, 25, AL

STRONE

(1)   Sarah M'Pherson, 55, Cirstie Cameron, 60

ULADAIL

(1)   Marjory Cameron, 75, Margaret Cameron, 30

ALTACHONAICH

(1)   Douglas M'Innis, 50, AL, Isabel, 45, Hugh, 13, Donald, 11, Alexander, 8, Anne, 6, Angus M'Kenzie, 20, AL

ULLIN

(1)   John Cameron, 70, AL
(2)   Hugh M'Master, 45, AL, Flora, 50, Anne, 20, Donald, 15, AL, Anne Robison, 7
(3)   Margaret M'Lachlan, 40, Jessie, 15, Lachlan, 12, Isabel, 6, Margaret, 3, Ewen, 1, Alexander Campbell, 25, AL

ATH BUIDHE

(1)   Duncan M'Grigor, 75, AL, Catherine, 45, Angus, 35, AL, Mary, 11

ARIENAS

(1)   Hugh M'Innis, 50, Mary, 45, John, 20, Catherine, 15, Cirstie, 15 Donald, 12 Sarah, 8, Flora, 6

LARACHBEG

(1)   John M'Lean, 55, AL, Flora, 45, Hector, 25, AL, Mary, 20, Anne, 12, Flora, 2, Alexander M'Pherson, 25, AL
(2)   Hugh M'Millan, 85, AL, Catherine, 60, Sarah, 30, Christina, 25, FS, William M'Dougel, 3, Jean Cameron, 6 months
(3)   Peter M'Lachlan, 80, hand-loom weaver, Mary, 70
(4)   Donald M'Kay, 55, hand-loom weaver, Sarah, 50, Mary M'Master, 15, FS
(5)   Hugh M'Kay, 20, AL, Anne M'Gregor, 85, Anne M'Gregor, 40

KINLOCHALINE

(1)   Donald M'Vean, 60, AL, Margaret, 40, Allan, 20, AL, Sarah, 15, Libby, 10, Jean, 8, Jannet, 4, Sarah Cameron, 80, Hugh, 14, MS
(2)   Donald M'Vean, 30, farmer, Peggy, 70, Duncan M'Master, 5, Peggy M'Innis, 20, FS

(3) Hugh Cameron, 45, AL, Katrine, 40, Katrine, 7, Dougald, 5
(4) Mary M'Intyre, 35, Katrine, 35, Anne Kater, 10
(5) Hugh Cameron, 30, AL, Jessie, 30, Anne M'Kinnon, 1
(6) Allan M'Donald, 40, spirit dealer, Flora, 25
(7) Duncan M'Intyre, 70, AL, Margaret, 60, Hugh, 25, tailor, Alexander Cameron, 12, Mary Cameron, 8, John M'Grigor, 3

ACHAFORS

(1) Alexander M'Callum, 45, AL, Anne, 35, Lachlan, 15, AL, Malcolm, 14, Jannet, 13, Isabel, 11, Mary, 9, Katherine, 7, Murdoch, 5, Colin, 3, Margaret, 1,
(2) John M'Intyre, 83, Mary, 70, Archibald M'Grigor, 14, AL, Angus M'Grigor, 12, Donald M'Grigor, 8

KNOCK

(1) Lachlan ?McMillan, 50, AL, Katherine, 35, Hugh, 15. AL Donald, 10 Anne, 8 Angus, 5 Margaret, 6 months Anne M'Intyre, 65
(2) Dugald Cameron, 40, AL, Cirstie, 35, John, 9, Mary, 4, Jannet, 1
(3) Hugh Cameron, 40, hand–loom weaver, Peggy, 55
(4) Donald M'Lean, 70, AL, Katherine, 30, Margaret, 30, Niel, 25, AL
(5) Alexander Campbell, 55, AL, Flora, 20, Sarah M'Innis, 70
(6) John M'Lachlan, 50, AL, Mary, 35, Robert, 12, Mary, 10, Flora, 8, Anne, 5, Dougald, 1 Mary M'Lachlan, 60
(7) Mary Heckman, 35, Mary, 14, John, 11, Catherine, 8, Jean, 5, Betty, 3
(8) Catherine Carmichael, 45, Anne, 15, Peggy, 8, Elizabeth, 4
(9) John M'Pherson, 45, mason, Mary, 40, Hugh, 10, Sarah, 5, Jannet, 35, FS
(10) Peggy Cameron, 60, Duncan, 25, AL, Sarah, 15, Donald, 10
(11) Donald M'Innis, 30, AL, Jannet, 60, Peggy M'Kenzie, 65
(12) Jean Blacklock, 40, Donald, 14, AL, John, 12
(13) Allan M'Lean, 45, AL, Jannet, 40, Angus, AL, Catherine, 12, Anne, 5, Flora M'Dougal, 30
(14) Archibald M'Intyre, 60, AL, Christina, 60, Norman, 15, Margaret, 4
(15) James M'Donald, 40, AL, Mary, 40, Duncan, 13, Ewen, 5
(16) Donald Cameron, 55, AL, Margaret, 50, John, 20, AL, Isabella, 15, Mary, 13, Sarah, 10, John, 4, John, 80. AL
(17) Myles M'Innis, 55, AL, Jannet, 55, Archibald, 15, AL, Mary, 10
(18) Catherine Kennedy, 90, Peggy, 60, Robert, 5, Catherine M'Quarie, 15, FS
(19) Alexander Currie, 20, AL, Jannet, 55, Jannet, 13, Cirstie, 8, Donald M'Fadyen, 50, shoemaker
(20) Hugh M'Lean, 50, AL, Mary, 40, John, 13, Anne, 11, Ronald, 9, Donald, 7, Catherine, 5
(21) John M'Calman, 75, AL, Anne, 65, James, 25, AL, James Cowan, 35, blacksmith, Anne Cowan, 25, Duncan, 1, Hugh M'Lean, AL
(22) Angus M'Eachern, 75, AL, Catherine, 70
(23) Alexander M'Gilvary, 55, army pensioner, Mary, 50, Margaret Groves, 15, FS

LOCHALINE VILLAGE

(1) David Bisset, 35, excise officer, Helen, 40, FS,
(2) Hugh M'Lachlan, 30, spirit dealer, Mary, 35
(3) Duncan M'Lachlan, 40, joiner, Flora, 35, Hugh, 15, AL, Catherine, 10, Cirstie,
      5, Mary, 3, John, 6 months
(4) Duncan Kennedy, 50, AL, Sarah, 50, Dougald, 10
(5) John Cameron, 40, spirit dealer, Marjory, 20, John, 3 months, Jean M'Eachern,
      60, Catherine M'Pharlane, 15, FS
(6) Donald M'Eachen, 60, hand-loom weaver, Anne, 50, Anne, 30, Betty, 15
(7) Duncan M'Lachlan 20, AL, Jean, 55
(8) Betsy M'Eachen, 35, dress-maker, Isabella, 8, Marjory, 6
(9) John M'Callum, 70, AL, Catherine, 35, Flora, 30
(10) Anne M'Phee, 35, Duncan, 15, AL, Mary, 12, Archibald, 8, Hugh, 6
(11) John Stewart, 30, shoe-maker, Mary, 25, Isabella, 4, Mary, 2, Allan, 1 month,
      Marion Cameron, 40, FS
(12) Angus M'Eachern, 20, shoe-maker, Marjory, 35, Margaret, 7 months
(13) Donald M'Eachern, 40, AL, Marjory, 65, Marjory, 35, Marjory Cameron, 8
(14) Angus M'Innis, 85, AL, Margaret, 70, Allan, 30, engineer merchant seaman
(15) Catherine M'Master, 80, Mary, 50, Cirstie, 35
(16) Donald M'Master, 45, AL, Mary, 40, Margaret, 20, Anne, 11, Duncan, 8,
      Alexander, 5
(17) Angus Kennedy, 50, tailor, Catherine, 80
(18) Robert Martin, 15, AL, Janet M'Lachlan, 55
(19) Duncan M'Lachlan, 45, joiner, Jannet, 40, Donald, 15, joiner-apprentice,
      Cirstie, 12, Mary, 10, Betty, 8, Duncan, 4, Anne, 60
(20) Allan Livingstone, 45, AL, John, 55, AL, Mary, 90, Jannet, 40, Patrick, 13,
      Catherine, 11, Duncan, 9, Alexander, 7, John, 5, Mary, 3
(21) Donald M'Innis, 60, army pensioner, Sarah, 50, Niel, 10
(22) Laurie M'Lauren, 35, wheel-wright, Catherine, 35, Mary, 12, Hugh, 10,
      Catherine, 8, Anne, 6, Lachlan, 4
(23) Cirstie M'Master, 55, Mary Sinclair, 20, John M'Master, 12
(24) Flory M'Eachern, 35, Anne, 11, Duncan, 9, Jannet, 7, John, 5, Angus, 2
(25) Donald M'Phee, 65, joiner, Mary, 50
(26) Mary M'Lachlan, 65, Catherine M'Lean, 60
(27) Peggy M'Niven, 35, Alexander Campbell, 10, John Taylor, 4
(28) Mary Livingston, 50, Jannet, 13, James, 10, Jean M'Dougall, 40, Niel
      M'Fadyen, 9, Anne M'Fadyen, 7, Allan, M'Fadyen, 5
(29) Catherine Cameron, 35
(30) Anne M'Lachlan, 70
(31) Flora Cameron, 80
(32) John Fraser, 60, tailor, Isabella, 55
(33) John M'Niven, 30, AL, Jean, 25, Hugh, 5
(34) Isabella Cameron, 35, Janet, 5
(35) Kenneth M'Innis, 70, AL, Angus, 35, mason, Anne, 30, Catherine M'Arthur, 5
(36) Angus Cameron, 30, AL, Mary, 25, Cirstie, 3, Mary, 1

(37) Andrew M'Donald, 45, hand-loom weaver, Harriet, 50, Alexander, 15, hand-loom weaver apprentice
(38) Mary Stewart, 45
(39) Patrick Doyle, 20, AL, Cirstie, 20, James, 11 months
(40) Catherine Livingston, 60, Flora, 20, FS, Allan, 10
(41) John M'Lachlan, 70, joiner, Marion, 70, John, 7
(42) Cirstie Currie, 30, Archibald, 4, Flora, 2
(43) Hugh M'Dearmid, 40, AL, Mary, 30, Catherine, 6, Dougald, 4, Jannet, 1
(44) John M'Grigor, 25, AL, Mary, 60
(45) Hugh Cameron, 35, tailor, Mary, 25, Peggy, 2, Archibald, 6 months, Donald M'Callum, 10, MS, Anne M'Lachlan, 15
(46) Donald Cameron, 30, cart-wright, Jean, 35, Anne, 2 months, Catherine, 2 months, Mary M'Pherson, 12, FS
(47) ?Sam Cameron, 60, AL, Cirstie, 50, Cirstie, 25, Duncan, 15, AL
(48) John M'Innis, 45, AL, Annie, 55, Allan, 15, AL
(49) Niel M'Donald, 55, army pensioner, Catherine, 50, Malcolm M'Lachlan, 2
(50) Christopher M'Callum, 45, AL, Agnes, 50

KYLE

(1) Sam Cameron, 60, parish schoolmaster, Mary, 60, Niel, 30, Alexander, 20, AL, Lexy M'Donald, 20, FS
(2) Donald M'Innis, 45, spirit-dealer, Catherine, 30, Allan, 15, AL, John, 13, Isabella, 11, Christina, 9, Catherine, 5, Mary, 3, Sarah, 10 months, Janet, 15, FS
(3) Donald M'Innis, 55, AL, Anne, 40, Mary, 12, Allan, 10, Anne, 5, Sarah, 3, Charles, 9 months
(4) Donald Livingston, 50, AL, Cirstie, 55, Mary, 35, FS, John, 15, AL, Cirstie, 11, Hugh, 9, Catherine, 7
(5) John M'Eachern, 35, AL, Margaret, 30, John, 9, Duncan, 7, Mary, 4, Alexander, 2, Christina, 6 months, Lachlan, 20, AL
(6) John M'Innis, 50, AL, Anne, 45, Allan, 12, John, 10, Lachlan, 5, Farchad, 3, Donald, 2 months
(7) Charles M'Lachlan, 40, AL, Mary, 35, Dougald, 14, Mary, 12, Ewen, 10, Catherine, 8, Anne, 6, John, 4, Flora, 2, Donald, 1
(8) Dougald Turner, 55, AL, Mary, 50, Mary, 12, Peggy, 9, Jannet, 7
(9) Allan M'Eachern, 50, AL, Catherine, 45, John, 15, AL, Anne, 7, Hugh, 5, Robert Cameron, 15, AL
(10) Robert M'Lachlan, 20, AL, Flora, 60, Donald, 15, AL, John Scouler, 10, Jannet Flaherty, 6, Robert Scouler, 6
(11) John M'Pherson, 50, AL, Mary, 45, Anne, 12, Angus, 7
(12) Hugh Cameron, 60, AL, Ann, 55, Archibald, 15, AL, Anne, 12, Jean, 7

ARDNESS

(1) Angus M'Innis, 30, carpenter, Cirstie, 65, Anne, 25, Sarah, 25, Dougald, 4, Mary, 2, John M'Kinnon, 2, Sarah M'Millan, 2

ACHABEG

(1) John M'Dougald, 40, AL, Angus, 35, AL, Catherine M'Leod, 35, FS, Donald Heckman, 15, MS
(2) Hugh Livingstone, 35, AL, Euphemia, 40, Hugh, 10, Christyine, 8, John, 6, Mary, 2, Catherine, 3 months
(3) Duncan Livingston, 30, AL, Catherine, 65, William Burke, 13, MS
(4) John Stewart, 60, AL, Margaret, 40, Jannet, 11, Mary, 9, Donald, 7
(5) John Henderson, 60, AL, Mary, 50, Sarah, 30, Cirstie, 25, Mary, 15, Flora, 7
(6) Duncan M'Kenzie, 35, AL, Mary, 60, Archibald, 20, shoe-maker, Alexander, 20, shoe-maker, Christina, 25
(7) John Cameron, 80, tailor, Emily, 70, Margaret, 35, Eneas, 25, Shoe-maker, Mary, 7, Archibald Rankin, 10
(8) Allan M'Lean, 40, AL, Anne, 75, Catherine, 35, Hugh, 12, Margaret, 9, John, 7, Alexander, 4, Donald, 1
(9) Donald Cameron, 20, AL, Mary, 40, Anne, 15, Alexander, 10, Duncan, 8, Sarah, 4, John, 1
(10) John Kennedy, 40, AL, Flora, 65, Donald, 35, hand-loom weaver, Niel Currie, 6, Sarah M'Lean, 20 FS, Archibald Campbell, 35, mason, Hugh Cameron, 40, hand-loom weaver, Catherine M'Kay, 35

ACHNAHA

(1) Allan M'Innis, 45, AL, Catherine, 45, Dougald, 15, AL, Jannet, 12, Mary, 10, Sarah, 8, Mary, 40, Peggy Campbell, 30, FS
(3) Margaret M'Lachlan, 45, Catherine, 15, Allan, 9, Anne, 6
(4) Anne Livingstone, 55, Jean, 15, FS
(5) David Smith, 25, AL, Elizabeth, 20, William, 6, Catherine, 4, Isobel M'Intyre, 20, Allan Watt, 25, AL
(6) Catherine Cameron, 65, John M'Lachlan, 14

SAVARY

(1) Duncan M'Master, 50, miller & spirit-dealer, Ann M'Kinnon, 45, FS, Hugh Cameron, 15, MS, Alexander Cameron, 30, AL,
(2) Allan Livingston, 70, AL, Marjory, 40, Duncan, 35, AL, John, 30, AL
(3) Mary M'Innes, 55, Charles, 25, tailor, Marjory, 20. Niel, 20, AL, Lachlan, 20, AL, Mary, 15
(4) Ann M'Lachlan, 40, Mary, 15, Lachlan, 15, AL, Robert 13, Donald, 8,
(5) Mary M'Innes, 40,
(6) Mary M'Innes, 40, Catherine, 6
(7) John M'Innes, 55, AL, Cirsty, 45, Allan, 20, AL, Ann, 15, Cirsty, 13, Sally, 7,
(8) Hugh Cameron, 65, farmer, Mary, 60, Donald, 25, AL, John, 30, AL, Cirsty, 20, Alexander, 6, Robert Livingston, 15, AL
(9) Dugald M'Lachlan, 50, farmer, Catherine, 40, Duncan, 15, Christina, 12, Catherine, 10, John, 8, Margaret, 6, Archibald, 20, MS, Isabel M'Intyre, 20, FS
(10) Donald M'Pherson, 55, AL, Mary, 40, Archibald, 15, Hugh, 13, Mary, 9

(11) Myles M'Innes, 60, AL, Catherine, 45, Betty, 20
(12) Malcolm M'Innes, 45, AL, Anne, 40, Niel, 9, Mary, 6, Angus, 3
(13) Donald Livingston, 45, AL, Sarah, 25,

LOCHALINE HOUSE

(1) John Sinclair, 60, IND, Catherine, 20, IND, John, 15, IND, Bell, 40, FS, Flora M'Fadyen, 30, FS, Peggy M'Master, 30, FS, Cirsty M'Millan, 15, FS, Peggy M'Master, 11, FS, Sally Cameron, 25, FS
(2) John Colquhoun, 20, MS, John M'Pherson, 20, MS, Archibald Turner, 14, MS, Malcolm M'Arthur, 13, MS

FIUNARY

(1) Donald M'Calman, 30, AL, Ann, 20, Dugald, 1, Peggy M'Lachlan, 12, FS
(2) Colin Cameron, 50, AL, Margaret, 35, John, 14, Norman, 9, Janet, 3, Archibald, 5 months
(3) John M'Leod, 40, clergyman, Margaret, 35, Jessie, 5, Norman, 3, John 2, Mary M'Lachlan, 50, FS, Ann M'Innes, 40, FS, Ann M'Phail, 25, FS, Marjory M'Niven, 40, FS, Ann M'Innes, 15, FS, Catherine M'Kinnon, 25, FS, Catherine Beaton, 80
(4) Lachlan Paterson, 30, AL, James Cameron, 20, AL, Archibald M'Pherson, 15, AL
(5) Alexander M'Leod, 25, AL, Catherine 25, Catherine, 75, Roderick, 9 months, Catherine M'Gregor, 6
(6) Archibald Sinclair, 45, AL, Ann, 35, Donald, 12, Catherine, 9, Helen, 9, Gilbert, 6, Christina, 3, John, 1
(7) Catherine M'Pherson, 70, Marjory, 20, Colin, 9
(8) Mary M'Lachlan, 70

SALACHAN

(1) Charles M'Lachlan, 50, AL, Margaret, 45, John, 15, Alexander, 12, Jane, 9, Mary, 6, Lachlan, 4

LAGAN

(1) John M'Gregor, 55, AL, Catherine, 40, James, 20, AL, Ann, 15, Jane, 15, John, 14, AL, Donald, 12, Ann, 8, Mary, 6, John, 4, Ewen, 1, John M'Kinnon, 6

KILLUNDINE

(1) Duncan M'Lachlan, 65, AL, Mary, 50, Alexander, 10, Samuel, 8, John, 6
(2) Angus Cameron, 35, AL, Ann, 35, Ann, 3, Catherine, 1, Catherine, 12, FS, Ann M'Innes, FS
(3) John M'Kay, 65, AL, Mary, 65, Alexander, 25, AL, John MacLeod, 16, Donald M'Leod, 14, Alexander M'Leod, 9

(4)   Margaret M'Eachern, 80
(5)   John M'Laine, 55, IND, Christina, 45, IND, Jane, 15, IND, Hugh, 15, IND,
      Flora, 15, IND, Ann, 11, IND, Ann, 11, IND, Alexander, 5, IND, Mary
      M'Kinnon, 45, FS, Catherine M'Laine, 20, FS, Isabel Morison, 20, FS,
      Ronald Campbell, 40, IND, Jessie Campbell, 15
(6)   Lachlan M'Eachern, 25, MS, Hugh M'Lachlan, 15, MS, Alexander
      M'Lachlan, 30, AL, Allan M'Pherson, 20, AL, Donald Cameron, 15, MS,
      Mary M'Neil, 45, FS, Ann M'Kinnon, 30, FS, Cirsty M'Millan, 20, FS,
      Archibald Sinclair, 55, joiner, Allan M'Donald, 45

CARNACAILLICHE

(1)   Hugh M'Millan, 65, AL, Mary, 50, Hugh, 20, AL, Donald, 20, Catherine, 15,
      Mary, 15, Angus, 13, John, 10, Archibald, 8, Dugald, 6
(2)   Hugh Cameron, 60, AL, Catherine, 45, Duncan, 20, AL, Hugh, 15, William,
      9, Christina, 7, Margaret, 55, FS
(3)   Mary Cameron, 40, Isabel, 10

FERNISH

(1)   Hugh Campbell, 35, AL, Mary, 30, Colin, 30, Angus, 25, Angus, 5, Donald, 1
(2)   John M'Intyre, 50, wheel-wright, Isabel, 40, Betty, 12, Archibald, 10,
      Duncan, 6, Margaret, 4, Joseph, 1, Donald Colquhoun, 75, hand-loom
      weaver.
(3)   Ann Livingston, 55, Catherine M'Varish, 20, FS
(4)   James Gray, 45, AL, Flora, 45, Flora, 20, Helen, 15, Helen Cameron, 15, FS,
      John M'Donald, 60, army pensioner
(5)   Alexander M'Niven, 30, AL, Christina, 25, Donald, 6, James, 3
(6)   Hugh Livingston, 60, AL, Elizabeth, 55, Angus, 40, AL, Donald, 35, AL,
      Duncan, 15, MS
(7)   Hugh M'Varish, 60, AL, Sarah, 45, Mary, 11
(8)   Catherine Livingston, 55

GLENMORVERN COTTAGE

(1)   John Beaton, 35, MS, Betty, 30, FS, Sarah Cameron, 15, FS

GLENMORVERN

(1)   John M'Donald, 40, gardener, Christina, 35, Donald, 15, AL, Margaret, 11,
      John, 8, Ann, 6, William, 4, Roderick, 2

BONNAVOULIN

(1)   John Cameron, 50, AL, Mary, 30, Susan, 15, Colin, 8, Jessie M'Pherson, 12,
      FS, Ann M'Kinnon, 80

(2) Alexander Cameron, 35, schoolmaster, Jane, 30, Catherine, 7, Allan M'Eachern, 45, tailor
(3) Angus M'Leod, 65, AL, Mary, 65, Betty, 25, John Smith, 5, Donald Smith, 3
(4) James Campbell, 35, blacksmith, Mary, 30, Sarah, 7, Mary, 5, Alexander, 1
(5) John Stewart, 35, miller, Margaret, 25, Hugh, 5, William, 3, Angus, 9 months
(6) John M'Donald, 65, AL, Mary, 55, Ann, 15, Catherine M'Dermid, 1, Mary M'Phee, 75
(7) Donald M'Lachlan, 50, wheel-wright, Catherine, 50, John, 20, AL, Mary, 20, John Cameron, 15, AL
(8) Flora Beaton, 30, Christina, 9, Flora, 7, Niel, 5, Margaret, 3, Donald, 5 months
(9) Martin Cameron, 45, AL, Isabel, 45, Sarah, 16, Hugh, 14, Ann, 12, Donald, 10, Isabel, 4
(10) David Kay, 55, AL, Betty, 50, Sarah, 15, Catherine, 12, Christina, 8, Flora M'Donald, 20, Janet M'Donald, 10
(11) Catherine Beaton, 40, Ann, 35,
(12) Margaret Cameron, 55

MUNGASDAIL

(1) Alexander Kirkpatrick, 35, farmer, Elizabeth, 40, Thomas Simpson, 40, AL, Margaret, 35, William, 15, Alexander, 13, Catherine, 10, Robert, 5, Margaret, 3, Thomas, 1, Jane M'Leod, 20, FS, Mary Kay, 20, FS

GLASDRUM

(1) Donald M'Lean, 40, AL, Mary, 35, Allan, 10, Duncan, 8, Janet, 4, Archibald, 2, Helen, 1
(2) Flory M'Lean, 40, Archibald, 15, Marjory, 12, John, 9
(3) Donald Cameron, 65, AL, Mary, 55, Alexander, 25, Mary, 9
(4) Allan M'Leod, 40, spirit-dealer, Sarah, 35, Ann, 15, Janet, 10, Helen, 6, Sarah, 2, NN, 2 days, Mary M'Kinnon, 40, Christian Morison, 50, Donald Morison, 25, AL
(5) Colin M'Leod, 30, AL, Mary, 60
(6) Alexander M'Donald, 60, AL, Catherine, 50, John, 11, James, 9, Christian, 7, Colin, 5, Mary, 2
(7) Angus M'Donald, 40, RC priest, Isabela M'Donald, 40, FS, Jessy M'Leod, 30, FS
(8) Hugh M'Donald, 50, tailor, Peggy, 40, Peggy, 12, Colin, 14, John, 8, Susan, 3

DRIMNIN HOUSE

(1) Margaret M'Donald, 35, housekeeper, Mary M'Nab, 85, IND
(2) Donald M'Pherson, 15, MS, Alexander M'Pherson, 20, MS, Donald Cameron, 15, MS, Alexander Cumming, 10, MS, Donald M'Nab, 35, packman

DRIMNIN

(1) Peter M'Nab, 55, farmer, Christian, 55, John, 15, Mary M'Niel, 35, FS, Mary Grant, 25, FS, Peggy Cumming, 10, FS, Roderick Cameron, 5, Catherine M'Lean, 65
(2) Catherine Cameron, 40, Catherine, 9, Donald, 7
(3) Mary Livingston, 20, John, 11, Donald, 8, Mary, 50
(4) Duncan Cameron, 60, hand-loom weaver, Christian, 40, Christian, 8, Colin, 4
(5) Donald M'Eacharn, 70, AL, Mary, 70, Flory, 60, Margaret M'Lachlan, 10, FS
(6) Charles M'Bain, 25, gardener, Grace, 25

ACHLEANAN

(1) David Corson, 25, farmer, John Ramage, 25, farmer, Mary Ramage, 35, Jane Ramage, 6, Helen Ramage, 3, Margaret M'Lean, 20, FS
(2) Alexander Alison, 30, AL, Euphemia, 25, Jane, 10, Alexander, 7, Jane, 5, John, 3, William, 1
(3) Duncan M'Innis, 45, hand-loom weaver, Catherine, 30, Janet, 9, Ann, 7, Christian, 5, Sally, 3, Mary, 1
(4) Hugh M'Donald, 70, tailor, Catherine, 50, Flory, 35
(5) John M'Lachlan, 35, AL, Janet, 35, Margaret, 13, Alexander, 11, Hugh, 6, Sarah, 4, Flory, 2

AULISTON

(1) Duncan Cameron, 45, AL, Catherine, 35, John, 15, AL, Catherine, 13, Alexander, 6, Donald, 3, John, 5 months
(2) John M'Leod, 50, AL, Catherine, 45, Alexander, 14, AL, Peggy, 10, Flory, 8, John, 5
(3) Alexander M'Gregor, 50, ground-officer, Ann, 35, Alexander, 10, Duncan, 3, Alexander M'Donald, 15, AL
(4) Donald Cameron, 50, AL, Margaret, 30, Sarah, 11, Margaret, 9, Mary, 7, Flory, 5, John, 3, Donald, 1
(5) Ann M'Leod, 40, Norman M'Leod, 20, AL, John M'Leod, 15
(6) Dugald M'Kinnon, 35, AL, Flory, 25, Mary, 2, Sarah, 1 month, Allan, 11, Christian, 12, FS, Duncan M'Leod, 13, MS
(7) Donald Livingston, 60, AL, Ann, 55, Ann, 80, Sarah, 80, Donald, 15, AL, Janet, 11, Niel, 8
(8) John Livingston, 35, mason, Sarah, 25, Janet, 6, Margaret, 1, Sarah M'Innis, 45, Peggy Campbell, 15, FS, Mary Livingstone, 6, Ewen Livingston, 5
(9) Colin M'Intyre, 90, farmer, Janet, 65, John M'Gilbhra, 40
(10) Donald Livingston, 60, AL, Peggy, 50, Archibald, 25, shoemaker, Alexander, 23, shoe-maker's apprentice, Donald Cameron, 15, MS
(11) John Cameron, 30, AL, Margaret, 60, Margaret, 30, FS, John, 12, MS, John Livingston, 35, mason
(12) Hugh Cameron, 40, AL, Flory, 25, Donald, 7, Allan, 6 months

(13) Allan M'Lachlan, 25, AL, Jane, 25, Mary, 1, Ann M'Intyre, 30, FS, Mary Livingston, 30, FS
(14) Archibald Cameron, 35, AL, Sarah, 35, NN, 2 months, Donald M'Kinnon, 8, John Livingston, 20, AL, Alexander M'Donald, 13, MS
(15) Archibald Livingstone, 60, AL, Christian, 60, Ann, 35, FS, Christian Given, 8, Elizabeth Morton, 11, James M'Kinnon, 5
(16) Hector M'Lean, 80, AL, Effy, 80, Lachlan, 35, MS, Sally, 35, Donald 4 months, Malcolm M'Lean, 15, MS
(17) Donald M'Kinnon, 35, AL, Betty, 35, Mary, 13, Catherine, 11, James, 8, Sarah, 6, Donald, 4, Duncan, 2
(18) Ann Gilles, 60
(19) Duncan Cameron, 25, hand-loom weaver, Alexander M'Intyre, 30, AL
(20) John Livingston, 70, AL, Betty, 35, FS, Betty, 15, FS
(21) John Cameron, 80, AL, Flory, 55

PORTABHATA

(1) John Campbell, 25, AL, Mary, 35, Donald, 1
(2) Mary Cameron, 40, Christina, 12
(3) Sarah M'Lachlan, 60, Hugh M'Laurin, 20, AL, Ann Frazar, 20, FS
(4) John M'Naughten, 35, AL, Jean, 25, Catherine, 4, Janet, 2, Angus, 6 months, Lucy M'Queen, 20, FS, Catherine M'Lean, 50, FS
(5) Allan Cameron, 40, AL, Mary, 40, Duncan, 14, Sarah, 12, Flory, 10, John, 8

SORNAGAN

(1) Sarah Cameron, 35, Hugh, 15, MS, Janet, 8, William, 6
(2) Isabella M'Donald, 40, Allan, 15, MS, Magnus, 10 FS (sic)

DOIRLINN

Hugh M'Innis, 60, spirit dealer, Donald, 25, MS, Catherine, 9, Ann M'Gregor, 25, FS

DRUIMBUIDHE

(1) William Blackleg, 35, farmer, Barbara Flint, 30, James Flint, 8, Wilhelmina Flint, 5, Donald Cameron, 18, MS, Margaret Cameron, 16, FS
(2) Catherine M'Donald, 60, Colin, 12
(3) John M'Phie, 55, AL, Donald, 45, AL, Ann, 60, Emily, 55, FS, Mary, 50, FS, Ket, 35, John, 11, Sarah, 9, Mary, 7, Duncan, 5, Colin, 3, Christina, 6 months

GLEANNAGUDA

(1) Donald M'Pherson, 65, army pensioner, James, 30, AL, Angus, 14, Mary, 56, FS

ORONSAY

(1) Mary M'Lachlan, 35, Sally, 80, Peter, 16, MS, Mary, 13, Sally, 9, Alexandra, 6, Ann, 3, Margaret, 1
(2) Peter Cameron, 25, AL, Peggy, 55
(3) Alexander M'Donald, 40, AL, Catherine, 30, FS
(4) Charles Cameron, 50, carpenter, Christina, 45, Donald, 15, carpenter's apprentice, Archibald, 15, AL, James, 13, Janet, 10, Christina, 2
(5) Mary Cameron, 50, Mary, 80, Archibald 20, MS, Cosmo, 15, MS, Allan, 8
(6) Ket M'Phie, 90
(7) Mary M'Donald, 35, Donald, 11, Sarah, 9, Christina, 6, Catherine, 4 months
(8) Rodrick M'Donald, 50, AL, Mary, 35, Alexander, 16, AL, Duncan, 13, Ann, 8, John, 6, Allan, 4, Lachlen, 1
(9) Mary M'Donald, 25, Ann, 1, Ann Cameron, 40, FS, Catherine, 12

BARR

(1) Duncan M'Kinnon, 50, AL, Ann, 40, Donald, 15, AL, Mary, 16, Sarah, 10, John, 8, James, 5, Margaret,
(2) Robert Kirkpatrick, 40, farmer, Alexander, 15, AL, Bell, 15, James, 14, Catherine, 13, Thomas, 11, John Simpson, 9, Archibald M'Leod, 20, MS, John M'Leod, 15, MS, Archibald M'Kinnon, 15, Morag Grey, 15, FS, John Cameron, 40, fox-hunter
(3) Hugh Cameron, 35, hand-loom weaver, Jean, 40
(4) Allan Sutherland, 45, AL, Sarah, 40, John, 15, Janet, 11, Helen M'Kinnon, 20, FS, Margaret M'Fadzen, 20, FS
(5) Dugald Cameron, 20, carpenter, Ann, 60, Donald, 20, AL, Mary, 60, Eugine M'Innes, 8
(6) Alexander Livingston, 55, wheel-wright, Margaret, 40, Mary, 15, Robert, 14, AL, Betty, 9
(7) John Livingston, 45, AL, Margaret, 30, Catherine, 9, Sally 7, Duncan, 4, Archibald, 8 months

ARDANTIOBAIRT

(1) Niel (?) Moreson, 60, Margaret, 60
(2) Katherine Cameron, 70, Mary, 40, FS
(3) Hugh Cameron, 50, AL, Katherine, 40, Hugh, 14

INNIEMORE

(1) James Cameron, 70, AL, Catherine, 72, John M'Call, 40, AL, Ann M'Call, 30, Hugh M'Call, 12, Ann M'Call, 10, John M'Call, 8, Mary M'Call, 6, Katherine M'Call, 4, James M'Call, 6 months,
(2) Flory M'Pherson, 6

Doire nam Mart

(1) Duncan M'Gregor, 35, AL, Catherine, 30, Gregor, 10, Peter, 4, Catherine, 2, un-named, 1 month, Jean M'Master, 15, FS

Kinlochteacuis

(1) Donald M'Naughtan, 25, AL, John M'Diarmid, 40, AL, Alexander M'Kenzie, 20, AL, James Cameron, 25, MS, William, Cameron, 12, MS, Mary M'Gregor, 25, FS, Mary M'Pherson, 25, FS
(2) Katherine Cameron, 55, John M'Millan, 12
(3) Mary M'Lachlan, 40, Katherine, 35, Ann Campbell, 13
(4) Alexander Mitchell, 75, blacksmith, Janet, 65, Marjory, 30, FS, Hugh, 25, AL, Anne Mac Turk, 17, Jessie M'Intyre, 13, Margaret Cameron, 50
(5) Allan M'Millan, 75, AL, Janet, 60, Catherine M'Kinnon, 15, Sarah, 10,
(6) Ann M'Pherson, 40, Ann, 15
(7) Alexander M'Lachlan, 80, spirit-dealer, Mary, 30, Ann, 25, Isabella M'Millan, 5, Duncan M'Millan, 12, James Glendining, 20, AL
(8) Flory Buchanan, 70, Mary, 35, Margaret Cameron, 16, FS, Ann, 8

Rahoy

(1) Donald M'Pherson, 35, AL, Ann, 38, Ann M'Donald, 80
(2) John M'Pherson, 40, AL, Angus, 25, AL, John, 6
(3) John M'Intyre, 40, AL, Mary, 35, Hugh, 12, Duncan, 10, James, 8, Mary, 6, John, 4, Flora, 2
(4) Christina Cameron, 40, Katherine, 15, Christina, 10, Margaret, 8, Hugh, 6
(5) Hugh M'Pherson, 65, AL, Mary, 25, Flora M'Intyre, 14
(6) Duncan M'Intyre, 80, AL, Flora, 75, Sarah, 25, Flora Blacklock, 16, ?Flory Blacklock, 14, John Blacklock, 10, Donald M'Donald, 14, MS

Glencripesdale

(1) Duncan M'Naughtan, 55, manager, Janet, 50, John, 13, Chirsty, 85, Mary M'Donald, 20, FS, Mary M'Pherson, 20, FS, Hugh Cameron, 35, AL, Alexander M'Donald, MS, James Robinson, 60, MS, James M'Pherson, 20, MS
(2) James M'Naughtan, 40, house-carpenter, Peggy, 40, John, 16, Eun, 14, Chirsty, 12, Donald, 10, Ann, 8, Mary, 6, Lachlan, 40, MS, John Cameron, 15, MS
(3) Ann Cameron, 45, Donald M'Dougald, 14, Duncan Robinson, 6
(4) John M'Pherson, 65, Ann, 55, James, 30, AL, Christy, 14, Archibald Clark, 6
(5) John Cameron, 40, AL

CAMAS SALACH

(1) Mary M'Lachlan, 55, Ann, 50
(2) Dugald M'Phie, 85, Hugh, 75, Mary, 45, John M'Gregor, 40, AL, Christy, 40, Catherine, 14, Ann, 12, Isabella, 8, Jessy, 5, Catherine M'Phie, 35, FS
(3) Angus Cameron, 70, AL, Mary , 60, John, 33, AL, Alexander, 25, AL, Mary, 22, Alexander, 15, Dugald, 5, Mary, 3
(4) Alexander Cameron, 45, AL, Grace, 35, Allan, 11, Alexander, 7, Colin, 4, Dugald, 2, Marjory M'Lachlan, 80
(5) Donald M'Lachlan, 40, pauper, Sarah, 35, Mary, 15, Colin, 13, Sarah, 10, Bell, 8, Jean, 6, Peggy, 4, Ann, 2, Alexander, 1 month

CARNA

(1) Angus M'Lean, 90, farmer, Mary, 70, Alexander, 25, AL, Katherine, 25, Archie MacLean, 16, Marjory, 5, Donald Cameron, 15, MS, Hugh Cameron, 12, MS
(2) Alexander M'Diarmid, 10, Elizabeth M'Diarmid, 8, John M'Diarmid, 5, Alexander M'Diarmid, 2
(3) Flory M'Lean, 60, Elizabeth, M'Lean, 15
(4) James M'Lean, 65, farmer, Margaret, 45, Hugh, 35, AL, James, 10
(5) William M'Pherson, 60, farmer, Sarah, 55, Ann, 15, Mary, 1, William M'Lachlan, 10
(6) Donald Cameron, 30, AL, Ann, 30, Donald, 6, Hugh, 4, Allan, 2, Alexander, 1 month, Sarah M'Donald, 35, FS
(7) Janet Cameron, 25, Jean, 5, John, 2, Hugh, 1, John Forbes, 14, MS, Bell M'Lean, 3
(8) Donald M'Lean, 60, farmer, Mary, 55, James, 30, AL, Hugh, 25, AL, Mary, 25, John, 35, Angus Cameron, 4
(9) Mary M'Lean, 30, Hugh, 11, Alexander, 9, Donald, 6, Mary, 4, Jean, 2
(10) Alexander Cameron, 60, farmer, Mary, 50, Lachlan, 30, AL, Mary, 25, John, 20, AL, Mary, 10, Ann, 3
(11) Hugh M'Pherson, 30, AL, Ann, 30, Robert, 5, Alexander, 1

ACHLEEK

(1) Colin Cameron, 30, AL, Peggy, 26, Mary, 24, FS
(2) Ewen Cameron, 30, AL, Luy, 24, Kett, 5, John, 3, Mary, 1, Kett M'Phie, 19, FS, Peggy Mitchel, 16, FS
(3) John M'Eachran, 40, AL, Sarah, 35, Ewen, 12, Mary, 10, Ann, 8, Margaret, 6, Jannet, 4, Allan, 2

GLASBHIL

(1) Samuel M'Donald, 30, AL, Christy, 25, Mary, 3, John, 10 months, Ewen, 8, Jean, 60
(2) Paul Graham. 70, AL, Kett, 70, John, 30, AL, Angus, 34, AL, Ewen

M'Pherson, 6 months, Ewen M'Pherson, 11, Ann M'Pherson, 25, Mary M'Pherson, 30 FS, Mary M'Pherson, 2
(3) John Cameron, 37, lead-miner, Kett, 33, John, 13, Ewen, 12, Donald, 10, Ann, 7, Mary, 6, Alex, 3

LIDDESDALE

(1) Alex M'Lachlan, 60, AL, Peggy, 60
(2) Archy M'Lachlan, 70, AL, Mary, 56, Lachlan, 15, MS, Dugald, 4, MS
(3) Mary Cameron, 74, Donald, 35, AL, Ann, 49, FS
(4) John Morrison, 60, AL, James, 20, AL, Allan, 17, MS, Mathew, 11, Alex, 11, Ewen M'Lachlan, 30, AL, Mary, 28, Kett, 2, Jean, 6 months, Janet, 6 months, Mary M'Phee, 12, FS

ACHAGAVEL

(1) Lachlan M'Lachlan, 50, AL, Saly, 45, John, 25, AL, Donald, 20, AL, Dugald, 4, Samuel, 12, Colin, 14, MS, Allan, 19, MS
(2) James M'Lachlan, 32, AL, Kett, 31, Ewen, 7, Saly M'Kay, 12, FS
(3) Samuel Cameron, 55, AL, Ann, 40, Kett, 25, FS, Ann, 23, FS

LIST OF OFFICERS FROM MULL AND MORVERN

MULL

Major Allan MacLachlan, Achnacraig, 75th
Captain Robert MacLachlan, his brother, 75th
Lieutenant Campbell MacLachlan, his brother, 75th
Colonel Fraser, Torosay, died Governor of Sierra Leone
Captain Alexander Campbell, Achnacroish (Greys)
Captain Murdoch MacLaine, Lochbuy, 84th
Lieutenant John MacLaine, his brother, 73rd
Sir Archibald MacLean, Scallasdale, 42nd (Commanding at Matagorda)
Colonel Hector MacLaine, his brother
Major MacLaine, his brother
Murdoch MacLaine, his brother
Colonel MacLean of Scour, 79th
General Campbell, Achnacroish (Marines)
Major Cambell, Knockmulligan
Captain Archibald MacLeod, Ross
Captain Donald MacLeod, his brother (killed at Corunna)
Lieutenant MacLean of Pennycross
General MacLean, his son (Dragoons)
Lieutenant Lachlan MacLean, his brother (Rifles)
Commissary MacLean, his brother
Colonel MacLean, Usigean, 86th
Captain John MacLean, his brother, 56th
Lieutenant MacLean, his brother, 56th
Captain Hector MacLean, Busnessan, 93rd
Lieutenant Allan MacLean, his brother, 91st, killed at Corunna
Charles MacLean, his brother, Inspector-General of Hospitals
Lieutenant Neil MacLean, Ardfinaig, RN
MacQuarrie of MacQuarrie
General MacQuarrie, 55th
Colonel MacQuarrie, 42nd
Captain Hector MacQuarrie HEIC
Captain Charles MacQuarrie, son of Colonel MacQuarrie, and a second son, un-named
Colonel Donald Campbell, Knock
Colonel Archibald Campbell, Knock, 46th
Captain Colin Campbell, Knock, RM
Captain Campbell, Killechronan, 92nd
Captain D Campbell, Killan
Colonel MacDonald of Inch, RA
Captain Duncan Stewart, Achadashenaig, 72nd
Captain Donald (or Colin) Stewart, 72nd
Captain Stewart, son to Captain Duncan, 72nd

Ensign James Maxwell, Aros, killed at Bergen-op-Zoom
Ensign John A Maxwell, Aros, 46th
Captain MacLean, Ceannagarthur
Major Duncan Campbell, Ardnacross, 42nd
Captaion John Cambell, Ardnacross, his brother, 91st
Lieutenant Alexander Campbell, Ardnacross, his brother
Lieutenant Angus Campbell, Treshnish
Major Dugald Campbell, Treshnish, 91st, his brother and a second un-named
    brother
Dr Neil Campbell, Freckadale
Captain Donald Campbell, Sunapol
Captain John Campbell, Sunapol
Captain Alexander Campbell, Sunapol
Major Donald MacLean, Lagamull
Dr Alexander MacLean, his brother
Lieutenant MacLean, his brother
Dr John MacLean, Callachoille
Lieutenant Neil Roy
General MacLean Torloisk
Captain Alexander MacLean of Coll
Captains Hector, Norman, Roderick and Hugh, (guards) his brothers

MORVERN

Major Charles MacLean of Drimnin
Captain John MacLean, his brother
Captain Hugh Beaton
General Donald Campbell, Barr
Captain Duncan Campbell, Barr
Lieutenant James Campbell, Barr
Captain Alexander Campbell, Barr
Lieutenant Duncan MacLachlan, Rahoy
Captain James Gregorson, Glen (Glencripesdale)
Captain Hugh Campbell, Killundine
Captain Donald Campbell, Killundine, his son
Captain Alexander Campbell, Killundine, his son
Lieutenant John Campbell, Killundine, his son
Captain Alexander MacLachlan (brother of Goa's), lived at Sallachan.
Lieutenant Robert MacLachlan, Goa
Captain Donald MacLachlan, brother, Goa
Lieutenant Finlay MacInnes, son to Fionladh Piopair
Colonel Donald Gregorson, 91st
Captain Dugald Gregorson, 42nd
Captain Alexander Gregorson
Commissary Eneas Gregorson
Captain Colin MacLean of Drimnin
Captain Cameron, Achacharn (Acharn)

Lieutenant MacInnes, Árdtornish
Colonel Lachlan MacLean of the Royals
Colonel Campbell of Possil (should be in the Mull List)
Dr Donald MacLean (in 42nd at one time)
Dr Allan MacLean, Ross (should be in the Mull List)
Captain 'Jack' Campbell, RN, Liddesdale, sailed as a lieutenant with Nelson
Lieutenant Donald Campbell, his brother

(MacLeod, J. N.; see also SWHIHR, *Notes & Queries*, March 1989, Series 2, No.3)